RINGSIDE

RINGSIDE

*Interviews with 24 Fighters
and Boxing Insiders*

DOVEED LINDER

Foreword by Greg Leon

McFarland & Company, Inc., Publishers
Jefferson, North Carolina

ISBN (print) 978-1-4766-6441-5
ISBN (ebook) 978-1-4766-2624-6

Library of Congress cataloguing data are available

British Library cataloguing data are available

Front cover: Muhammad Ali and Leon Spinks in their first
boxing match on February 15, 1978, in Las Vegas, Nevada
(Steve Lott/Boxing Hall of Fame)

Manufactured in the United States of America

*McFarland & Company, Inc., Publishers
Box 611, Jefferson, North Carolina 28640
www.mcfarlandpub.com*

In memory of Daniel Linder

Contents

Acknowledgments

While writing this book, I was fortunate to cross paths with a lot of great people. The journey began when I first put on the gloves, and continued when I started training fighters. Just a few of the people (and places) who have impacted my life within the sport and assisted me along the way include Matt Brown, Rob Clark, Jamie Mushlin, Panda Athletic Club, Jose Ponce, Steven Fitzpatrick Smith, and Sweat, St. Louis.

The writing of this book was ignited by the generosity of Evan Dick, who is Larry Merchant's son-in-law. He offered to set up the interview with Merchant over lunch and he even picked up the tab!

Boxingtalk.com publisher Greg Leon gave me my start in this business, shared all of his contacts with me, and was gracious enough to write the foreword. Boxingtalk editor Scott Shaffer has also been a huge source of support for my boxing writing.

Two of my go-to guys for securing interviews or asking questions were Michael Schmidt and John Scully, whom I couldn't have done this without.

Other people who either arranged interviews, gave me phone numbers, referred me to a photographer, contributed photographs, or were involved in the making of this book in some way include Johnathon Banks, Jeff Brophy, Ryan Burton, Marie Souza Cunningham, Stephen Edwards, James Akhir Fisher, Heather Hummel, Jackie Kallen, Yale Kim, Dr. Stuart Kirschenbaum, Christopher Klapp, Darrell LaMontre, Dr. Billy Lathan, Julie Lederman, Samuel Leonard, Steve Lott (Boxing Hall of Fame Las Vegas), Rick Perez, Fred Rusche, Tarick Salmaci, Steve Smoger, Ryan Songalia, Virginia Souza, Randy Speight, Dino Spencer, Sylvia Steward-Williams, Patricia Stich, Matt Stolow, Tom Tsatas (5th Street Gym), Carlos Varela, Jr., Volunteer Lawyers & Accountants for the Arts in St. Louis, Steve Weisfeld, and Adie Zuckerman.

Photographers who contributed their top-notch work to this book include Bob Barton, Claudia Bocanegra, Craig Eagleson, Dan Graschuck, Bret Newton at ThreatPhoto.com/Pound4Pound.com, and Marty Rosengarten/RingsidePhotos.com.

Darrell LaMontre, Barbara Madison, and Steve Yu read this book before it was published and offered a great deal of input and encouragement along the way.

Barry Hamilton is the "technical genius" who helped me organize all of the materials for this book and bring this thing home.

In addition, the following people gave me a lot of help and support throughout this process: the Cooper Family, Ric Dark, the Gerbin Family, Pam Goss, Bill Hoffman, Lloyd Jowers, Lena Kozina, Noah Linder, Mary Minton, and Dave Rutherford.

My mother and father, Katie and Daniel Linder, have always stood beside me and supported all of my artistic endeavors.

Most of all, I want to thank each of the 24 people who were kind enough to allow me to interview them. They are the true authors of this book.

Foreword
by Greg Leon

Boxing has always been a part of my life. My father was an amateur boxer and the sport was prominently featured in my house. When I was a kid, I remember watching Pryor-Arguello and all the other classic fights from the '80s. I loved the sport and wanted to be a part of it in some way. In 2002, I had a chance to interview one of my boxing idols, Sugar Ray Leonard. It was one of the coolest experiences of my life to that point. I submitted the interview with Sugar Ray to various websites, including Boxingtalk.com. From there, I became part of the Boxingtalk team and over time, I started developing close relationships with all of the movers and shakers in the sport. My Rolodex continued growing and I eventually became the owner of the site. Boxingtalk was the forum for the fighters. They could say whatever they wanted, knowing that their words wouldn't be taken out of context. A lot of the biggest fights of the 2000s were made on Boxingtalk. The fighters would challenge each other and negotiate through the interviews. Some of these fights include Roy Jones, Jr.–John Ruiz, Antonio Tarver–Roy Jones, Jr., Oscar De La Hoya–Bernard Hopkins, Oscar De La Hoya–Floyd Mayweather, Jr., Floyd Mayweather, Jr.–Zab Judah… The list goes on and on.

Since I found myself assisting in putting these fights together, I saw a new career opportunity as an advisor. I took what I learned as a writer and used it to guide the careers of fighters. I wasn't spending as much time doing the interviews, but I still owned the site, which gave me a chance to give other people the opportunities I had when I was first starting out. A lot of die-hard fans want to be up close and personal with the people in boxing. That's usually what draws people to boxing journalism in the first place. Over the years, I've had quite a few writers submit material, some who went on to take their craft very seriously. One of these writers was Doveed Linder. He made a strong first impression and his work was always excellent, so I started sharing my contacts with him and giving him assignments. I would send him a list of names of people to call. He would knock it out the next day and ask for more. At one point, he mentioned that he was going to write a book of interviews. Like his work on Boxingtalk, he jumped in head-first. Since meeting Doveed, I've seen him go from a fan, to a journalist, and now to a published author. I couldn't be more proud.

I don't recall any piece of literature that covers the sport as thoroughly as *Ringside*. This is a book that explores unchartered territory. There's an interview with Angelo Dundee, an iconic trainer who worked with some of the best fighters of all time. You've got Bob Arum, who has promoted everyone from Muhammad Ali to Oscar De La Hoya to Manny Pacquiao. But then there's an interview with Monte Barrett, a heavyweight who never won a world championship, but a true warrior who fought everybody. And then you've got Exum Speight, a guy with a record of 9–39, who fought all the champions when they were just getting started. The media never highlights people like that. This book has interviews with officials, announcers, managers, trainers, prospects, suspects, champions… We wouldn't have a sport if it wasn't for these people. The purpose of an interview is to ask questions that will give people the answers they want. But if you really go in depth, a reader will feel like they've gotten to know the person who has just been interviewed. That's what this book is—a chance to meet the people of the sport.

Greg Leon is a veteran journalist who has interviewed the sport's most notable figures and is the owner of Boxingtalk.com and CEO of Jean Pascal Promotions, based in Quebec.

Prologue:
Appreciating Fighters

The first fighter I ever idolized was Rocky Balboa, the Sylvester Stallone character from the *Rocky* movies. From there, I watched Mike Tyson, George Foreman, Evander Holyfield, and Oscar De La Hoya. After I saw the documentary *When We Were Kings* about Muhammad Ali's 1974 "Rumble in the Jungle" with George Foreman, I was hooked. From that point on, I began to develop a strong appreciation for, not just the greatest fighters in history, but everyone who has ever stepped inside the ring. At one of the first live fights I attended, I saw a welterweight with a record of 3–12 get absolutely hammered by an undefeated prospect who was padding his record. After the fight, I went up to the 3–12 fighter, told him what a great job he did, and bought him a Diet Pepsi. Nobody else approached this guy, but for some reason, I was just so proud of him.

In 2009, as a hobby, I began writing for Boxingtalk.com. I was inspired by the interviews of Boxingtalk publisher Greg Leon, whose work I had been following for years. After a while, I wanted to do an in depth interview with HBO boxing analyst Larry Merchant. I reached out to some people I knew in the boxing world to see if they could introduce me to Merchant, but nobody knew how to get in touch with him. One morning, I was at a gym, wearing a boxing-related t-shirt. Someone walked past me who was also wearing a boxing t-shirt. We started talking and it turned out that he was Merchant's son-in-law. I told him what I wanted to do and he offered to set up the interview over lunch. The interview with Merchant was so much fun that I started doing the same thing with other people in the boxing world, eventually finding myself writing this book.

These twenty-four interviews come from a variety of perspectives, yet they all have a similar theme. They offer strength of character, hope, and wisdom. They are stories of accidental involvement and humble beginnings that grew into something bigger than the people themselves could have ever imagined. You don't have to be a boxing fan to draw inspiration from the people of the sport, especially the fighters who inspire the "Rocky Balboa" in all of us. *Ringside* is a book that I would describe as incomplete, as there are countless people in boxing who have a story to tell. Some of these stories date back to the 1960s with the emergence of Muhammad Ali, whose profound impact on the sport is still felt to this day. Angelo Dundee, the trainer of Ali, was among the last of the living figures of that era. He passed away shortly after he was interviewed for this book, as did trainer/manger Emanuel Steward, cutman Joe Souza, and former cruiserweight/heavyweight Exum Speight. Regarding the state of boxing today, Dundee said, "Our world is a smaller place. The worst thing that can happen in this business is silence. Right now, boxing is having a lot of silence, but I'm not the least bit concerned. Boxing is always going to come back."

1

Larry Merchant:
Lunch with a Legend

While announcing fights on television, boxing analysts are often encouraged to follow an "agenda" set by the network. Certain fighters and upcoming events are sometimes presented in an overly positive and even artificial way. But every once in a while, someone comes along who speaks his mind and is willing to take risks, regardless of the powers that be. Born and raised in New York City, later relocating to Philadelphia, Pennsylvania, Larry Merchant is a former sportswriter and longtime boxing analyst for HBO. A graduate from Lafayette High School in Brooklyn, Merchant grew up at a time when the sport was heard on the radio, read in the headlines, and talked about by the general public. Like most fans, he was caught up in the drama that only a sport like boxing can bring. Merchant covered several historical fights over the years, notably the 1965 rematch between Muhammad Ali and Sonny Liston. A famous photograph was taken from that fight, featuring Ali standing over Liston, who had just been knocked down in the first round. In that photo, Merchant can be seen in the background with his mouth wide open in shock. Merchant retired from broadcasting in December 2012 after thirty-five years on HBO. He is known for his poetic use of words and his blunt honesty, regarded by many as one of the best television boxing analysts of all time. In March 2011, I met Larry Merchant for lunch at 17th Street Café in Santa Monica, California. At the time of this interview, Merchant was looking forward to his next assignment, which was the Victor Ortiz–Andre Berto fight, scheduled for April 16th.

What is your background in boxing? How did this sport work its way into your blood and become such a big part of your life?

I grew up in the '30s and '40s, and boxing and baseball were the dominant sports. I was and still am a baseball guy, but there was no way you could avoid boxing because it was in the air. Whether it was people talking about it or headlines in the newspaper… Boxing on the radio… Actual fights on the radio… I was among many in my generation who was allowed to stay up late for the first time to listen to the Louis-Schmeling rematch in 1938. I was seven years old. I tell people that Louis didn't want kids like me staying up

Television boxing analyst Larry Merchant (courtesy Patricia Stich).

late, so he knocked him out in the first round. Uncles would give you boxing gloves. Parents's friends would show you pictures of a boxer who was a distant relative. An uncle who had been an amateur fighter took me to my first fight at the Garden. But I was no more interested in boxing than I was in baseball and also football, but boxing was a part of my culture.

As I got into journalism, I realized how writers loved boxing because of the drama, because of how fighters like Johnson, and Dempsey, and Louis were, and how they were presented. These were huge, popular cultural events, because of the man-to-man aspects of the sport and how it revealed character. They were colorful guys to write about. The first fight I ever covered was the Robinson-Basilio fight at Yankee Stadium. The first *big* fight I should say. When I was in the Army, I wrote for *Stars and Stripes* in Europe, and I was assigned to cover fights between division teams in Germany. As I got into being a newspaper journalist, I started to cover boxing. I was in Philadelphia where there was a very deeply imbedded infrastructure of boxing. There were many fighters. When I covered that first major fight, I was sitting ringside with two of my heroes, Ernest Hemingway and Joe DiMaggio. They were right there. It was a glamorous world and a world that revealed not only the characters of the fighters, but the characters at ringside. It was a world that was written about by the most famous journalists of their time, as well as novelists like Hemingway. It was an important part of the world I grew up in.

On May 25th, 1965, Muhammad Ali had the rematch with Sonny Liston. He knocked him out in the first round, and there's the famous shot of Ali standing over Liston, which is one of the most well-known sports photos ever. In that photo, you can be seen in the background. What was going through your mind at that particular moment?

I was sitting at a place where you could actually see the punch land, so I never believed all of the suspicions of fixes, and all of the conspiracies. I saw the punch land. I was as stunned as everybody. It was a fight that was a very big event. There was a tremendous build up toward the fight and it ended in the first round, so everybody was stunned no matter what. I was surprised that he knocked Liston out, because Liston presented himself over time as a guy who seemed almost immune to being knocked out like that. He had never been knocked out like that. I was stunned, shocked, and you didn't mention that my mouth was wide open, which expressed that. It was a moment that will outlive me by hundreds if not thousands of years.

In March 1971, Muhammad Ali and Joe Frazier squared off in a battle of undefeated heavyweights, a fight that Frazier won via unanimous decision. At the time, Frazier was the reigning heavyweight champion. What do you recall about that particular event?

I remember it quite vividly. It was a very powerful visceral feeling. That visceral power was palpable in the arena. We're talking about a fight that was one of those larger than life and bigger than boxing fights. Two undefeated heavyweight champions. The turmoil of the '60s and '70s in terms of social change, civil rights, human rights, anti-war—they all seemed to be embodied by Ali. Ali was assigned the role of the anti-establishment figure and Frazier was the establishment figure. Frazier was admired and respected as a pure fighting guy. Nobody didn't like Frazier, but to some people, he was never going to be the hero that Ali was. To those people who saw Ali as the hero, they saw a threat in Joe Frazier. The build up was Ali building the fight and trying to provoke Frazier. What Ali did, as with most fighters—it's about themselves and their own fears and anxieties.

The world saw Ali as this kind of pied piper who had been unfairly treated in American society, which I agreed with. I once saw Ali perform in a play on Broadway, but he couldn't perform in Madison Square Garden. Frazier was the most honest of workers. I knew him from Philadelphia. I had invested in him. When Frazier was supported by Philadelphians who bought shares in him so that he could fight full time, I bought a share in him. I watched all of his fights. This was a collision of all kinds of forces. You could hardly be in the world and not know the fight was happening. In the Garden that night, you could almost light a match and the place would explode. It was filled with celebrities, important political personages, underworld figures… What makes it really so memorable is the fight itself. You

HBO commentators Larry Merchant (left), Jim Lampley, and Lennox Lewis, 2006 (courtesy Marty Rosengarten/RingsidePhotos.com).

couldn't have higher expectations for a fight and the fight exceeded those expectations, which is a rare thing.

In October 1974, Muhammad Ali defeated heavyweight champion George Foreman via eighth round knockout in Zaire, Africa, in "The Rumble in the Jungle." You were in Africa before the fight, and if I'm correct, you broke the story that the fight was going to be postponed due to a cut that Foreman suffered in sparring.

I sort of did break the story. I was at the sparring session when Foreman's eyelid was cut. I knew instantly and intuitively that the fight could not go on. I literally ran for about a half a mile to the communications center, because I knew that my paper at that time, the *New York Post*, that given the time difference, there could still be time to get it into that afternoon's paper. I got on the line and I called them and I told them. There was a plane in New York ready to take off, filled with newspaper people to cover the fight. I probably went out on a limb, but I didn't think it was much of a limb, to say that this fight couldn't happen. So much had been invested by the government and the promoters and such that they probably really felt that it would go on. They got their guys there, but it didn't go on. They had to wait six weeks. It was an amazing scene being in Africa, seeing Ali cavorting amongst the Africans and picking up their chants. Few people gave Ali a serious chance to win the fight. It was assumed that this was his last hurrah. I came home and when I tried to go back I was not allowed back in the country for the fight, primarily because I had written some stories including breaking the news that the fight couldn't go on. Maybe the government was upset with that and maybe Don King was upset with that as well.

After the Ali era, Larry Holmes took over as the heavyweight king. His reign wasn't as historically significant as Ali's, but many consider Holmes to be an underrated champion.

He had an impossible act to follow, obviously. He was always going to be compared to Ali, not just as a fighter but as a figure and a presence. That was a mismatch, but he was an outstanding fighter, a terrific fighter, and I don't think he's underrated anymore. I think he's regarded as one of the best heavyweights. That's pretty good. That's all you can do is be the best of your time and he was. He didn't have that crowd-pleasing style or appeal, and it also turned out to be the era of Sugar Ray Leonard and Tommy Hearns and Hagler and Duran. That was the center of boxing attention, but Holmes fought a lot and he was a respected figure. There were some very big fights. The fight with Gerry Cooney was a big fight. It was simply that Duran was well known as a great Latino who was on television and was about as good as it got as a lightweight champion. Leonard came shooting out of the '76 Olympics as a star and then they fought and fought again. Hagler worked his way through, and then Hearns exploded out. The Leonard-Hearns fight was like a big, huge heavyweight fight. It was one of those times where the heavyweight champion didn't blot out the world of boxing. That's why Holmes might not be considered on the level of legendary important heavyweight figures like Johnson, Dempsey, Louis, and Ali, but he was a damn good fighter.

After Larry Holmes, three heavyweights who really stood out were Mike Tyson, Evander Holyfield, and Lennox Lewis. When Tyson first came onto the scene, many considered him to be the best thing since Ali. What were your initial thoughts about Mike Tyson, and what is your final assessment now that his career is over?

Tyson had an aggressive, take-no-prisoner style like Dempsey, Marciano, and Frazier. He was electric, but there were questions, as with any fighter of that style, as to how he will do against a pure boxer and what happens if he walks into some punches. He was a sensation. He won the title when he was twenty, so for that generation of sports fans, they saw him as their heavyweight champion. For their generation, he could stand up as well as any of the famous champions of the past. They wanted to own him in that respect, and they still do, to some degree. He was not a very stable athlete off the field, which undoubtedly influenced some of the things that happened in the ring. He probably was never the same after he was upset by Buster Douglas and he never beat the top guys. He lost to Douglas, he lost to Holyfield twice, and he lost to Lewis. It's hard not to acknowledge the profound impact he had on the world that still exists out there. There was this undisciplined personality who was going to grow up and self destruct in front of our eyes. He was like a walking reality show with his antics and issues. He's still remembered fondly, understandably so. I'm not a ring historian and I'm not good at lists, but I don't think that those of us who have been around for a while consider him to be one of the best champions.

Of the three heavyweights I mentioned, Evander Holyfield was probably the most embraced by the fans, because he had such a tremendous heart. At this time, Holyfield has spent more years

Former four-time heavyweight champion Evander Holyfield, 2006 (courtesy Marty Rosengarten/ RingsidePhotos.com).

fighting past his prime than he did in his prime. Do you think all of these fights after the fact have hurt his legacy in any way?

There are many fighters, great fighters, who fought well beyond their prime. Sugar Ray Robinson is widely regarded and rightly regarded as the best fighter ever pound-for-pound. He lost seventeen fights, almost all of them well past his prime. My feeling about that is that fighters like all athletes are judged by what they do in their prime. I remind people that Babe Ruth hit something like .170 in his last season, but nobody remembers that or even cares. I think that that's how fighters will be remembered in history. What did they do in their primes? Sometimes they need to go on fighting, whether it's because they need to be on stage or they need the money. That's as old as prize fighting itself. You see it in all sports, particularly now when there's so much money. When a fighter like any athlete has built up his reputation and his marquee value simply because of his name and what he's accomplished, it can be very difficult to walk away.

Between Tyson, Holyfield, and Lewis, Lewis was the most dominant of this bunch. He had a lot of very good wins on his resume, though he never had a career defining fight. When he beat Holy-field and Tyson, they were both arguably past their primes. What are your thoughts on Lennox Lewis's legacy?

I think he was the best heavyweight of his time. Maybe Holyfield and Tyson were past their primes when he fought them, but so was he in a way. Since he wasn't a huge attraction, not everybody wanted to fight him. I thought Riddick Bowe was the best short-time heavy-weight champion in boxing history. He lost to Lewis in the Olympics and he didn't want to fight him as a pro. I think a case can be made that Lewis was the best of his time, which is all that a fighter can really do. He was from Britain. Born in Britain and raised in Canada, but he fought out of Britain. I think he lead a resurrection of boxing in Britain, which is still ongoing. There was a time when American heavyweights would swim across the Atlantic to fight European heavyweights, but Lewis changed that.

At this time, Wladimir and Vitali Klitschko are sitting on top of the heavyweight division. What are your thoughts on the Klitschko brothers and how do you think they would match up with heavyweight champions of the past?

First and foremost, they are a phenomenon that never existed before and probably won't exist in our lifetime again. Two brothers who have done what they've done and have maybe between them a 90% knockout ratio… That's an amazing phenomenon. They are the best of their time, regardless of whether Americans like them and whether we boxing people like their styles or not. How would they have done against the other champions of the past? Jack Dempsey weighed 188 pounds. Is it fair to say how he would have done against these athletic giants of the modern era? It's only what you do in your time. I can't compare the great running backs of the modern era to the great running backs of forty or fifty years ago. They're bigger and they're faster. I think they would probably be too big and too good for most of those guys, but that doesn't make them better fighters.

You mentioned how Jack Dempsey was a smaller heavyweight at 188 pounds. Nowadays, heavy-weight champions are 6'5", 6'6", 6'7", 250 pounds, where as they used to be 6'2" 215. Has the time come to create two divisions? Can a small heavyweight who is 210 pounds realistically com-pete with these modern day giants?

It would take an exceptional smaller heavyweight to beat the top guys, but I believe in the axiom that there ain't a horse that can't be rode or a rider that can't be throwed. Fighters get older and they become vulnerable and somebody comes along and shocks the world. That's the nature of boxing. I don't believe in two divisions, because I don't think people would support it. If a smaller heavyweight comes along who has stood out and

Wladimir (left) and Vitali Klitschko, the dominant heavyweight champions of their time, in 2005 (courtesy Marty Rosengarten/RingsidePhotos.com).

raised public expectations, then they're going to get their shot and one of these years or decades, one of them will do something unimaginable.

Switching gears, the welterweight showdown between Sugar Ray Leonard and Thomas Hearns in September 1981 is considered to be one of the most important fights in boxing history, right up there with Frazier-Ali I. Leonard won the fight via fourteenth-round TKO. What made this fight such an all-time classic?

What made Leonard and Hearns, as well as Duran and Hagler, was Leonard. He was an outstanding fighter who America fell in love with during the '76 Olympics. Television fell in love with him and watched him rise to the top, and here comes Tommy Hearns knocking everybody out and building a huge following in Detroit, where Joe Louis came out of. A fire built under them, and there again, the actual fight exceeded the highest expectations. They were two hungry-to-be-great champions colliding at the peak of their powers and giving us an unforgettable drama.

Another classic was the middleweight fight between Marvin Hagler and Thomas Hearns in April 1985. Hagler won the fight via third-round TKO. This fight seems to be the standard for what a great fight is all about.

I can sort of plug into the electricity that existed around the time of that fight. I find myself thinking of the day of the fight, hanging out at the pool at Caesar's Palace, and people were in kind of a blazed frenzy waiting for this to happen. The fight itself was one of those really rare occasions where two elite fighters, both of who had real abilities to box, decided to test each other's will and courage. Hagler thought because he was the naturally bigger man as a middleweight that he was just stronger and that he could impose his strength on Hearns, which he did. It was eight minutes when you couldn't breath. Again, it's one of those indelible dramas that stand out in boxing history.

Fights like Leonard-Hearns I and Hagler-Hearns were the classics of their day. What would you consider to be the classics of the last fifteen years?

I think the round robin of fights among Mexican featherweights. Morales-Barrera I was as intense as anything I've ever seen. Manny Pacquiao entered that picture, so we had kind of a featherweight version of the Leonard-Hagler-Hearns-Duran series. It was important culturally in a way that it brought to life vividly the domination of Latino and especially Mexican fighters. Before that, Oscar De La Hoya and Roy Jones, Jr., were important figures. De La Hoya was one of the transformative figures in boxing, because he was sort of the figure head for the Latino domination of the sport. He was an American gold medalist. He was sort of the next Ray Leonard in terms of the popularity that he was able to generate. Earlier in the '90s, Riddick Bowe had five amazing fights, three against Holyfield and two with Andrew Golota. Holyfield is one of the great fighters of our time or any time. He went from cruiserweight up to heavyweight. George Foreman became an important figure in his return to boxing. It was like the fans threw themselves a party having George Foreman back, lifting them on their shoulders and putting him into a position to have big fights. In the '90s, going into 2000, the first Mosley–De La Hoya fight was a really big deal in Los Angeles. Two young, outstanding Los Angeles area fighters… Those are the things that come into my head recently, but I probably missed something.

You mentioned Oscar De La Hoya and Roy Jones, Jr., as important figures of recent times. With everything said and done, what are your thoughts on Oscar De La Hoya's career?

I think he stands out as a guy who was a terrific fighter, who fought everybody, and who didn't duck anybody. He was mostly a transformative figure in terms of his extraordinary popularity. Maybe because of that popularity early on, the expectations of how great he would become were unrealistic, but he had a terrific career. Fighters become superstars because they have some appeal to the public. It's like what I would call the sixth tool in baseball. Five-tool ball players can hit, can run, can field, can throw… They're rare, but some of those guys have that sixth tool which is their magnetic performance that puts asses in seats. In boxing, there are many champions. God knows how many champions there are these days, but how many superstars are there? They are rare. They are the rarest thing in boxing. He was a superstar in terms of everything he did. Whether or not he was as good as that guy was, or the next guy was, he was a damn good fighter.

Some believe that Roy Jones, Jr., was unbeatable in his prime, while others feel that he was untested. What is your assessment of Jones's career?

He had extraordinary athletic ability. He was completely dominant for a number of years and would do things with his athletic ability and hand-speed that were incomparable.

Win or lose, Oscar De La Hoya was always a fan favorite, as was the case after his 2007 split decision loss to Floyd Mayweather, Jr. (courtesy Marty Rosengarten/RingsidePhotos.com).

He was also, as he moved up in weight, kind of a cautious fighter who wasn't interested in closing the show in a crowd pleasing fashion, but for what he did in his prime, beating Bernard Hopkins, beating James Toney, and anybody else… Pretty damn good. There were some people who thought so highly of him that it got carried away. When he got knocked out twice in a row, even though he was a little past his best, I think it brought him down to Earth, and it brought some fans down to Earth as well, as far as where he stood. But there's no denying how good he was in his prime.

The mega fight between welterweights Manny Pacquiao and Floyd Mayweather is this generation's equivalent to Ali-Frazier I and Leonard-Hearns I. At this time, the fight hasn't materialized, and there are doubts that it ever will. Who has the better resume at this point? And if both fighters were at their absolute best, who do you believe would come out on top?

I don't think there's any doubt that Pacquiao has the more impressive resume. In every division he's fought, he fought virtually the best guy who was available. Not only did he not duck any opponents, but he went out of his way to find guys to not duck. I think arguably he's this generation's Henry Armstrong. He's a guy who moved up in weight divisions as a pro. I say as a pro because I don't think it's widely known that when both of them were sixteen, they weighed the same amount, 112 or 115. Pacquiao was a pro and Mayweather was an amateur. Now, Mayweather is actually bigger than Pacquiao, who is really 140 pounds. For whatever reason, Mayweather, in my mind, wasn't eager to make the fight with Pacquiao. What would have happened if they both fought? I think Mayweather would have been favored, because he is a defensive wizard in a style where he has been successful in turning every climactic event into an anti-climactic event. He's brilliant at what he does and I think he would be hard to beat, but if anybody could beat him, it probably would be Pacquiao. No matter what would happen in the fight, in my view, Pacquiao has had a greater career. There are too many fighters Mayweather found a reason not to fight when he could have or should have fought them.

In no particular order, who do you consider to be among the best fighters of all time?

I think Ali and Robinson stand above everybody. As great athletes, as giant figures in their time, as important cultural figures… Robinson is the quintessential fighter of the Jazz Age, and Ali of his time. There have been many other great fighters. Henry Armstrong certainly stands out. At a time when there were thousands of fighters, Armstrong was arguably the best fighter from featherweight to middleweight. He held three titles at one time, which today would be like six titles at one time. How good is that? In boxing history, figures like Johnson and Dempsey and Louis were profoundly important and great athletes. I don't know how to separate them. Harry Greb was arguably one of the best middleweights. I've never seen him fight and I don't know how to put that in context. There was a British fighter named Ted "Kid" Lewis who started as a fourteen-year-old bantamweight, became the welterweight champion of the world, was fighting the top light heavyweights of the world by the time he was through, and had almost three hundred fights. Where do you put that? In the modern era, I don't think anybody was much better than Duran and Leonard. I have a personal favorite in Carlos Ortiz, the great lightweight champion. Who knows? Maybe "Canelo" will be among them some day.

What do you consider to be the best fights of all time? What are your personal favorites?

I've seen so many, but my mind immediately goes to Hagler-Hearns and Leonard-Hearns I. Those were great fights and melodramas, but where do you put the Gatti-Ward trilogy? Those guys may not have been the best fighters in the world, but they had hearts

Emanuel Steward presents Larry Merchant with a plaque at Merchant's 2009 induction into the International Boxing Hall of Fame; announcer to right is unidentified (courtesy Bret Newton—Threat-Photo.com/Pound4Pound.com).

that were almost too big for their bodies. The Bowe-Holyfield trilogy was amazing for the drama of each fight. The tenth round in the first fight, the "Fan Man" in the second fight, the knockdowns in the third fight… Floyd Patterson and Ingemar Johansson fought fourteen rounds in their three fights and there were just as many or more knockdowns. Were they the best fights? I don't know. I've seen nothing fiercer than the first Morales-Barrera fight, and there's been nothing quite like the Ali-Frazier fights, particularly the first and the third. But there have been too many. I've lived too long to either single them out or list them.

2

Ray Charles Leonard:
Coffee with Sugar

In boxing, the nickname "Sugar" originated from "Sugar" Ray Robinson, a former welterweight and middleweight champion, who fought professionally from 1940 to 1965. Many consider Robinson to be the greatest fighter of all time. His nickname is considered sacred—something that only fighters with special qualities should be allowed to use. Born and raised in Wilmington, North Carolina, eventually moving to Palmer Park, Maryland, Ray Charles Leonard, also known as "Sugar" Ray, carried on the tradition. Having won a gold medal at the 1976 Olympic Games and having captured world titles at welterweight, junior middleweight, super middleweight, and light heavyweight, he is one of the best fighters to ever put on the gloves. Like his idol Muhammad Ali, Leonard had Angelo Dundee in his corner for most of his career, notably during his 1981 welterweight unification bout with Thomas Hearns. Going into the thirteenth round, it was anyone's fight. In between rounds, Dundee told Leonard, "You're blowing it now, son! You're blowing it!" Leonard flipped the switch and won the fight via fourteenth-round TKO in one of the most dramatic moments in boxing history. Sugar Ray Leonard, Thomas Hearns, Marvin Hagler, and Roberto Duran are four legendary fighters who faced one another in a number of memorable battles throughout the '80s. Leonard holds victories over all three of his fellow competitors and he was named "Fighter of the Decade" for the 1980s, eventually retiring in 1997 with a record of 36–3–1, 25 KO's. In November 2011, I called Ray Charles Leonard and had coffee with "Sugar." At the time of this interview, he was promoting his book *The Big Fight: My Life In and Out of the Ring*.

When did you first put on the gloves? How old were you and what were the circumstances?
When I first started boxing, I was probably seven or eight years of age. I went to the gym mostly out of curiosity. I put the gloves on and I took them off real fast. I wasn't the kind of kid who liked to get punched on. Once I felt the power of those punches, I quit and I didn't start back till I was fourteen. My older brother Roger introduced me to boxing the second time. Like most kids who will follow their brothers anywhere, I followed mine, and it just happens that I followed him into a boxing gym. I was there for pretty much the

rest of my life. It was one of those things where I found *it, it* found me, and we found each other. I had to convince my parents to let me do it, because I was such a quiet kid. I was such an introverted kid. As I recall, in my first fight, my first boxing event, I was nervous and it was kind of a life and death experience. But once I got through it and I won, it was everything to me. Boxing was my safe haven. It was that sport that was like a counselor, like a teacher, like a protector. I look back and I try to figure out how all this happened. All I know is that it was a blessing and every time I went to the gym, I felt better about myself.

From what I understand, you weren't a violent person outside the ring. What was it that compelled you to fight?

I think you just have to have a certain mentality. You have to have a certain edge to be a successful fighter, to be a great fighter. It takes a certain soul and spirit to take it to the next level. If you talk to people who know me, they'll tell you I'm very non-confrontational. I'm quiet and almost always typically shy, but in the ring, I could flip that switch and do my thing. I think it was just inside me. It was an instinct. It was a certain quality I had that boxing stimulated for me.

When did you get the name "Sugar" and how did it come about?

A few years after I started boxing, I was getting better and people would say how good my left hook was or my jab or my hand speed. I was getting a lot of compliments on my physical attributes, and I started to read and watch films of other boxers. Muhammad Ali, "Sugar" Ray Robinson… When I saw "Sugar" Ray Robinson, that's when I knew.

So, you are a self-proclaimed "Sugar"?

Yes. I'm a self proclaimed "Sugar." I gave it to myself. When I met "Sugar" Ray Robinson, I said, "Sir, can I use your name?" He said, "It would be an honor if you use my name." It was a bold move, but when the real "Sugar" said it was okay, that's all that mattered.

In 1976, in Montreal, Quebec, Canada, you were on a very successful Olympic Boxing Team. What stands out in your mind about that experience?

That Olympic Boxing Team was so special. It was just an amazing honor to participate. As a team, we took home five gold medals. The general consensus was that we had a small chance to bring home just one, but that team with Leon and Michael Spinks, and Howard Davis, and Leo Randolph—it was amazing what we did that year.

Former four-division world champion and Olympic gold medalist Ray Charles Leonard (courtesy Marty Rosengarten/RingsidePhotos.com).

From what I understand, you turned professional as a way to support your family. Tell me about that decision and what your intentions were.

My friend and mentor Janks Morton knew how badly off we were financially. He knew my dad was in the hospital, and he knew how much it bothered me that we didn't have any money. He saw the desperation and frustration in my face and he said, "Son, if you want to make a difference and help your family, you can turn pro and make some money." That's all he had to say. I had no intentions of becoming a professional fighter. I had heard so many horrible stories of fighters being taken advantage of and mismanaged. I didn't want to do that, but I *had* to do that. It wasn't because of my love of fighting. I loved my amateur career, because of the Olympics and what have you, but I had no love and passion for professional boxing. I did it out of necessity.

At what point did Angelo Dundee begin training you?

Once I decided to turn professional, we put together a team and Angelo was a major asset of that team. I was a big fan of Muhammad Ali and all you heard about was Ali and Angelo Dundee. Angelo was his trainer, so that was a big time feather in my cap. For me as a young man, it didn't get any better than that. I met Muhammad when I was nineteen years old. I gave him an award at this ceremony when I was living in Washington, D.C. I introduced him and he hugged me and gave me advice. He asked me if I was going to turn pro. I told him that I wasn't going to, but he said that if I did change my mind and turn professional, there's one guy I had to get in my corner and that's Angelo Dundee. He said that he has the right connections and the right complexion. Those were his exact words. Angelo Dundee was such an integral part of my career. We had a connection. He didn't have to say much to me. I could just look into his eyes and I would know what he was thinking. He always had the perfect sound bites. He said just enough to get me started, but not frighten me or discourage me. Like when I fought Tommy Hearns, he said, "You're blowing it, son!" He said the right thing at the right time. Right then, I knew I had to pick it up. I had to be the man. I had to want it more than Tommy Hearns, and that right there is something that separates contenders from champions. It's the one who has more desire.

In June 1980, you defended your welterweight title (that was captured by defeating Wilfred Benitez via fifteenth-round TKO) against Roberto Duran, a fight you lost via unanimous decision. This was your first loss as a professional. What stands out in your mind about that fight?

I watched Roberto Duran fight when I was still an amateur boxer. I saw how good he was back then and I never could fathom that I would one day fight him. But three and a half years after I turned pro, there I was fighting the same guy I looked upon when I was a kid. It was a huge fight in Montreal for a ton of money. I was no longer thinking about how I'm going to pay for my father's hospital bills, I'm thinking about what house I'm going to buy next. I was experiencing the fame and the fortune and everything that comes with fighting a guy of this caliber. I was in awe of the situation.

Was this the first time as a pro that you were perceived as an underdog?

Yes, it was, but as far as the odds were concerned, it was kind of close. I had matured by then. I was a welterweight and Duran was coming up to my division. People thought I was faster and stronger, but it was a big fight and I just lost perspective. I got suckered in. I lost the fight based on the whole appearance. He got in my face and talked trash and I

Ray Charles Leonard (right) goes to war with Wilfred Benitez en route to a fifteenth-round TKO victory in their 1979 fight (courtesy Steve Lott, Boxing Hall of Fame Las Vegas).

had never experienced that before. I was fighting at a whole new level. It was a huge crowd and it was just mind blowing. That's when you realize that boxing isn't just physical. It's psychological. He was a bully and he was pushing and shoving at the press conferences. He cursed me out and he cursed my wife out. He got under my skin. Looking back, if I had a little more poise and a little more experience with that kind of trash talking, I would have handled it

Former four-division world champion Roberto Duran, who gave Leonard his first loss as a professional, shown here in 2005. Leonard and Duran fought three times, with Leonard winning twice (courtesy Marty Rosengarten/RingsidePhotos.com).

better. But I was a twenty-four- year-old kid fighting a guy like Duran who was already a legend. He knew the tricks of the trade. He knew how he could get into a young guy's head and it worked.

You took an immediate rematch with Duran in November 1980, which was the famous "No Mas" fight, a fight you won via eighth-round TKO, because he elected not to continue.

What happens with most fighters when they lose, it takes a little therapy to get them back. They lose a little confidence and their self -esteem drops. But with me, after I fought Duran, I knew I could do better. I knew I could out-box him as long as I didn't get suckered in, so I went out there and frustrated him to the point where he just threw his hands up without realizing the ramifications it would have on his legacy. I don't speak Spanish, but I later learned that "No mas" means "No more." I could tell what was happening by his expressions and by the referee's actions. It was really crazy. The infamous "No mas" is one of those things they talk about all the time. It's become a cliché, the butt of all jokes.

The fight that really defines your career came against Thomas Hearns in September 1981, a welterweight unification bout that you won via fourteenth-round TKO.

The fight with Tommy Hearns was without question my most defining moment. In my life, in my career… At the time, Tommy was considered so unbeatable. My own brother didn't even think I was going to win. People were afraid, because Tommy had displayed so much power and destruction. He was 6'1", 147 pounds. He was a freak of nature. He was an anomaly. When I'm challenged and viewed as an underdog, I tend to soar. I tend to beat the odds. I tend to defy logic, because that's what drives me. That's what stimulates me. I trained so hard for that fight. I had sparring partners who were clones of Tommy Hearns.

They were all tall guys who had fast left jabs and powerful rights. That was the prerequisite of the fighters I sparred with. I prepared for that fight like it was my last fight. Walking into that ring, I was so confident that I was going to win. It was one of the biggest fights ever. It was a fight that challenged me to the utmost. I was sitting in that corner and Angelo Dundee said to me, "You're blowing it!" For that fight, if I wanted to win, I had to go through the pain. That's what was asked of me and I answered the question.

After the fight with Hearns, you drifted in and out of boxing and seemed to be indecisive about your career. What was going through your mind at that time?

That fight with Tommy Hearns just took so much out of me. You can't reach that level too many times. It will take the life from you, physically, mentally, and spiritually. You can only go to the well so many times, because it takes its toll. I loved it though. I ate that up. I loved that challenge, but that's when I was diagnosed with a partial detached retina. I was twenty-five, twenty-six. I sat out for a couple of years and went through a state of limbo. There's no book, there's no manual to tell you how a man can go from a truly humble beginning to all of a sudden find himself on the cover of *Sports Illustrated* and *Ring Magazine* and then have it all end. I was a boxer who was at the top of his game and all of a sudden it was over. I didn't know how to deal with that. I tried the best I could with whatever I could use, whether it was cocaine or alcohol or women. I tried every conceivable thing to pamper the pain and suffering I was feeling. I just didn't know what to do at the time.

From left: James Toney, Jackie Kallen, Ray Charles Leonard, and Roy Jones, Jr. Jones and Toney eventually fought in a battle that would determine who the best boxer in the world was, a position that Leonard once held (courtesy Jackie Kallen).

Your final career-defining moment came in April 1987 when you faced and defeated middleweight champion Marvin Hagler in a fight you won via split decision.

Nobody thought this fight was doable. To go from welterweight to middleweight is not that easy, especially with a guy like Hagler. Before that fight, I was doing commentary for HBO, so I was always at ringside, watching Hagler and Hearns and Duran. When I sat ringside, I studied these guys. I knew their styles. I was sitting there two feet away from them. The more I saw Hagler, the more I thought I had the style to beat him. Hagler was a beast. He was strong and powerful and ambidextrous. When I saw him fight Tommy Hearns in that three-round destruction mode, I said that there was no way I would fight him. One night, I watched him from ringside when he fought John Mugabi, and I saw certain things that I could take advantage of. When I announced my decision to fight him, people figured I had just taken too many punches. A lot of the governing bodies wouldn't sanction the fight. Only the WBC did. If the WBC hadn't sanctioned it, it wouldn't have happened.

Ray Charles Leonard, 1979 (courtesy Jackie Kallen).

Everybody thought it would be a mismatch and that it would hurt boxing. I understood their concern, but I wanted the fight. I believed I had the magic it would take to beat a guy like Marvin Hagler, so I went in there and I did my thing.

3

Bob Arum:
Inside the Iron Gates

Top Rank is one of the premier promotional companies in the fight game. Over the years, they have promoted several legendary fighters, including Alexis Arguello, Joe Frazier, Carlos Monzon, Larry Holmes, Ray Mancini, Terry Norris, James Toney, Floyd Mayweather, Jr., and Erik Morales. Ironically, this company was founded by a man who grew up knowing very little about boxing. Born and raised in Brooklyn, New York, Bob Arum was once an attorney for the United States Department of Justice. In the 1970s, his life changed courses when he was introduced to Muhammad Ali. He wound up becoming Ali's lawyer and promoter, eventually starting Top Rank and finding himself promoting some of the biggest fights in history. In the 1980s, Arum promoted classic match-ups with several high profile fighters, including Sugar Ray Leonard, Marvin Hagler, Thomas Hearns, and Roberto Duran. In the 1990s, he handled the comeback of George Foreman and guided Oscar De La Hoya to superstar status. In the early 2000s, he promoted Manny Pacquiao who went on to become the face of boxing. Arum came along around the same time fellow promoter Don King was making his mark. Arum and King became rivals over the years, but they gradually developed a mutual respect for one another, as both men knew how to promote a fight. In July 2011, I arrived at Bob Arum's house in Beverly Hills, California, pressed a buzzer, and was allowed inside the iron gates. At the time of this interview, Arum's key fighters were Manny Pacquiao, Miguel Cotto, and Julio Cesar Chavez, Jr.

What is your background in boxing and what led you to become a promoter?
    I was a lawyer and I was with the United States Justice Department. When I left the justice department, I went into private practice. I was introduced to Muhammad Ali and I became his promoter and his lawyer. Up to that point, I had absolutely no interest in boxing and had never seen a boxing match. My early experience with boxing was only promoting Muhammad Ali and I had very little interest in the sport, but gradually, I became enmeshed in the sport. That was in the 1970s. I remember particularly with the success of the 1976 U.S. Olympic Team in Montreal—that led to a series of matches I did in the '80s with Hagler, Leonard, Hearns, and Duran. I put together some fights with some of these guys in the

lighter weight classes and I eventually handled the comeback of George Foreman, which segued into the career of Oscar De La Hoya. Finally, after promoting many, many fights in the '90s and at the turn of the century, I hooked up with Manny Pacquiao and I now promote Pacquiao as my major fighter.

In front of the cameras, Muhammad Ali was a comedian and jokester. What was he like behind the scenes?

Behind the scenes, he wasn't a jokester. He was a great, great promoter, but he

Boxing promoter and Top Rank founder Bob Arum (courtesy Marty Rosengarten/RingsidePhotos.com)

also had an underlying political message which resonated. At first, people were antagonistic towards him, but people later came around. He opposed the Vietnam War when many people didn't. He was in the forefront of the Black Power Movement. Muhammad Ali was a very, very serious guy for all of his antics. He was and still is a very good and caring person.

In 1978, Ali's fight with Leon Spinks was a unique match-up, given the fact that Spinks only had seven professional fights under his belt. It turned out to be a historic event, because Spinks pulled off the upset and won a split decision. Tell me how this match-up came about.

Leon was a Marine, he was an incredible talent, and he was also very self-destructive. We realized that if we didn't get him into a major match very quickly, he would self-destruct against a secondary opponent. When the opportunity came, Ali was looking for an easy fight, Spinks was an Olympic champion, and so we made that fight and Spinks got the upset. In that era, I had this kid from New York, Davey Moore, who won the junior middleweight championship in only his ninth professional fight. Asian fighters, Japanese and Thai fighters win titles when they've had very little professional experience. The Cuban kids, because of their great amateur background, don't have to have a lot of professional fights before they can fight for a title, so it wasn't all that rare for a younger fighter to win a title.

You and fellow promoter Don King were both making your mark right around the same time. From what I understand, it wasn't always friendly.

King operated differently from the way I operated. We came from different backgrounds, but I always recognized, and still do recognize, that King was a great promoter. King can stir up an event. He knows how to promote. He did a number of things that I wouldn't do, but again, we came from different backgrounds.

Bob Arum and fellow promoter Don King, 2006 (courtesy Marty Rosengarten/RingsidePhotos.com).

King was once quoted as saying that the two of you were "close to fisticuffs." Is there any truth to this or is that just an exaggeration?

There were a number of times when we came close to a physical confrontation, but I wouldn't say fisticuffs. King was a lot bigger than me, but yeah, we had a couple of incidents that got a little out of hand. There was one incident that I can recall where he was trying to get in the ring after the Hagler-Leonard fight. I wouldn't let him and I grabbed him and pulled him down, and there was almost a physical confrontation, which a security guard broke up. But generally, it didn't go to that extreme.

In April 1985, you promoted the fight between middleweight champion Marvin Hagler and Thomas Hearns, a fight that Hagler won via third-round TKO. What do you recall about that particular promotion and the fight itself?

For the first time in history, we did a two-week tour of the United States. We had two planes and we flew all over. I think we did close to twenty-five cities in two weeks. With that type of itinerary, the fighters got on each other's nerves, particularly Hagler who had a very short fuse. I remember in St. Louis, they almost went at each other, until we broke it up and told them they were being stupid because they wouldn't get paid this way. By the time the bell rang at Caesar's Palace for their fight, they hated each other. There was going

Marvin Hagler hammers Thomas Hearns on the ropes en route to a third-round TKO victory in their 1985 fight (courtesy Steve Lott, Boxing Hall of Fame Las Vegas).

to be no boxing and no playing around. They just went after each other. Hagler was wide open and Tommy, who was a tremendous puncher, hit him with his best shot. Hagler was stunned for a second, but he kept coming. At that point, they knew the fight was over.

You promoted the April 1987 fight between Marvin Hagler and Sugar Ray Leonard, a fight that Leonard won via split decision. Even people outside the boxing world knew that the fight was happening.

We hit the right chord, and the chord was that we equated Leonard as the yuppie and the guy with the silver spoon because he had won a gold medal, while Hagler was the blue collar guy who had gone up unrecognized and fought his way up through preliminary fights and so forth. That type of symbolism caught on. It wasn't like it was today, because Leonard and Hagler were known to the public because they had been on network television so often. The whole country, the whole world was caught up with that fight.

You promoted George Foreman shortly after he began his "second career," which lasted from 1987 to 1997. What led you to promote Foreman during his comeback?

When Foreman came to see me, I hadn't promoted any of his earlier fights. He had about a ten year layoff when he became a pastor. He called me one day, while I was doing ESPN shows. He wanted me to promote him and put him on ESPN. He had just started his comeback, but Foreman was horrible his first time around. He was just a terrible person and I didn't want anything to do with him. I told him, "George, I don't really want to promote you." Again, I had no ties to him, but he said, "Well, I'm coming out to see you." I was doing the Hearns-Barkley fight and he came out on his own dime. He was sweet as hell and I figured he was conning me. Finally, I realized that I had a show on ESPN prior to Christmas, and that's a horrible time to put on a boxing show. I said, "Ok, George, I'll put you on that show." I figured we'd do no business anyway, so what difference did it make? But lo and behold, Foreman sold the place out.

I was sort of intrigued by him, so we linked up together and we did a lot of crazy things. George was embarrassed about his weight and I told him to make a joke of it, so we started serving him hamburgers before the fights and we got him a lot of commercials that way. That led to the Foreman Grill, which made him a fortune. Gradually, he worked himself back into contention. After he knocked out Gerry Cooney, we got him a fight with Evander Holyfield and he gave Holyfield a very, very good fight. He wouldn't quit. He was a huge attraction on HBO. Finally, we put him in with Michael Moorer and he knocked Moorer out after losing every single round. He became the heavyweight champion of the world again and it was a marvelous story. George demonstrated to me that he wasn't a con man. He had really become a great and caring person.

Lucia Rijker fought professionally from 1996 to 2004 and she is considered one of the best female boxers ever. You took a gamble when you promoted some of her fights in the sense that women's boxing doesn't have a strong track record for commercial success. How do you feel about it now?

Former six-division world champion and Olympic gold medalist Oscar De La Hoya, who rose to stardom under the Top Rank banner, 2007 (courtesy Marty Rosengarten/ RingsidePhotos.com).

What was demonstrated to me is that there is no future in women's boxing and that it can't be commercialized. Men look at it sort of as a diversion. I don't think there's any type of market for women's boxing. We gave Lucia a few fights. She had a nice personality. A lot of these women boxers are terrific. Christy Martin is a terrific person. Mia St. John is a terrific person and was very glamorous, but there's no market for it.

In the 1990s and in to the turn of the century, Oscar De La Hoya was boxing's biggest star. Tell me a little about when you first signed De La Hoya and how his success took off from there.

Oscar De La Hoya was the only American Olympian in Barcelona to win a gold medal. He had a very compelling story, because his mother had just died and he dedicated the medal to her. In addition, he was a very, very good looking, charismatic kind of kid, and he was bilingual. The Hispanic population in the United States was growing by leaps and bounds, and because Oscar was bilingual, he could play to this emerging

Hispanic audience, while at the same time appeal to the general, English-speaking audience. Oscar was perfect for that. He was a very good fighter and he could have been better, but it's very, very hard when guys have a lot of success. It's hard to remain as dedicated as they were when they first started. Oscar fell victim to that, which is understandable, because he came from a poor background and suddenly he had great riches. He took his foot off the gas pedal a little too much. In my opinion, he didn't reach his potential. He was a very good fighter and he had a lot of talent, but it's hard when you're making that money and you see for the first time the nightclubs, the women, the golf… It's hard to be as dedicated as you need to be to remain a world class athlete. That distinguishes him from someone like Bernard Hopkins, who doesn't have near the talent as Oscar, but Bernard is in training every day of his life.

How does a boxer become a superstar? Is it something the fighter either has or doesn't have?

Certain athletes, who are very good, appeal to the public or appeal to big segments of the public. Oscar had a great appeal to women because of his good looks and because of his personality. We built on that and we built on his Hispanic base and people became intrigued by him. Floyd Mayweather is looked upon by most of the public as being, I don't want to say a thug, but being a little rough around the edges. People are intrigued by the way Floyd acts and a lot of people tune in to his fights hoping that he gets beat. A lot of people watched Mike Tyson because he was so fearsome as a puncher and he intimidated his opponents, but once Buster Douglas knocked him out, his ability to instill fear in an opponent was diminished. Tyson kept trying and his behavior turned out to be very bizarre, so people were clamoring to see him. Part of it was that they wanted to see him get beat and part of it was that they realized that anything could happen. It turned out to be a freak show. Manny Pacquiao attracted an entirely different audience to boxing. He attracted the ninety million people who live in the Philippines and the fifteen million Filipinos who live around the world, including the six million in the United States. From that fan base, the general population in the United States became intrigued with him because of the kind of person he was, the fact that he ran for congress, the fact that he became a congressmen, and because of the humble way that he conducts himself. He became a big cross-over star. Around the world, he's now the face of boxing. It's all different.

As you said, Manny Pacquiao is now the face of boxing. Pacquiao is a man who literally went from rags to riches. Did you ever imagine that he would get so big?

Saying that Manny Pacquiao went from rags to riches really understates the case. Manny lived in a cardboard shack on the streets of Manila for many years. This was abject poverty that American kids, no matter what their circumstances are, don't experience. If I had known him then, I would have said that there's no chance. When I met Manny Pacquiao, he was well on his way as a good, exciting fighter. Not as good as he became, but he was still very, very good. I can't answer the question as to if I would have believed this would have happened, because I wasn't around at the beginning. If I was, I wouldn't have believed it.

Fighters leave legacies, trainers leave legacies, and as a promoter, you have created a legacy of your own. How do you want to be remembered when all is said and done?

Manny Pacquiao, Bob Arum, and Joshua Clottey, surrounded by Dallas Cowboys Cheerleaders at a press conference for the 2010 Pacquiao-Clottey fight (courtesy Marty Rosengarten/Ringside Photos.com).

I have enjoyed doing what I've done. I have enjoyed putting on the events. As long as I keep doing this and for many years after, I'm sure Top Rank will continue, but to say that it's my legacy is stretching it a little bit. It's the fighters who make the fights. I've been fortunate to promote some of the great fighters and some of the great fights, but as far as legacy is concerned, it doesn't concern me. When you're dead you're dead. When people look back at the Hagler-Hearns fight, they're going to look at Hagler and they're going to look at Hearns, and maybe they'll look at the corner people, but probably not. They'll probably just look at the two fighters. They won't remember who the referee was, and they won't remember who the promoter was, and that's the way it should be. That's exactly the way it should be.

4

Naazim Richardson:
The City of Brotherly Love

The city of Philadelphia has a long tradition of boxing. Many fighters from Philly have made their mark on the sport, including Joe Frazier, George Benton, and Matthew Saad Muhammad to name a few. Just as this city is known for producing great fighters, it is also known to have many great trainers, or "teachers," if you will. Born and raised in Philadelphia, Pennsylvania, Naazim Richardson, also known as "Brother Naazim," is one of the city's key trainers, as he has spent several years working with Philadelphia boxing icon Bernard Hopkins, among other top fighters in the sport. Richardson was with Hopkins for Hopkins's twelfth-round TKO victory over Felix Trinidad, a historical event that took place at Madison Square Garden just weeks after the devastation of 9/11. Richardson learned about working with fighters by watching the great Philadelphia trainers before him, particularly English "Bouie" Fisher, who brought Richardson in to Team Hopkins. The time Richardson spent learning under the top trainers of Philadelphia has served him well, as was demonstrated in January 2009 when he prepared Shane Mosley for his bout with Antonio Margarito, a fight that Mosley won via ninth-round TKO. Before the fight, Richardson discovered plaster in the handwraps of Margarito, which was one of the most shocking and controversial incidents of the modern era. In addition to Hopkins and Mosley, Richardson has also worked with his sons Rock and Tiger Allen, Karl Dargan, Steve Cunningham, Miguel Cotto, Beibut Shumenov, Ivan Robinson, Travis Kauffman, Buster Drayton, and Nate "Mister" Miller, among others. In July 2011, I called Naazim Richardson to discuss his background in the City of Brotherly Love. At the time of this interview, Richardson's key fighter Bernard Hopkins was set to face Chad Dawson on October 15th.

What is your background in boxing and what led you to become a trainer?
I come from the fighting city of Philadelphia. I fought as an amateur and I've been around the gyms for years, watching legendary trainers like English "Bouie" Fisher, Harold McCall, Al Fennell, Stan Williams and all these guys that raised fighters. As I moved around in the gyms and started helping out, they started telling me to go talk to fighters. I was looking at them like, "Are you sure you want *me* to talk to them?" These guys had trained

31

eyes, and when they had confidence in me, it made me believe I could do it. I started reaching out and helping fighters, and I had the privilege of working with guys like Buster Drayton and Nate "Mister" Miller. I saw Nate develop from an amateur fighter to a world champion. The time I spent working with them guys was like an internship you develop in Philadelphia, and that love just fuels that boat.

English "Bouie" Fisher was a legendary Philadelphia trainer who passed away in June 2011. Tell me about what Fisher meant and still means to Philadelphia boxing.

Bouie Fisher was a great man. He was bigger than boxing. I learned more about family and patience from Bouie than I did about boxing. Bouie would teach you about demeanor and about how to conduct yourself. He was just a good human being, man. Philadelphia is a fighting city. I tell these young guys at the gym that their reputation as Philadelphia fighters was crafted by guys like Bouie Fisher. All we can do is try to live up and add to that legacy.

Fisher started out as Bernard Hopkins's head trainer. How did you become involved in the Hopkins camp?

I started working with Bernard around '96 or '97. Bouie would ask me to work the mitts with him and everything else. He kept telling me, "I want you to start helping me with this guy and going out to the fights with us." I'd be making excuses, "No, I can't. My job, my kids…" He was like, "No, man. You know what you're doing. I want you to come with us." To be honest, I wasn't sure I could. But I trusted him and started helping.

Boxing trainer Brother Naazim Richardson (courtesy Marty Rosengarten/ RingsidePhotos.com).

In September 2001, Bernard Hopkins defeated Felix Trinidad via twelfth-round TKO in a middleweight unification bout. Leading up to the fight, there was a lot of animosity between Hopkins and Trinidad, followed by the tragedy of 9/11, and also followed by a controversial situation surrounding Trinidad's handwraps on the night of the fight. What do you recall about this time?

Bernard was focused on the middleweight title. That was key. We had camp out in Las Vegas, and just the discipline of being out in the desert and wanting to win the middleweight tournament with Felix Trinidad, William Joppy, and Keith Holmes—he was just absorbed. Bernard wasn't a factor in that tournament and he wanted to prove everybody wrong. They called us to have a press conference in New York. I walk up on the press conference and Bernard grabbed the Puerto Rican flag and threw it on the ground. He was supposed to go to Puerto Rico after that. I was like, "Man, when you go to Puerto Rico, they're gonna try to

From left: James Akhir Fisher (Bouie's son), Naazim Richardson, English "Bouie" Fisher, and Bernard Hopkins at a press conference for Hopkins's 2002 fight with Carl Daniels (courtesy James Akhir Fisher).

kill you!" I wasn't gonna go, but I made the trip at the last minute, because I felt like I had to look out for my guy. We were in Miami and I had to go buy clothes at a Walmart, just so I had something to wear the next day. We got there and I said, "Bernard, don't throw no flag down. We're in Puerto Rico." He said, "You think I'm crazy?" We're there at the press conference and he wound up grabbing the flag from Don King and throwing it down again in front of all those people. The people went off in that place, man! They started tearing up the joint, tearing our limo up, and tearing up everything else. I'll never forget the energy. Right after that, they were trying to get us out of Puerto Rico and get us to the airport. Cars were literally following us along the expressway, making gestures at us and driving alongside us. One guy was giving us so many fingers I wondered how he was steering the car! It was a crazy sight.

We got out of there, got the camp going, and went to New York on September 7th. We got set up and we were training at a gym about a block away from the Twin Towers. On the morning of the 11th, my son Rock came in and said, "Yo! There's something going on up the street. There's all this smoke." I went outside to look and that's when the second plane came and hit the tower. I said, "Whoooooa!" Nobody knew what was going on at the time. It was just chaotic. We got back to the room and got back downstairs, and word started going around about what happened and that it was Muslims behind it. I'm a Muslim and I was wearing my kufi. This man runs up and says, "Take your kufi off! They're attacking Muslims! Take your kufi off!" My sons were with me and they were wearing their kufis, too. I had told my sons their whole life that they've got nothing to be afraid of, because Allah protects us when we've done nothing wrong. I didn't take my kufi off, because I had to let them know that. We got that squared away and we got up there with crazy Bernard, and do you know what he says? Bernard says, "Let's go to the gym and train. They're not gonna bomb the gym." The plane crashes into a building and he's thinking about his fight! He goes to train that day! That's why I say his focus is extraordinary. It's just peculiar. That's the best word for it. It's actually peculiar.

That night, we got into the van and got back to Philadelphia. Naturally, the fight was postponed, but with the kind of focus Bernard had, when the fight went back on, he went right back into fight mode. When we got to Madison Square Garden on the night of the fight, it was just like when we were in Puerto Rico. I was looking for the Philly supporters, but everybody was there for Trinidad. We're getting ready and I went into Trinidad's dressing room to watch them wrap his hands, and one of his hands was already wrapped. One of the commissioners told me that he had watched them wrap it. I said, "Are you in the Hopkins corner? I need to see the hand re-wrapped." The way they wrapped his hand was illegal in the state of New York. They were taping and gauzing and taping and layering the hands several times over. It looked like a cast. You could actually do that in other states, but in New York, it's illegal. We got to arguing back and forth and Papa Trinidad was like, "The fight's off." Everybody started panicking and going crazy. They said I was creating a ruckus, and they brought Donald Trump into the room. Why? I have no idea. I guess they thought I would get intimidated and fold under that. They got Don King in the room, too, and he cussed all them dudes out, and said that he had nothing to do with no handwraps. Finally, the commissioner with the New York State Athletic Commission came into the room. He heard everybody's story, and he said you've got to go by the law and re-wrap the hands. That's the law.

Trinidad was one of my favorite fighters. I liked watching him, because when he came to the ring, he looked like he was enjoying himself. He looked like he was having the best time of his life. Sure enough, when he got in the ring against Bernard, he had that same look on his face. Before the fight, I had a conversation with Bernard and I told him that he could beat Trinidad with the jab. Sometimes the most difficult puzzle can be solved with a simple answer, and sometimes the fighter doesn't trust the fact that the answer is that simple. Bernard cussed me out for about a half an hour when I told him that, but the minute he stepped into that ring, he tried it. That's when you know you have

Naazim Richardson and Bernard Hopkins at a press conference for Hopkins's 2006 fight with Antonio Tarver (courtesy Marty Rosengarten/RingsidePhotos.com).

a connection with an athlete. He went out there and he tried. He probably did it just so he could come back to the corner and prove me wrong, but at least he trusted me to try it. I knew that when he threw that jab that he would throw everything else off of it. He was boxing and controlling him with the jab, and Trinidad couldn't throw his hook like he wanted to. Before the twelfth round, Bernard sat down in the corner and looked at me and asked me, "What round is this?" I said, "It's the twelfth round." He said, "Now, I'm gonna knock his ass out." That's what he did. He went out there and knocked him out.

Your first fight as Shane Mosley's trainer was in January 2009 when he faced and defeated welterweight champion Antonio Margarito via ninth-round TKO. Tell me about your experiences leading up to that fight, particularly the controversy surrounding Margarito's handwraps.

I've known Shane for years. I remember taking my guys to an amateur tournament years ago. Shane came down to the tournament to watch my guys fight. They were going on and on about "Sugar" Shane Mosley this and "Sugar" Shane Mosley that. They just thought he was something. Before the Margarito fight, I got a phone call from Shane's people, asking me if I would be interested in working with him. I said I would, because I always liked Shane. Everybody was counting him out against Margarito. He had just fought Ricardo Mayorga, and people were really giving him a tough time. Even though he won, he didn't do as good as some people thought he should. When we got into camp, I saw a fighter who was still willing to learn and try new things. I said to myself that I was going to take full advantage of the commitment he was showing, because I had never seen that kind of

Shane Mosley (right) breaks down Antonio Margarito en route to a ninth-round TKO victory in their 2009 fight (courtesy Bret Newton—ThreatPhoto.com/Pound4Pound.com).

devotion and dedication from an established fighter like that. He was so focused and I felt extremely confident going into the fight. We had a game plan and he was willing to follow it like a soldier.

On the night of the fight, I was in the dressing room, watching them wrap Margarito's hands. In California, you can have a small bit of tape directly on the skin, but he had it wrapped all down his wrist. I approached them about it and I was like, "Yo…. You can't have that much tape on his hand." We went back and forth and they brought in the top commissioner of California. He made them re-wrap the hand, and they had the cushion on the table. I reached out and I picked up the cushion and squeezed it. I was like, "Yo, man, this knuckle pad feels pretty hard." I gave it to the deputy commissioner and he said, "It feels okay to me." I said, "Well, it don't feel alright to me." I gave it to the commissioner and he said, "Yeah, that does feel pretty hard." When he opened it, a block fell out. I was like, "He's got to unwrap that other hand, too." They were like, "No, no, that hand is already cool." I said, "Listen, y'all want to wait till after the fight and we find something in that knuckle, too?" They unwrapped it and another block fell out.

For me, that was like finding somebody breaking into my house. My natural reaction was to respond, but if we got to fighting and wrestling in that back room, those two blocks would disappear, and it would just be my word against theirs. I scooped up the blocks and the commissioner said, "I need those as evidence." I said, "Dig this. I work for Shane Mosley. Get his lawyer in here." Judd Burstein, his lawyer at the time, came in and wrapped them up in a box. Later, Shane's doctor felt the block and he said that that's the same stuff they make casts out of. To be honest, I thought they were going to take Margarito and them away in cuffs, but they started wrapping Margarito's hands. We had to go through a few more things, because they were taping up his wrist again. I said to the commissioner, "Will you please put your finger on the wrist and show him where the cut off line is?" The trainer would look right at me and go right past the cut off line. We argued back and forth, but we got that squared away.

People have said that the whole handwrap thing got to Margarito's head before the fight. They say the same thing about some of the guys Bernard Hopkins fights. They say Bernard is a master of mind games and he gets in their head. I'm like, "Yo! Can he fight? Does he have a right hand and a left hook? You think all these guys do is get in their head and pick up a check?" I think we lose sight of how talented these athletes are. You have to be special to get to this level. Margarito had never been knocked out before he fought Shane Mosley and he hasn't been knocked out since. He's been in there with some real killers. Manny Pacquiao hit him with everything and he didn't go down. He eats punches like they're Skittles. You can't say that Margarito got knocked out because it got to his head. He got knocked out, because Shane Mosley went out there and fought his butt off. There was a lot of controversy in that fight because of Margarito's handwraps. People have asked me since that fight if I think Margarito had done that in the past. I can't say what he's done in the past, because I don't know. We all have things we think, but if I don't have any proof, I'm not going to point my finger at anybody.

A lot of people call you Brother Naazim Richardson. Why do they call you Brother?
    It's the same reason they call you mister. People ask me what Brother stands for and

I ask them what mister stands for. This is my attribute. This is my name. Brother Naazim. This is who I am.

Some of the nicest people you'll ever meet are in the boxing world. It seems ironic that you'll find people who are so loving and caring in the most brutal game known to man.

Boxing is just a sport. It's gladiators competing against each other. People say violence, but it's only violence when you violate the rules. Once you violate the rules, you implement the violence. When everybody understands and respects the rules, then we're on an even playing field. Everything is balanced and fair. When we sit down to the chess board, your queen can't do anything my queen can't do, but if you have two extra rooks and an extra queen, now we're outside the confines of the rules. Now, I'm being manipulated. Now, I'm being taken advantage of. That's when we start dealing with what's right and what's wrong. Our sport is rough enough as it is. If you go outside the guidelines, it can become deadly. That's not gonna happen against my guy. Not if I can help it. All I want to do is please God, because I have to answer to God with everything I do. When I look back sometimes, as mad as I can be at some of the things people say and do, I can honestly say that I have a good feeling about the people in this sport. Sometimes we yell and cuss each other out from across the ring, but I have such a great deal of respect for what everybody's doing.

You always hear about the pessimistic side of boxing these days. There's no more trainers no more, the fighters aren't what they used to be… I call this "The Microwave Era." They're taking talented athletes and just throwing gloves on them. A lot of the trainers aren't taking the time to teach boxing anymore. For this sport to get back to what it was, we have get back to the basics. We have to work together and care for these athletes. I come out of Philadelphia, and we have such a big reputation for boxing. It's the City of Brotherly Love, and we love to get in the ring and show you how brotherly we are. I've been blessed to work with some of the best athletes of this era. I always say that they're tremendous human beings who just happen to know how to fight. Shane Mosley is one of the greatest human beings you'll ever meet. Steve Cunningham, who I also train—his wife is his manager. This woman had a baby and twenty-three days later, she was overseas with the baby in her arm, negotiating his title fight. I applaud that! She works so hard for Steve and that makes me want to work hard for him. When Steve comes to the gym to train, his whole family comes with him. They set the baby up on the table, and his son and his daughter and everybody's hitting the bag. These are just the stories you tell as time passes on.

I hope people appreciate Bernard Hopkins and recognize what this guy is doing and what he's accomplishing. We argue all the time, but I'm telling you, man, I'm so impressed with this guy. When we were on the press tour for his fight with Chad Dawson, I gave him back the check he wrote me for training him for the Jean Pascal rematch. He went to Canada in that fight and became the oldest man ever to win a world title. Few Americans have actually traveled outside the country and won world titles. Bernard stood by me when I had the stroke, and I just wanted to show him how much respect I have for him and how much I appreciate everything he's done. He's cut from a special cloth. I've been blessed to work with some great trainers, too, man. I've worked with John David Jackson, who was a heck of a fighter, as well as an outstanding coach. I've worked and communicated with Freddie

Naazim Richardson (far right) looks on as Bernard Hopkins jumps rope, preparing for his 2011 fight with Chad Dawson. Two other men unrelated to Team Hopkins observe the workout (courtesy Bret Newton—ThreatPhoto.com/Pound4Pound.com).

Roach, Emanuel Steward, Angelo Dundee and the late great Bouie Fisher and Eddie Futch. These are great human beings who just happen to be the masters of their craft. There are a lot of great, hard-working trainers out of Philadelphia like Buster Custas, Sharron Baker, Brother Khalil, Danny Davis, and Sloan Harris—trainers who people outside of Philadelphia don't know about. They're the background brothers and that's the world they prefer. There are some young, up-and-coming trainers like Robert Hines, Stephen Edwards, Hemsa Muhammad, Billy Briscoe, and "Big" Chip Hart who will be carrying on the Philadelphia tradition years from now, alongside teams like the Concrete Jungle Boxing Tribe and The Untouchables.

When I'm at the gym, I always mention Bouie Fisher, so these young guys don't forget their history. We're out of a gym called the James Shuler Memorial and I'm hoping these kids know the history of James Shuler. He was a tremendous amateur and an outstanding pro, who we lost too early. He was killed in a motorcycle accident and it's another reason why boxers and bikes don't go together. You can't talk about Philadelphia without saying the name Joe Frazier. His daughter Jacqui checks in at the gym all the time. She spoke at Bouie's funeral. Jacqui's a judge now. She's so supportive of these athletes it's ridiculous. Whenever you see a problem with young people, you see Jacqui Frazier. These kids got it tough, man, and they're doing what they can to make something of themselves. They see guys with more money than them and sometimes it hurts. I always tell them, "We're all gonna eat, we just can't sit at the table at the same time." I tell kids that all the time. Sometimes they come up to me years later and remind me of that after they won the big one. We're just blessed with these people, man, and I've been blessed to do the things I've done. All of the success is Allah's, only the mistakes are my own. Man can't determine who we are and what our place is in life. I look at the whole journey and it boggles your mind what God asks of you. It's been a ride, man.

Former heavyweight world champion and Olympic gold medalist Joe Frazier, 2008 (courtesy Marty Rosengarten/ RingsidePhotos.com).

5

Leon Spinks: From the Vault

In 1978, heavyweight champion Muhammad Ali was at the tail-end of his career. At that time, he was looking for a tune-up as a way to keep busy and defend his titles. As it turned out, the opponent Ali chose wound up scoring one of the biggest upsets in the history of the sport. Born and raised in St. Louis, Missouri, Leon Spinks is a former gold medalist, who had a professional record of 6–0–1 when he out-worked Muhammad Ali on February 15, 1978, to earn a split decision victory. In September of the same year, Spinks lost the title in a rematch with Ali via unanimous decision, but he became the first of his family to put the "Spinks" name in the history books of professional boxing. The Spinks family is one of the most accomplished families to ever put on the gloves. Leon and his younger brother Michael both won gold medals at the 1976 Olympic Games. Michael Spinks went on to establish himself as one of the best light heavyweights of all time, eventually moving up to defeat heavyweight champion Larry Holmes via unanimous decision. Leon's son Cory Spinks is a former two-division champion himself, having won world titles at welterweight and junior middleweight. Leon Spinks retired in 1995 with a record of 26–17–3, 14 KO's. In May 2004, I attended a Spinks family gathering at a hotel in Earth City, Missouri, where I conducted several videotaped interviews, the first being with Leon Spinks. In May 2011, I went into my closet, took an old Betacam SP "from the vault," and transcribed the video. At the time of this interview, Leon's son Cory had just successfully defended his welterweight titles via unanimous decision against Zab Judah.

We were just talking about St. Louis a second ago and you said that I wouldn't like it so much if I was from your neighborhood. What was it like growing up in your neighborhood?

Well, my neighborhood was pretty rough. It was tough, I mean… My father wasn't at home and my mother was raising five kids. And then plus, people always seemed to beat up the oldest guy. And I was a real skinny guy. At the time, people just beat me up all the time. Took my money… I would go to the store and come back and whatever… I went through a lot of changes with my mom, because my mom and my dad would have arguments and whatever. That's basically what I had to go through. It was hard, it was real hard. When I got to the age of fourteen, fifteen, I started boxing. Boxing was a big thing then in St. Louis. In the amateurs… It was the only way you could make it out. But there were different

Former heavyweight world champion and Olympic gold medalist Leon Spinks (courtesy Steve Lott, Boxing Hall of Fame Las Vegas).

gangs then and me being tall and skinny then, gangs would jump on you and beat you up and take your money and I would go home and go crying to my mom, "They took my money!" So, when my mom had seen that, I had decided to go into the ring. So, I started at a gym called Capri. After that, I started boxing and I started beating who I can. And then I saw that I could travel as long as I beat my opponent and I did very well doing that.

So, you basically started boxing because you had to.

Well, it wasn't what I *had* to do, it was my best escape. It was my best respect in the neighborhood I stayed in. So, the guys knew that I boxed and how good I did at it. And the guys that would jump on me wouldn't jump on me no more.

When you first started professional boxing, what level did you see yourself reaching? Ultimately, you became a champion. What did you see for yourself when you first started?

I didn't see nothing. The only thing I seen at the time I started boxing period is it was important that I had a good opportunity to travel and see the world. When I was an amateur and as long as I was still fighting, I did boxing to see the world and I had a jacket and come back with trophies and what not. Then I heard that the Marine Corps never had a gold medal in boxing. And I thought the Marine Corps was better than anything. So, I joined the Marine Corps. The Marine Corps was even better for me, because it taught me self-respect and it taught me to learn things, to teach myself things. It taught me more than school. I got educated more so. Then I heard that the Marine Corps never had a gold medal-ist, so I joined.

Speaking of gold medals, I'd like to talk about the 1976 Olympics when you and your brother Michael both won gold medals.

Yeah, but see, my brother Michael was inspiring to me. You know how it is when the younger brother goes farther. My younger brother Michael won the national Golden Gloves. So, I said I'm going to win the AAU Golden Gloves. Me and my brother was always in competition against each other. I wanted to be better than him and he wanted to be better than me.

You inspired each other.

Yeah, we inspired each other. And I was in the Marine Corps at the gym and when I heard my brother won the national Golden Gloves, I said, "What's better than that?" And they said the AAU, so I won the AAU.

Now, it was at the Olympics where the nickname "Spinks Jinx" originated. How did the name "Spinks Jinx" come about?

Because me and my brother used to knock 'em out with overhand rights. My brother gave me the name "Spinks Jinx" and I just carried on with it. Carried on… And we both carried on with it. That was the overhand right and we just kept knocking people out and it worked. You fight Leon Spinks or Michael Spinks, you're liable to get hit with an overhand right.

When you turned professional, you had just a small handful of fights and then you were thrown into the big fight with Muhammad Ali. How did that come about?

Ali told his promoter, Butch Lewis at the time, he said, "I will fight Leon if he gets in the top ten." I trained at Joe Frazier's Gym and I had a good trainer at the time. And I was strong and young and silly, as usual. But I went for that. And so I beat these guys and it got me in the top ten.

Going into that fight with very little experience, it seemed like you didn't have a worry in the world. You were smiling and ready to go, where most people in your position would be a little apprehensive about getting in with the best in the world.

See, I grew up watching Ali fight all the time. Even when they had him on the radio. Or when he would fight on *Wide World of Sports*. He was inspiring to me. He was the big mouth from the South. So, I'd see him talk 'em into the fight and talk 'em out of the fight. He was yappin' his mouth and people was scared of him. And I said, if it were me... You can't be no more than what you can be. You do your thing and I'll do my thing. And then I won that way.

And what was your thing that night when you got in there with Muhammad Ali? How were you able to beat him over fifteen rounds?

I had to keep punching and make him fight more than what he had to. Fighters hug on each other and dance with each other... I'm a boxer-puncher. Steady puncher. I don't stop. Most guys fight for a little while and then stop and hug each other. But the military taught me to punch all the time and stay busy. I always liked Ali, but the point is, when it comes down to fighting, you got to do your job. That's the bottom line.

I would assume your life changed significantly after you beat Ali. Tell me what your life was like after that win.

Leon Spinks out-works Muhammad Ali en route to a split decision victory in the first of their two 1978 encounters (courtesy Steve Lott, Boxing Hall of Fame Las Vegas).

Top: Left to right: Leon Spinks, Davey Lee Armstrong, Emanuel Steward, Prentiss Byrd, Jackie Kallen, and Thomas Hearns, 1979 (courtesy Jackie Kallen). *Bottom:* Leon Spinks hammers Alfredo Evangelista on the ropes en route to a fifth-round knockout in their 1980 fight (courtesy Steve Lott, Boxing Hall of Fame Las Vegas).

Well, a lot of people tried to take advantage of me. A lot of people *did* somewhat. But you make mistakes like a human being does. People make mistakes. I have made mine.

You were saying before how you and Michael inspired each other's careers. Do you think your victory over Ali inspired him when he went on to beat Larry Holmes?

Yeah. But the main thing is, you have two heavyweight champions of the world in the same house. The only thing we had to compete on is he said I can't beat him and I said he can't beat me. But hey… He's my brother, I love him, and he's the heavyweight champion of the world. My brother's career was great because he was undefeated as light heavyweight champion. And he kept knocking people out. Then he became heavyweight champion. I mean… I love him. I love him and I wish the best for him.

Switching gears, your son Cory is now the undisputed welterweight champion of the world. How did you feel that night on December 13, 2003, when the referee raised his hand in the air and it was announced that he was the new champion?

I felt great. I said, "Cat off the old block!" Because St. Louis is like an amateur fighting town. We got some good fighters out of St. Louis. And my son, he came out and blazed.

Before the fight, I know Ricardo Mayorga said some things that were very offensive to your family (Mayorga made some derogatory remarks about Cory's mother and older brother Leon, Jr., who are both deceased). How did you feel about that?

That didn't bother me. Because they'll say anything to upset you. And a mad fighter cannot fight. So, I said, "As long as you know in your heart and in your mind that it's not true, then why bother? And you know what he's trying to do."

When Cory first started fighting, did you think he would become a champion some day?

Well, I didn't really judge Cory when he fought. Because I didn't know how much he wanted to fight. In the fighting game, you got to fight from your heart, not from your mind. Because your mind can tell you anything. Your mind can tell you to quit. But if you fight from your heart, nobody can stop you. Especially when you believe in yourself. And God. Believe in yourself and believe in God. Let God take you the way. You can't miss out.

Leon's son, former two-division world champion Cory Spinks, 2007 (courtesy Marty Rosengarten/Ring sidePhotos.com)

Where do you see Cory's career going from here? Do you believe he will continue defending his title successfully?

If he listens. Only if he listens to somebody that really cares about him and does everything right. Then the sky's the limit.

Why do you think Cory and his trainer Kevin Cunningham are such a good team?

Because they love each other. That's it. When a man loves you as much as Kevin does… I've never seen no fault in it yet, but you never know what happens when you go down the road. But they love each other. And if Cory believes in him the way he believes in Cory, they can't lose.

Of all of your experiences in boxing, what is your proudest moment?

My proudest moment was winning in the Olympics. Because you see, when I fought Ali, it was just me. But when I fought in the Olympics, it was me and Sugar Ray and Howard Davis, my brother, Leo Randolph… We were representing the United States. And that was our big gift of giving back.

If you had one wish, what would it be?

One wish… That's a heavy answer. I really can't answer. I really can't tell you. (long silence) I got three other boys. I just hope they come through and their dreams come true and I hope I be there to see it.

6

Michael Buffer:
The Ring Announcer

Before every boxing match, ring announcers set the tone for the evening. It's their job to excite the crowd, introduce the fighters, and bring energy to the room. In the history of the sport, no words have brought more excitement to a crowd than "Let's get ready to rumble!" Born and raised in Philadelphia, Pennsylvania, Michael Buffer started out as a car salesman. He then gravitated toward modeling, but he always had a passion for boxing. After watching a ring announcer in Atlantic City, New Jersey, do a less than spectacular job, his son encouraged him to give announcing fights a shot. In 1982, Buffer made his debut as a ring announcer and began working in lower profile events. He got his break in big-time boxing in June 1983 when Bob Arum hired him to announce the Roberto Duran–Davey Moore junior middleweight bout that took place at Madison Square Garden. From there, Buffer started working all of Top Rank's shows, as well as every bout that took place in Donald Trump–owned casinos. In 1984, Buffer began using the catchphrase "Let's get ready to rumble!," which has become a world-recognized phrase for which he acquired a federal trademark for. While Buffer is known for his popular catchphrase, very few people know that he was the first ring announcer who said, "It's Showtime!" before a boxing event. In February 2012, I called Michael Buffer to discuss his experiences as a ring announcer for some of the most significant fights of the modern era. At the time of this interview, he had just announced Julio Cesar Chavez, Jr.–Marco Antonio Rubio.

What is your background in boxing and what led you to become a ring announcer?
    As a kid, I was a big sports fan. Growing up in Philadelphia, I dreamed of playing for the Phillies. I was also an insane football fan, but boxing was always there. I remember watching Sugar Ray Robinson in the final years of his career. When I was really young, my dad let me stay up late and watch the rematch with Rocky Marciano and Joe Walcott, where Marciano knocked him out in the first round. I was a big Floyd Patterson fan, too, and it broke my heart when he lost to Sonny Liston. In 1960, I took notice when this young, flashy kid named Cassius Marcellus Clay won a gold medal at the Olympics and I thought he was just the greatest. Years later, everybody started calling him "The Greatest" and he

later changed his name to Muhammad Ali. I was a big, big Muhammad Ali fan. I was still living in the Philadelphia area when he started training at Deer Lake, which was about a two hour drive from me. I started going up there and I was kind of a regular face. I got to meet Ali and Angelo Dundee and Drew Bundini Brown and Walter Youngblood, who later became Wali Muhammad. One time, I rode my motorcycle up there. Ali hopped on the bike and took off, and Angelo just about had a heart attack! This was around '72, '73 and I never even dreamed of being involved in boxing. As it turned out, years later, I was introducing Muhammad Ali as a retired three-time heavyweight champion at ringside.

After a period of being the worst car salesman in history, I started doing some modeling and found myself doing it for a living. At the time, I was working in Philly and New York City, right around when boxing came along to Atlantic City with the opening of the casinos. There were three or four shows per weekend, and one or two shows a night during the week. One night, I watched a fight where the ring announcer gave the scores for a split decision. With a split decision, you're supposed to say how one judge has Fighter A winning, another judge has Fighter B winning, pause, take a breath, and then announce the winner. In this case, the announcer read the two scorecards for Fighter A first, so you already knew who won before the third score was announced. My oldest son, who was about thirteen at the time, said, "Dad, you could do that." I had done a few commercials, but that was in a

studio where you can do re-takes if you make a mistake. I had never worked as a deejay, never worked a live event where you're put on the spot, but I thought, why not? I fished around and looked into it and got my license. In October of '82, I worked a show that was on USA cable. I saw the replay and I was ridiculously bad. I was given another chance six months later and I improved quite a bit. It was fun and it was great to be part of the sport that I love. I had been such a huge fan and I love that feeling of being ringside around the fighters and trainers.

It took off from there and I started doing a fight almost every week in Atlantic City. Gradually, it became a full time job. An early turning point in my career came in June of '83 when Roberto Duran faced Davey Moore at Madison Square Garden. Top Rank was promoting the fight. With less than a

Ring announcer Michael Buffer (courtesy Marty Rosengarten/RingsidePhotos.com).

year's experience, I wrote Bob Arum a letter and told him that I thought I could do the job. He gave me the opportunity and it turned out to be a monster night and a monster fight. It was a sold out crowd at the Garden and it revived Duran's career all over again. It was so electrifying to be there. Before the fight, I had a list of fighters to introduce—Ray Mancini, Marvin Hagler, Larry Holmes, Gerry Cooney, Muhammad Ali… I saved Ali for last. In the older tradition of the Garden, the fighters would come up and wave and step out of the ring, but when Ray Mancini came up, I said, "Stay in the ring." There were about eight guys altogether and they all lined up next to each other. It was like royalty meeting royalty. The place went nuts. It was one of my favorite nights ever.

I started at the Garden where a decade earlier, Muhammad Ali and Joe Frazier had one of the biggest fights in boxing history. Just a few months ago, Joe Frazier passed away. Even still when I talk about this, it becomes hard because I really got to know Frazier quite well. I did the ten-count at a couple of different events for Joe. We did a tribute at Cotto-Margarito II, and presented his son Marvis and his daughter Jacqui with a special photo that was taken. When the lights went down and they started playing this video segment on Joe Frazier, I actually started weeping in the ring. Just recently, I found myself struggling to stay composed once again when we did a ten-count for Angelo Dundee. Sometimes it's hard to keep the emotions under control when I'm up there. Sometimes things are sad or absurd or I become the bearer of bad news. I don't always agree with the scorecards I have to read, but what can I do? I just keep my opinions to myself and hope that they don't kill the messenger. Boxing never fails to surprise. It's part of what makes this sport what it is. I love every minute of it. Even after almost thirty years of announcing fights, it's still a thrill. It still has that special quality. It's especially exciting in my case when it's time for me to say what has become my trademark. It sets the tone for the whole evening.

At what point did you begin to say "Let's get ready to rumble" and how did this come about?

At the big fights, there's all this anticipation when the fighters come to the ring. It's a production, it's a presentation. In the late 1970s, early 1980s, ring announcers would introduce virtually everybody on the commission. It became a standard. Two timekeepers, three judges, three doctors, the executive director… I can remember one event where there were nineteen names before I introduced the fighters. When that happens, it takes all of the electricity and excitement out of the room. It kills the energy in the crowd. What I wanted was something that would be comparable to the Indianapolis 500 when after all the proceedings, somebody says, "Gentlemen, start your engines!" It's the phrase that means, "Now!" I wanted something that would let the crowd know that they were about to meet the stars of the show and that the fight is going to start. I tried "Man your battle stations!" and "Fasten your seatbelts!" On the ESPN broadcasts, Sal Marchiano used to say, "We're ready to rumble from Resorts International!" and Muhammad Ali always used to say, "Rumble young man rumble!," so I started saying, "Let's get ready to rumble!"

Through the years, I fine-tuned it and it evolved into what I wanted it to be. I met a guy in Louisiana named Jody Berry. He had been a singer in the '50s and '60s and he had this flair for showbiz. He was a big fight fan and we would hang out together and he said to me, "When you say 'Let's get ready to rumble,' shut up." I said, "What do you mean?" He said, "People want to react to that." I used to say, "Let's get ready to rumble, twelve rounds

Michael Buffer poses with ring card girls at a 2006 fight (courtesy Marty Rosengarten/RingsidePhotos. com).

of boxing…," and there was no pause. I just continued with whatever I was going to say next, but Jody said, "Please believe me. Do what I say and you'll get a good response." I took his advice and it changed everything. I started to see "Let's Get Ready to Rumble" in the headlines before big fights and I realized that it was becoming a popular phrase. There's another well-known pre-fight phrase, and I'm sure a lot of fans will be surprised to learn this, but I was actually the very first announcer to say, "It's Showtime!" That line has been around forever, but one of the first times it was used for a boxing match, if not *the* first, was at Trump Taj Mahal for Thomas Hearns vs Michael Olajide in April of 1990. I may have said it before then, because I had done a lot of fights on Showtime before that one. The late Jay Larkin, who was the head man at Showtime at the time, decided to plug the network by having it said before the main event.

In June 1988, you were the ring announcer for the showdown between heavyweight champion Mike Tyson and Michael Spinks, a fight that Tyson won via first round knockout. What stands out in your mind about that night?

Tyson-Spinks was a spectacular event. That night, before the fighters came into the ring, Butch Lewis complained about Tyson's handwraps as a ploy to psyche Mike out.

There was a big delay and there were all these rumors going around. Somebody said that Spinks wasn't coming out, somebody said that Tyson wasn't coming out… To this day, there are probably like three or four different stories about what happened, but this is the fight where Tyson put his fist through the wall in his dressing room. People were coming up to the ring saying, "Tyson just punched the wall and broke his hand!" We were all ready for the main event and it turned out to be thirty, forty minutes before it happened. They were playing music and I was making introductions as a way to make this delay seem normal. The crowd was going insane and nobody knew what was going on. Eventually, the fighters came to the ring. In this particular fight, based on a gut feeling, after I did the introductions and held the microphone in front of referee Frank Cappuccino, I didn't go to my seat. I just went down and sat on the bottom step, because I had a feeling that this wasn't going to last past the first round. As it turned out, it was over in ninety-one seconds. You could just feel the brute force and the energy. You ever look down a desert road and see those ripples on the horizon from the heat? That night, you could see the heat coming off of Tyson's shoulders. It was quite scary. It was passionate, it was exciting… It was everything you would want in a big fight atmosphere.

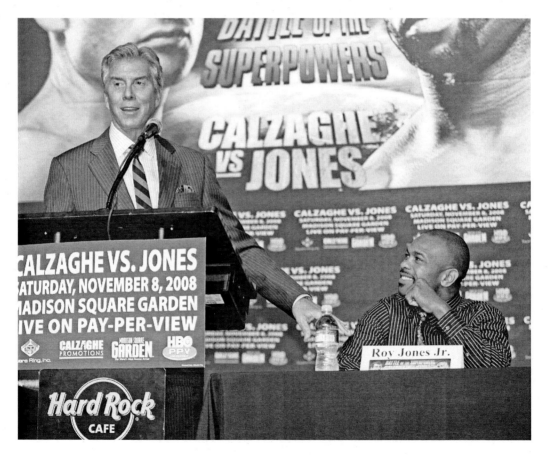

Michael Buffer and Roy Jones, Jr., at a press conference for the 2008 Joe Calzaghe–Roy Jones, Jr., fight (courtesy Marty Rosengarten/RingsidePhotos.com).

In November 1993 when Evander Holyfield defeated heavyweight champion Riddick Bowe via majority decision in their second fight, a man known as "Fan Man" parachuted into the ring during the seventh round.

Before it happened, there was a murmur in the crowd, because the guy was circling above. I didn't even notice. I was watching the fight, which was one of the best fights ever. All of a sudden, there was a crash and I see this parachute or a canvas or a silk, hanging from the stands that are holding the ring lights up. I realized that something wasn't right and I went right into safety mode and tried to keep things under control. I had the microphone in my hand, because I keep it with me during the fight. The very first thing I did was address the crowd and say, "Everything is under control. Please stay in your seats. We'll have security take care of this." Thank God this guy had a helmet on, because Bowe's security people looked like the offensive line from Wisconsin. There were so many of them trying to hit him. To this day, I believe this guy actually pretended to be unconscious so he wouldn't get beat up. I don't think he was out. I think he pretty much played possum and just prayed for the best. It was a crazy night, but it worked out and they got him out of there and we got things underway.

Speaking of Bowe's security people, right after the first fight between Riddick Bowe and Andrew Golota in July 1996, members of Bowe's team were involved in a situation that resulted in a full-scale riot when Golota was disqualified in the seventh round for repeatedly throwing low blows.

Golota was completely dominating the fight. It was very one-sided, but at the same time, he was going south with his punches. There were a lot of warnings and point deductions for low blows. When the final low blow came, Golota was disqualified and Bowe's people ran across the ring and one guy hit him in the back of the head with a cell phone. After that, people started fighting in the ring. Literally, hundreds of people from the crowd were rushing the ring and getting in the middle of it. Lou Duva fell down on the ring apron and everybody was worried about him. When I got on the PA system, I said, "Please stay in your seats and remain calm." I said that if there were any members of NYPD out there to please come to ringside. All we had was Garden security. While all of this was going on, I just stayed at ringside. It was like when I spent three years in the Army during the Vietnam War. They were sending soldiers over, but somehow I never went west of Fort Knox, Kentucky. The same thing happened here. Pure luck! I just stayed where I was with the microphone in my hand and tried not to get clobbered. Eventually, the cops came into the building and they started getting people out of there.

In November 1994, you announced to the world that George Foreman was the oldest man in the history of the sport to become heavyweight champion, after he knocked out Michael Moorer in the tenth round.

Up until the tenth round, George lost every minute of every round. When the moment happened, it wasn't just one punch. It was a one-two, one-two. He stuck his jab between Moorer's gloves and that right hand came in behind it. He did it one time and then instantly did it again. He got those gloves open and stuck that right hand down the pipe. It was a work of art. When you look at the replay, especially the overhead replay, you can see he had total torque in his punch. It was like Tiger Woods teeing off. Nobody is going to survive

HBO commentator Jim Lampley and Michael Buffer, 2008 (courtesy Marty Rosengarten/Ringside Photos.com).

that punch. As it happened live, as soon as Moorer went down, you knew that was it. The punch landed, there was a millisecond where everybody was in disbelief, and then there was this huge roar from the crowd. It was probably the most exciting and most dramatic thing I've ever experienced. It came out of nowhere. I was heading for the steps before Joe Cortez counted to ten, because I knew it was over. I was really blown away, but I also felt really bad. I've known Michael Moorer since he was nineteen years old. He was undefeated at light heavyweight. After he moved up to heavyweight, at one point, he was 26–0 with 26 knockouts. I knew his mother and his family and I was just as heartbroken for Michael as I was elated for "Big" George.

Americans today view this as a weak era of heavyweight boxing, but when you go over to Europe for a fight with either of the current heavyweight champions, Vitali and Wladimir Klitschko, I would imagine the fans feel differently.

They do. The Klitschkos both put forty to fifty thousand fans into a stadium. Fights in Europe seem to generate a lot more excitement. There's a greater fan base, not just for the sport of boxing, but for the individuals. Joe Calzaghe put 50,000 people in an indoor stadium in Wales. Ricky Hatton had 50,000 fans show up at Manchester Stadium. It's just

Wladimir Klitschko and Vitali Klitschko, 2009 (courtesy Marty Rosengarten/RingsidePhotos. com).

another day at the box office. They really pack 'em in. The only American fight that could reach that level would be if Manny Pacquiao and Floyd Mayweather were to face each other. They could probably draw 100,000 people.

As you said, the dream fight of the modern era is Manny Pacquiao versus Floyd Mayweather, Jr. (presumably at the welterweight limit). It would be this generation's Ali-Frazier and Leonard-Hearns. Have you, yourself, fantasized about this fight? Have you thought about how you might feel when you introduce the two fighters and say, "Let's get ready to rumble"?

Yes, I have. It's one of those things when I'm taking a shower and if I've got the right echo, I might say, "Let's get ready to rumble!" and introduce both fighters in a fantasy world. I've been doing this for almost thirty years and it never gets old when it comes to the really big super fights. It's something you want to do and you want to be a part of. I still have enough of the fan left in me that I think of these dream fights and imagine the excitement of being there. I'd like to retire soon and I sure hope this fight happens while we're all still in the game.

As a ring announcer, when it's time for you to speak on the night of the fight, what do you want to give to the thousands in attendance and the millions watching around the world?

When I would watch black and white TV as a kid, I was always excited when I would see a major league baseball game and the announcer would introduce the players. They would line them up along the first base and third base lines and it was so thrilling to see the crowd react when each guy came out. It was the same thing with the fights. Sometimes Johnny Addie would introduce Sugar Ray Robinson in the audience and call him into the ring. I have fond memories of that. If I can deliver a moment like that to somebody, I know I've done my job. I like to think that somewhere in a car in the traffic leaving the arena, there's a kid who went to his first fight with his dad, and he says, "Dad, remember when that guy said, 'Let's get ready to rumble'? Remember how exciting that was?" Going into a fight, I try to put that image in my mind and hope that I do a good job and that I send somebody away with a great memory.

7

Jackie Kallen:
The First Lady of Boxing

Very few women have the gumption to make their mark in the sport of boxing. Those who try are usually not taken seriously, given the chauvinistic perceptions that exist. However, it has been proven that a lady can walk right in to this male-dominated sport and do what most people believe they can't do. Born and raised in Detroit, Michigan, Jackie Kallen started out as a sports journalist. This path led her to Emanuel Steward's Kronk Gym, where she wound up learning the ins and outs of boxing. Kallen developed a love of the sport and went on to manage fighters. This seemed to be an uphill battle, as many in boxing refused to give her the time of day because of her gender. Regardless of the pre-judgments of others, Kallen was determined to guide a fighter to a world championship. In 1989, Kallen joined forces with an up-and-coming prospect by the name of James Toney. Kallen detected greatness in Toney from the start and believed he had what it took to make it to the top. She was so confident that in May 1991, she took a huge gamble and put Toney in the ring with middleweight champion Michael Nunn. Most people thought that Toney was in over his head, but he wound up winning the fight via eleventh-round TKO. For the next few years, the team of Jackie Kallen and James Toney produced outstanding results. During their run together, many regarded Toney as the best fighter in the world. Their success came to an end in November 1994, when Toney lost his super middleweight title to Roy Jones, Jr., via unanimous decision. In addition to managing Toney, Kallen has also managed Bronco McKart, Pinklon Thomas, Tom "Boom Boom" Johnson, Tarick Salmaci, Damian Fuller, Joseph Kiwanuka, Michael Dallas, Jr., Bobby Hitz, Scotty Buck, Dorell Van Horn, Jr., Jeanine Garside, Bridget Riley, Yvonne Trevino, Nonito Donaire, Jose Celaya, Arthur Saribekian, and Bernard Harris. In December 2011, I called Jackie Kallen and asked her how she became known as "The First Lady of Boxing." At the time of this interview, Kallen had just moved from Los Angeles, California, back to her roots in Detroit.

What is your background in boxing and what led you to start managing fighters?

In 1978, I started out as a sports writer for the Oakland Press, and boxing became one of my beats, so to speak. I really enjoyed covering it. I covered Sugar Ray Leonard's fights,

I covered Larry Holmes's fights… I wound up working for Emanuel Steward at the Kronk Gym. I was their publicist for ten years. I did press kits for fighters like Thomas Hearns and Milton McCrory. I covered weigh-ins, press conferences, victory parties… It just fueled my love for the sport even more, because Kronk is such an illustrious gym. There were so many great champions coming out of there and I found myself wanting to learn more and more about the sport. The Kronk Gym was like college for me and Emanuel Steward was my professor. He taught me how to wrap hands, how to stop cuts, how to run a sparring session… I learned all of the little intricacies of boxing that I never would have learned as just a spectator, watching from my living room.

What really got me hooked was the time I saw Thomas Hearns fight Rudy Barro. Tommy knocked him out in the fourth round and it was the first live fight I ever saw. I was fascinated with, not only the sport, but this huge dichotomy that is common with fighters. Tommy was a very quiet, shy boy and he turned into

Boxing manager Jackie Kallen (courtesy Jackie Kallen).

this animal that got in the ring and annihilated people. I thought, "How could this possibly be the same person?" This mild mannered young man just turned into something else. What I found is that a lot of boxers have this switch that they can just turn on and turn off. I don't know where they get it. I guess it's just something that's inside them, but the psychology of it really fascinated me. Of course, I was very intrigued by the amount of discipline that a sport like boxing requires. It was just amazing to me, so I found the sport compelling on many levels.

In 1988, after spending ten years at Kronk, I decided that I wanted to start managing fighters. At the time, I was doing PR for a promoter here in Detroit. He was promoting a George Foreman fight. The young fighter who came to fight Foreman was a kid from Chicago named Bobby Hitz. Bobby didn't have any management, so I asked him if he was looking for a manager. He said, "Why? Are you looking to manage someone?" I told him that I was, so I started managing him and getting my feet wet. From there, I met James Toney who became my first of several world champions. I also managed Bronco McKart, Tom "Boom Boom" Johnson, Pinklon Thomas, Joseph Kiwanuka and Jimmy Lange, among others. It just became my love. The first thing I would do every day is get up and get on the phone, find fights for my fighters, and get an idea of the who's who in every weight class. I really did my homework.

For me, the job of being a manager was probably different than it was for a lot of other managers. Everyone has their own style. I became a big sister, a surrogate mom, a cook… On many occasions, I had to take over the cooking because one of my fighters had to make weight and he wasn't eating properly. I was also a financial advisor, because I didn't want them to squander all of the money they were making. At times, I was a babysitter. I would sometimes watch my fighters's kids when they were training. I was a social director, because I would plan the activities that they would go to. I was even a speech therapist, because I had a couple of fighters who needed a little work with their enunciation, so they could do a proper interview. I took on many diverse roles. It wasn't just about getting them fights and handling their money. I covered all the bases.

You take pride in being an honest and forthright person, but when you became familiar with the world of boxing, I'm sure you found that not everyone was the same way. How did you maintain your integrity in a business where some people have a reputation for being dishonest?

When I first started in this business, it was a big learning experience for me. I just assumed that because I was a certain way that other people would be that way, too. That wasn't the case and I learned the hard way. There were times I made deals for my fighters for ten thousand dollars, but then I found out later that the actual number for the fight was fifteen and that the person who got me the fight pocketed five. Of course, I was stunned and shocked and dismayed. Who does that? I realized that a lot of people do that. To me, that's just unconscionable. If there's fifteen thousand for the fight, why wouldn't you just give it to the fighter? I was a little dismayed at the beginning at how the business was, but I figured that I would just stick to who I was, follow my own voice, and do whatever it told me to do. Never mind what everybody else was doing. I couldn't control what other people did, so I just dealt with people the way I would want to be dealt with. Just because the next guy was a liar and thief didn't give me a license to do the same. I still had to adhere to my core values.

Being that you were a woman in a world that is dominated by men, did people treat you differently? If so, how did you overcome some of the prejudgments that some people might have had?

Obviously, the difference in gender was noticeable from day one. People would look at me and wonder what a girl like me was doing in a sport like this. Sometimes they thought that I was fronting for someone or that I was just somebody's girlfriend. They just assumed I had some kind of ulterior motive, because they couldn't fathom that a female would be doing this for the love of the sport. Initially, I was disregarded by a lot of people I came in contact with. On a number of occasions, I would call up a promoter to get my fighter on a card. Every time, they would tell me that it was locked off or that there was no room. I knew they were lying, because that same promoter had just called the gym looking for a welterweight. I would call them back with a welterweight who was all ready to go, but they would say, "Who are you again?" I would say, "I'm his manager." They'd say, "You're his manager? Who are you calling for? Who's behind you? Who do you work for?" If we ever got past that, they would assume that I didn't know anything. They didn't think I had any business doing this. A lot of people are used to stereotyping, whether you're black, Jewish, Mexican, or female. I took it for what it was. I didn't take it personally. All I could do is prove them wrong.

From the late '80s to mid–1990s, you managed James Toney, who captured world titles at middleweight and super middleweight while you were working together. When did you first meet Toney?

I was at a small community gym in Livonia, Michigan, in the basement of a fighter's apartment. I was there with Bobby Hitz, the fighter I was managing. James was there and he sparred that day. I guess he wasn't happy with his performance, because he kicked over the spit bucket and cursed everybody out and went into the locker room and started banging his fists into the lockers. It was just a horrible scene. I said, "Who the heck is that?" They said that he was just some guy who worked out there. I said, "Why is he so mad?" This guy, who was with James, said that he was upset because he didn't like how he trained that day. He said that he was a perfectionist. I thought that wasn't necessarily a bad thing. It was a good thing. We started talking, and little by little, I learned that his original manager had been shot and killed recently. He was looking for a new manager and I liked what I saw in him. He was a very driven young man. I could see that he had a heck of a temper, but I thought that he could use that to his advantage in the ring. James liked the way I worked with Bobby. He thought I was a caring person and we started talking. One thing led to another and we joined forces in 1989.

In front of the cameras, Toney had a lot of attitude and defiance. What kind of person was he behind the scenes?

He was exactly what you said. With James, what you see is what you get. He has a foul mouth. He's very temperamental and very confrontational, but he's also a very lovable guy. He's a blend of a lot of different personality traits. He can be the sweetest person you've ever met. He can also be your worst enemy. He's just a very complex person. You never know which James you're going to get. He can flip on a dime. You'll be laughing and joking around with him one moment, and then you'll say something that he takes the wrong way, and then all of a sudden, he's throwing a temper tantrum. His behavior would just change so drastically. James was like a son to me. He stood up for my son's wedding, and both of my boys stood up for his first wedding. Today, he's like the estranged son who moved away. I don't speak with him on a regular basis, but he's still like a son. If I were to see him, I would run up and hug him because he's my boy. That's how I feel about him. He's still part of my life and he always will be.

At one point, Toney began wearing the Star of David on his trunks as a tribute to your Jewish heritage. When did this come about and what compelled him to do that?

That was from the very beginning. Tommy Hearns did that for me for one of his fights. He wore the Star of David and I thought that was such a nice tribute. I don't know if James talked to Tommy or how it came up, but he said that he would like to do that as well. Bronco McKart started doing it, too, and most of my guys in my stable did it. It seemed to be a good luck charm, because everybody was winning. Why change something if it isn't broken?

In May 1991, Toney established himself as an elite fighter when he defeated middleweight champion Michael Nunn via eleventh-round TKO. What stands out in your mind about that particular event?

We were given that opportunity, because Nunn's original opponent pulled out due to an injury. When I was given the opening, I said that we would absolutely take it. James was a big underdog in that fight and I was ridiculed for making that decision. A lot of people thought it was a ridiculous move at that time in his career. They thought that there was absolutely no way that James could beat Michael Nunn, especially in Nunn's hometown. When James won the fight, all of a sudden I was a genius. All of a sudden, I knew what I was doing. Sometimes you just have gut feelings about these things. I believed that James would beat Michael Nunn. I did not have a doubt in my mind. I just knew he could do it, but I must admit, when James was falling behind on the scorecards, it made me second-guess myself. We got into rounds six, seven, eight and it was not going the way I anticipated. Nunn was winning the fight, but after a while, James started to turn it around and apply the pressure and get past the nervousness and the magnitude of the whole situation. He became the James Toney that I knew he could be.

I thought the fight with Nunn would put us on the map and it did. For the whole first half of the '90s, James was the dominant force at middleweight and super middleweight. He was just an incredible talent. His defensive skills were unequalled. When he got in there, he could deal with any opponent. He was a brilliant strategist, along with his trainer Bill Miller. Bill Miller was an amazing trainer. With those two working together in the gym, we just had a machine that was cranking out wins for a number of years. But it wasn't always easy. James was a challenging person to work with. Right after he won the title from Michael Nunn, I opened Galaxy Boxing Gym in Detroit, basically because James had been thrown out of a few other gyms in town. His behavior was very erratic. He was very unpleasant at times, so I thought it would be better to open up our own facility, so we could train and not have to worry about offending other people. All of the other fighters I had at the time liked having a gym of their own. We all came together under one roof and it worked out very well, unless James was having one of his bad days. When that happened, it was rough for everybody. If he was having a bad day, he took it out on everybody else.

Jackie Kallen and James Toney, early 1990s (courtesy Jackie Kallen).

Toney remained undefeated until November 1994 when he lost his super middleweight title to Roy Jones, Jr., via unanimous decision.

Going into the fight with Roy Jones, I thought it was a pretty even match-up. I wasn't as sure of this fight as I had been with Michael Nunn and Iran Barkley and some of the other fights. I was very respectful of Roy Jones's ability. I thought that whoever wanted it more and whoever came into the fight in the best shape would probably be the one to win it. As it turned out, the one who was in the best shape was Roy Jones. I'm not saying that Roy wanted it more, but he certainly displayed more of a winning attitude from the get go. As we got close to the fight, James was very overweight. We had to do all kinds of things to get him to make 168. There was a fear that if he didn't make weight, he would lose his title. Weight was a big issue for James throughout all of his years at middleweight and super middleweight. Losing a lot of weight in a short period of time is bound to affect you. I saw it happen before when he fought Dave Tiberi, so I had my concerns before this fight.

Former three-division world champion James Toney, 2005 (courtesy Marty Rosengarten/RingsidePhotos. com).

I think James was overconfident and that he didn't think that Roy was going to be as difficult of an opponent as he turned out to be. I think he felt that he could do what he wanted when he wanted, and somehow pull it off as he always had in the past. James had never tasted defeat, so it was something he wasn't familiar with.

When he lost, it was a turning point for all of us. Our relationship was never the same after that. I don't think *he* was ever the same after that. He had been a very confident, cocky kid. After the fight, he was very bitter and very angry. Instead of owning the situation, he blamed everybody else for what happened. He accepted no responsibility whatsoever and I think it was very hard for him to acknowledge that he lost. It was a very painful awakening. At the time, we had a huge deal on the table with HBO. Had he won the fight, it would have made a big difference in all of our lives. The sky was the limit, but because he didn't win, everything went downhill from that point on. That fight was in November. The following June, our contract ran out and that was it. There was no major blow up. We just went in different directions.

A lot of people refer to you as "the First Lady of Boxing." How do you feel about that title and the fact that you are distinguished because you are a female?

I accept it now, because it's a fact. I'm not one of the boys. Through the years, traditionally, boxing has been a male dominated sport, and nothing is going to change that. When James won the title back in '91, I thought that more women might follow in my footsteps and do what I'm doing. As it turned out, that hasn't been the case. There are a few young women who come along every so often and pursue careers in managing and

Bronco McCart and Jackie Kallen (back), and Damien Fuller, Thomas Hearns, and Tarick Salmaci (front) at the 2015 movie premiere for *Southpaw* **(courtesy Tarick Salmaci).**

promoting fighters, but as a rule, you don't see it very often. I wear that title very proudly, because I went where few other women have dared to go, so to speak. Being considered "the First Lady of Boxing" is a wonderful honor, but will there ever be a second, or a third? I'm proud of the fact that I showed that a person can do what they want and be whoever they want to be, without any restrictions. There have been a number of minorities who have gone into fields that they don't normally go into and have had success. When that happens, it serves as a lesson to other people.

When I first started in this business, nobody thought I would have a world champion, but I refused to believe that. After a few years, sure enough, I had a world champion. I think a lot of it had to do with my ability to detect greatness in a fighter. When I met James Toney, I knew there was something special about him. I happened to get lucky and find myself at the Kronk Gym and learn from Emanuel Steward, one of the greatest trainers who ever lived. I had a chance to watch Thomas Hearns, one of the all-time greatest champions. When I left Kronk, I knew what to look for in a fighter. The fighters I gravitated to, the fighters who caught my eye—they were the kids who I felt had the potential to be at the top echelon of the sport. That's the playing field I chose and that's what made it even harder. Not only was I a woman, but I was choosing to manage the elite. I set my goals very high. I wanted world champions. Those were the fighters I sought out. Taking a kid right out of the amateurs and guiding him to a world title is a three to four year process. If it's meant to be, I want to do the whole thing all over again. That's on my bucket list. I'll keep doing this as long as I'm physically and mentally able, because I love this sport so much. I love the process of developing fighters. When you do what you love to do and you believe in yourself, you're bound to have success.

8

Gerry Cooney: The Fight

A fighter's toughest opponent is usually himself. Unlike the fighter standing in the opposite corner, this is not an opponent you can train for. It's a battle that most people don't want to fight—fought in a dark hole against their own personal demons. Born and raised in Huntington, New York, "Gentleman" Gerry Cooney started boxing as a way to distract himself from his father's alcoholism and abusive nature. In 1977, Cooney turned pro as a heavyweight, remaining undefeated as he was coming up in the ranks. He was known for his trademark left hook, which was one of the most devastating left hooks in boxing. This was punctuated by his knockout of Muhammad Ali conqueror Ken Norton, a fight that ended fifty-four seconds into the first round. On June 11th, 1982, Cooney faced heavyweight champion Larry Holmes in one of the biggest and most anticipated fights in the history of the sport. Before the fight, Cooney's manager Dennis Rappaport and Holmes's promoter Don King began a racially toned campaign as a way to stir up some controversy and sell tickets. This approach was blown out of proportion and was not the intention of either fighter. Having never previously fought past the eighth round and having been inactive for over a year, Cooney gave it his all, but he lost the fight via thirteenth-round TKO. Cooney retired in 1990 with a record of 28–3, 24 KO's. In December 2011, I called Gerry Cooney to talk about his fight with Larry Holmes, as well as "the fight" he fought outside the ring. At the time of this interview, Cooney was co-hosting a radio show called *Friday Night at the Fights*.

When did you first put on the gloves? How old were you and what were the circumstances?

When I was about thirteen, fourteen years old, I used to box in the back of the school bus with the other kids. If you want to call it boxing. I didn't have any lessons. There was no skill. We were just messing around. I started hitting the heavy bag when I was about fourteen, fifteen. My older brother used to hit the bag, so I did it, too. I thought I was pretty good, so I went to a boxing gym. I was 6'4" 160 pounds and they put me in with this little tiny guy who kicked my ass. I went back home and I realized that my opponent was going to come at me. A heavy bag is just a stationary target, but in boxing, they hit back. I thought about what I had to do and I worked on it and went back to the gym. When they put me in with that kid again, he couldn't do anything with me.

I used to go to the gym three days a week. We didn't have a ring. We would box in a gymnasium. I was always pretty good. I could always punch, especially with the left hook. I was always telling people that I was going to fight in the Golden Gloves. I never realized that I was actually going to do it, but when I was sixteen, there I was, showing up to get my physical. I got in the elevator and I get to the top floor and I heard this big guy say, "Whoever is fighting novice at 160 might as well go home right now." Two weeks later, I fought that guy. It wasn't the greatest of fights, but I beat him and I went on to win the New York State Golden Gloves at middleweight. Seven fights with five knockouts. At that point, it was like I was made. I had my place. I found something that was good for me for the first time in my life. It gave me light, it gave me hope—all of those things that people need.

Former heavyweight world title challenger Gerry Cooney (courtesy Marty Rosengarten/RingsidePhotos.com).

What were your intentions when you first started boxing?

I really didn't know. I liked what it did for me, because I grew up in a very distressed household. My father was an alcoholic. He was physically and emotionally abusive and he taught me five things that I carried around with me for most of my life. He'd say, "You're no good, you're a failure, you're not going to amount to anything, don't trust nobody, and don't tell anybody your business." My oldest brother left the house when he was sixteen because he couldn't take it anymore. He started going to the gym, so I did the same thing. Boxing was a way to express how angry I felt. I was an angry kid and I didn't know how to channel that. I hated bullies and I was getting into fights anyway. When I started boxing, I stopped fighting on the street. I liked boxing because I didn't have to depend on anybody. That's how my life was anyway. I always had to depend on myself.

My father was just a very abusive man. He always wanted to be a fighter, but he was in World War II and he didn't get a chance to, so he used to push us to go running and go

From left to right: Steve Cooney (Gerry's brother), Bruce (Dennis's cousin), Mike Jones, Gerry Cooney, Harry Bollhoffer, and Dennis Rappaport after a successful night in the ring, early 1980s (courtesy Gerry Cooney).

to the gym and all that. But it was out of selfishness. It was out of his own need. My father grew up in an abusive house and that's how he lived his life. People can go two roads. They can change it or they can repeat it. He repeated it. He had six kids and a house payment and a lot of frustration or whatever it was, but it all stopped with me. I didn't take that road. I did start drinking for a while there and losing control of things, but I put the bottle down and found a way to turn my life around. That was my biggest fight. That was my toughest opponent. I was told a lot of things when I was a kid and I had to change my mindset.

What led to your decision to turn professional and how did your career evolve from there?

I had a lot of international fights in the amateurs. I was invited to the Olympic Trials, but my father was sick and dying, so I chose not to go. I had a school teacher who told me that I should stay home and stay close to my mother. When I was eighteen, most of my friends were going away to college and I had to think about what I was going to do with my life. Boxing just fell into place. At the time, I was approached by these two real estate brokers, Dennis Rappaport and Mike Jones. They signed Howard Davis after he won the gold medal in 1976. I had talked to a lot of different people who wanted to represent me, but I liked them the best. They ended up managing me and they put me in touch with my trainer, Victor Valle, Sr. Victor and I hit it off right away and I think he's one of the best trainers ever. I sometimes teach kids how to box, and I show them a lot of the things that Victor would show me.

My pro debut was at Sunnyside Garden in Queens and I knocked the guy out in the first round. Every fight I had coming up was my toughest fight, 'til I got to the next one. They just got tougher and tougher, and then I was fighting guys like Eddie "The Animal" Lopez, John Dino Denis, Ron Lyle, and Jimmy Young. Ron Lyle was a little bit older when I fought him. He couldn't absorb my power and I stopped him in the first. When I fought Jimmy Young, I knew it was going to be tough. Nobody looked good against Jimmy Young. When I got in there, I could see that he was looking out for my left hook, so I turned my hook into an uppercut and gave him a two-inch split between his nose and stopped him in the fourth round.

In 1981, I knocked out Ken Norton in fifty-four seconds of the first round. I was a twenty-three-year-old kid and there I was facing this guy who had beat Muhammad Ali. I was scared to death, but on the night of the fight when we got to the center of the ring, I said to myself, "This guy's not that big." At the start of every fight, I always liked for guys to feel my power, so I went at him and I caught him with a body shot. I saw his legs buckle a little bit and then I caught him with a shot on the ropes. I didn't even know he was out. I remember I looked over at the referee and he didn't say anything, so I kept swinging. In all the papers the next day, they said he was "four punches from death." Looking back on that night, it was really horrific, but I'm a fighter. In the fight game, when you've got a guy hurt, you can't let up on him.

After my fight with Ken Norton, I was ranked number one in the world. I was on my way to fight for the heavyweight championship, but after that fight, my career ended. The light just went off. I don't know what it was. Maybe it was a fear of success. You see, I never learned to trust people. The people who I was supposed to trust in my life had already betrayed me. When I started winning fights, people had all of these expectations of me. I remember my managers were trying to get my name out there and they were having me walk into the ring with leprechauns and making me out to be all these things. To me, it was very silly. All I wanted was to fight for the championship, but with everything I had been through in my life and everything that was going on at the time, it was hard for me. I didn't want to let everyone down, but part of me felt like I didn't deserve it.

Even before you signed to fight heavyweight champion Larry Holmes, he seemed to have an issue with you. Where do you think the animosity came from?

You've got to understand, here's a guy who followed in Muhammad Ali's footsteps. He was the sparring partner for Ali and he saw all the attention Ali got. When he became heavyweight champion of the world, people didn't acknowledge him the same way and he was bitter because of that. When I came along, a lot of people were able to relate to me and he was a little envious. That's just how it was at the time. When it came right down to it, I don't think he had a problem with me. It was the situation we were in. It didn't have anything to do with us. On the night of the fight, we went to the center of the ring and he said to me, "Let's have a good fight." That's what boxing is all about right there. We did have a great fight. We're forever entwined because of that night and we're good friends to this day.

The promotion of the fight between you and Larry Holmes was based on the idea that it was a fight between two races, because of the fact that you were white and he was black. Did you have any idea that everything would get blown out of proportion the way it did?

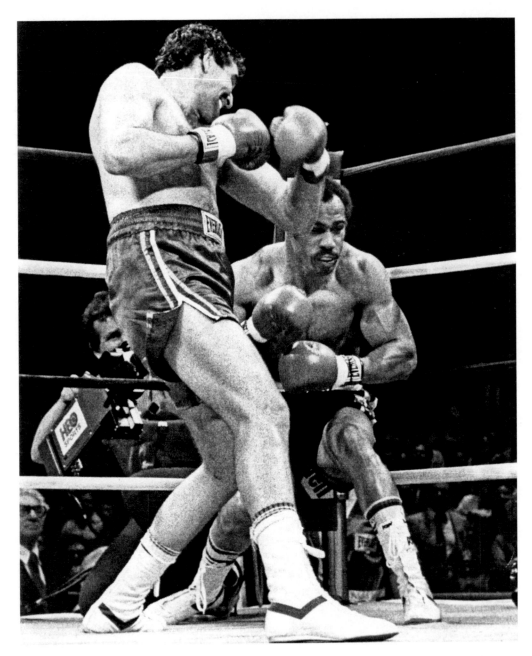

Gerry Cooney hammers Ken Norton in the corner en route to a first-round TKO victory, 1981 (courtesy Gerry Cooney).

I never paid any attention to it. When all that was going on, I was hanging around a bunch of kids who I grew up with, and we never got caught up in all that. There was some hate mail that came in. Some people were calling me a white supremacist and stupid stuff like that. One time, we got a box in the mail and we opened it up and it looked like a dead rat. As it turned out, one of the guys who worked for us forgot his wig in Palm Springs and they put it in a box and sent it to us. Can you believe that? He forgot his toupee! I opened it up and I thought it was a dead rat, but it was his hair piece! I didn't pay any attention to that stuff. This was a dream come true for me. I was fighting for the most prized possession in sports and I was having a great time.

On June 11th, 1982, you lost the fight with Larry Holmes via thirteenth-round TKO. What stands out in your mind about that night?

Going into the fight, I wished I could have had more fights leading up to it. I wanted to fight Tim Witherspoon and Mike Weaver and all those guys, but they were with Don King. I wouldn't sign with King because he had a bad rep, and because I wasn't a Don King fighter, he wouldn't let me fight them. After the fight with Ken Norton, I was out of the ring for thirteen months. Now, take a baseball player and have him sit out for thirteen months, then put him in to pitch in the fifth game of the World Series. That's what it was like for me when I fought Larry Holmes. You can't perform at the highest level when you've been out thirteen months. I really needed two or three fights during that time, but my team had a plan and my best chances to win were taken away so they could get a payday. There were things that were done that weren't right. I wasn't really in tune with what was happening at the time, but I trained hard for the fight and I did the best I could.

Gerry Cooney rocks Larry Holmes in their 1982 fight (courtesy Gerry Cooney).

I actually didn't really learn how to fight until I finished fighting. I didn't know how to sit down and relax and get some rounds in. I was all about taking 'em out and going after them. That's what I did with Holmes. When that bell rang, I went out there and stood in front of him. I got knocked down in the second round and I was kind of embarrassed. I said to myself, "What the hell are you doing here?" I got back up and fought back even harder. I always figured, don't get mad, get even. We went back and forth and up and down. I had never gone past eight rounds before, and I fought for thirteen rounds for the heavyweight championship of the world. That was the first time I ever lost a fight and I felt like I let my fans down. I was really disappointed and I remembered all the things my father used to say to me—"You're no good, you're a failure, you're not going to amount to anything, don't trust nobody, and don't tell anybody your business."

I knew I could have done better than that. I knew I was a better fighter than what I showed. I wanted to win and be the heavyweight champion and that was my chance. Maybe with a tweak here and there, I could have changed the outcome, but I did the best I could with the tools I had. If I had won that fight, I might not be here today. With all the fame and everything that comes with being a champion, I don't know if I could have handled it.

Larry Holmes and Gerry Cooney (shown here in 2006), became friends after their 1982 fight (courtesy Marty Rosengarten/RingsidePhotos.com).

I was on a wheel back then. My life was crazy. I was in a lonely place and I had no one to share it with. But that was then and this is now. I fight the better fight today. In 1988, in a moment of clarity, I put down the bottle and started to come to my senses. I had to go into that dark hole and look at everything. I didn't want to, but it was the only way to set myself free.

I wish things could have been different. I wish I had the self-esteem to feel that I deserved the things I wanted, but it is what it is and I can't change it. I made some mistakes in life, but I pulled through. I'm a fighter through and through and I still fight for what's right. I was fortunate enough to hold on to most of my money and most fighters don't have that luxury. That's why I've tried to reach out to other fighters and help them transition out of boxing. I want to keep helping people as much as I can. I want to live my life as best as I can. I want to grow. I want to be closer to my family. I want all those things that Americans are supposed to have. I'm grateful for everything that's happened to me in my life and in my career. I haven't had a drink in twenty-three years and I've got my family here with me. My life is beautiful and I'm a very lucky man.

9

Joe Souza: The Cutman

In June 2003, heavyweight champion Lennox Lewis defeated Vitali Klitschko via sixth-round TKO, due to a cut Klitschko suffered in the third round. This was one of the worst cuts ever suffered by a boxer in a major prize fight. However, Klitschko's cutman controlled the cut for three more rounds, giving the fans the best heavyweight fight of the first decade of the twenty-first century. Born and raised in New Bedford, Massachusetts, Joe Souza first learned the art of stopping a cut from the teachings of Whitey Bimstein, who many consider to be one of the best cutmen of all time. He was later mentored by Ace Marotta, who is also a highly regarded cutman. Souza went on to become a legendary cutman, as there was rarely a major prize fight from the mid–1990s through the early 2000s where he wasn't in one of the corners. He worked as the cutman for numerous high-profile fighters, including Arturo Gatti, Jesse James Leija, Andrew Golota, Evander Holyfield, Pernell Whitaker, and Fernando Vargas, among others. Following a career in the Air Force, Souza relocated to San Antonio, Texas, where he began working at the San Fernando Gym and devoting himself full-time to boxing, first as a trainer, and eventually as a cutman. Souza retired from boxing in the mid–2000s due to prostate cancer. In July 2011, I called Joe Souza to talk about his experiences as the cutman for several top fighters of the modern era. At the time of this interview, Souza was full of pep and vigor. Joe Souza, who was a friend to many in the boxing world and a father figure to several young fighters in the San Antonio area, passed away on November 14, 2011, at the age of seventy-seven.

What is your background in boxing and what led you to become a cutman?
As a kid, I fought as an amateur, and then I went into the military. I did twenty years in the Air Force and that's when I gained quite a bit of experience, fighting all over the world, mostly in Europe. Once I was transferred to San Antonio and my career in the military was ending, me and my wife decided to stay here. I got involved in boxing and became very successful, up until a couple years ago when I took sick. I've had to retire. Being a cutman was a total accident. There were a couple of kids fighting and they needed a cutman. I didn't know much about it, so I started reading. Whitey Bimstein wrote several books about it and that's how I first learned how to do it. Bimstein could stop a cut when nobody else would. The thing that Bimstein said that very few people know about is that the trick

Joe Souza gives a thumbs up after a successful night in the ring, 1990s (courtesy Rick Perez).

is pressure. You clean the cut and you put pressure on it. Just plain pressure. You use whatever you're allowed to use, which of course is a bunch of bologna. We used whatever we mixed. One day I got a hold of the book and after about a page and a half, it says to do this and to do that and I said, "Oh, shit! I think I can do this!"

In June 2003, you were Vitali Klitschko's cutman when he challenged heavyweight champion Lennox Lewis, a fight that Klitschko lost via sixth-round TKO because of a cut he suffered in the third round. What do you remember about that fight?

The thing with Klitschko, he didn't do what he was told. If he set down and boxed, I think he could have won that fight. Once he got cut, he went bananas. I had to use my experience to keep the cut in check and try to control it. That's all you can do with a cut like that. Just slow it down and control it. I kept him in the fight and kept the cut controlled as best I could. I can almost count the few fights I worked that got stopped on me. I didn't have too many fights stopped, even with the bad cuts. As a matter of fact, after one fight, the referee came up to me and said, "I didn't stop the fight because I knew you were in the corner." That's a hell of a compliment.

Former super featherweight and junior welterweight champion Arturo Gatti was a notorious bleeder. Tell me a little about your experiences as Gatti's cutman.

One time, I got busy with some preliminary fights. In fact, I worked the whole damn card. Seven fights. He's in his dressing room and I open the door and walk in and he's saying, "Where the hell is Joe Souza? Where the hell is Joe Souza?" I said, "I'm right here. Sit down. We'll take care of everything." Most of the time, he won his fights, but he gave Lou Duva more grey hairs than anything else. Lou loved him. Lou had a lot of fighters, but he sure as hell loved Arturo. Arturo was one hell of a fighter and he would never try to let anybody down. He was a great fight person. It was easy with Arturo, because he would listen. Once he got cut, I would get up in the ring and I would say, "Settle down, listen to the corner, and I'll take care of the rest." That's it. You just have to keep the fighter in check and then you work.

From May 2002 to June 2003, Arturo Gatti and Micky Ward had three fights at junior welterweight, which are considered to be some of the most exciting fights in the history of the sport. What stands out in your mind about the Gatti-Ward trilogy?

Boxing cutman Joe Souza (courtesy Rick Perez).

It was just a job. The bell rings and you're up there. That's it. I believe I was very successful because before every fight, I would get things ready. I would put this in my pocket, I would keep this away from the referee... Come on! We mixed stuff and we knew what we had to hide. You know for a fact that if we followed the rules, none of us would have been successful. Wouldn't you agree? What I would do is find out who the hell the referee was. He'd come up to us and say, "Keep it clean." I said, "Oh, shit." Before I left the house, I always made sure that I had all my equipment in my bag. Once I had my bag, you couldn't get nowhere near it.

What was in the bag?

What are you talking about what was in the bag? What the hell you think was in the bag? Bandages, tape, gauze... That and whatever the hell else I put in it! I always made sure I had plenty of gauze and tape. Some of these so-called managers were supposed to bring the gauze and the tape, and we get there and they say, "Uh.... Where is it?" I always made sure I had that. One time the guy didn't want to pay me for the gauze and the tape. I said, "That's bullshit! He's your fighter! You're supposed to bring the gauze and the tape!" It's common sense.

You were the cutman for heavyweight Andrew Golota, who was known to lose focus in the ring and even panic. What is your assessment of Golota?

The problem with Andrew is that he was always concerned with too much around him. Andrew grew up at a time in Europe when things were pretty rough. I always thought that he never trusted nobody. Whoever was with him had his hands full. Andrew and I got along very well because I wouldn't take his shit. I would tell him that. Once he got to know me and once he found out that he couldn't bologna me, we never had any problems. Now, if you think Andrew was tough, you should see his wife. She couldn't have weighed more than a hundred pounds and she wouldn't take *anybody's* shit. You just knew that she was the boss. She loved him. Her and I got along real good. She would ask me how much I wanted and I'd tell her and she'd make sure I get it. I had no problem with them.

In Golota's two 1996 fights with Riddick Bowe, he was disqualified both times for low blows. Why do you think those fights resulted the way they did?

I think the moment just overcame him. I don't think he could have controlled it. There was too much around him and he just lost it. I remember after the fight he was all busted up. He was looking at me with them eyes and he said, "What are you doing? Why are you poking your finger at me?" I said, "Andrew, take it easy! I'm cleaning out the cuts!" You see what I mean? He was just a wreck. One thing with Golota, I never had to chase my money. With some people, especially with the promoters, they try to be slick. You hear, "I'll pay you later, I'll get back to you…." No, no, no… I'd tell 'em, "You know what I wanted coming in and that's what I want going out. I didn't say I was going to work tomorrow or I'll work later. I did the work tonight and I want to get paid tonight. You give me the damn money *now*!" That's the way I felt about it, so I made it clear to them. I've only been burned a couple of times. Usually, I never had any problems with money.

You worked with Vernon Forrest, who won world titles at welterweight and junior middleweight. What do you remember about working with Forrest?

Vernon himself was a good person. He knew where he was going in life. He was a good person and it's tragic what happened to him. There's no other way of saying that. He had that organization where he worked with kids and he worked hard at that. He believed in those kids. He believed in what he was doing. I was over there before and let me tell you, those kids loved him. They *loved* him!

Pernell Whitaker, who won world titles at lightweight, junior welterweight, welterweight, and junior middleweight, is considered to be one of the best fighters of all time. Tell me about your experiences as Whitaker's cutman.

Whitaker was a man within himself. He was such a professional. He was the type of person who didn't like people falling all over him. I remember one time he walked into my gym in San Fernando downtown and people were all over him. He said, "Hold it! I'm here to train. When I get done training, I'll sign all the autographs you want. Right now, I'm here to train." That was it and that's what I liked about him.

Former two-division world champion Vernon Forrest, who was killed by an armed robber in 2009 (courtesy Marty Rosengarten/RingsidePhotos.com).

Tell me a little about some of the other people you've met and worked with in the boxing world. Who stands out in your mind?

You know Ronnie Shields, don't you? Ronnie and I became good friends and we stay in contact with each other. We kind of clicked for some reason. We used to travel all over and work together as a team. That's something I know about boxing. When you become friends with someone, it's like a lifetime commitment. I almost feel like Ronnie's my brother. We talk all the time.

Trainer Ronnie Shields and Joe Souza, late 1990s (courtesy Rick Perez).

I understand that you built a boxing museum in your garage. What does this consist of?

I got more crap than I know what to do with. There's too much to even explain. I've got a lot of posters. That's one thing that I would get after the fights. I love posters. I was just in there yesterday. Sometimes I go in there and straighten it out and look at all the stuff and think about everything I did. That's my successful part of life. I was successful for the fact that I had my family behind me. My family was always there. When I got called to do something and I wasn't sure it was the right thing, I sat down with my wife to discuss it and she would tell me yes or no. I'd say, "Well, that's it." If it wasn't for my wife, I wouldn't be successful. My problem in life was that I would tell you the way it was. One day, my wife sat me down and made me realize that I'm not the only person in the world. There's other people doing their job and you can't go walk all over everybody. I think that every man, no matter what business they're in, you have to learn how to get along with people. My wife made me realize that. I'm a lot better now than I was then.

What are some of your best boxing memories?

There are a lot of things that stand out in my memory. I could tell you one thing, but I'm sure something else would come to me later. You know, the fight business is no longer what it was years ago. Back then, you could turn on the radio or the TV and there were fights every day of the week. Now, there's a couple of fights here and there and that's it. I miss the fight game. I *miss* it. It's been my life. I still go to the gym once in a while, but it hurts to go there. When I go to a boxing show, people still remember me. They come up to me, "Hey, Joe. How're you doing? How're you feeling? What's your medical situation?" The thing I have to learn is that I get in these moods sometimes and I get bitter. Why did I have to get sick? Why did this happen to me? I'm fortunate to have had the life I had. I have to remember that I still have a lot to be thankful for. I'll tell you one thing that I'm very proud of. When I was working, I'd come home and I'd have a bucket full of money. I'm on the plane with a bunch of people and there's five, six, seven, eight, sometimes even ten or fifteen thousand dollars in my pocket. I got cash, because that's how the fight business is. When I'd come home, I'd walk in the door and I laid it all on the table. I would take fifty dollars for myself and my wife would take care of the rest. I've never been a selfish person. I did my job, she did her job, and that's why we were successful. She's been with me all these years. I've got two wonderful children, I've got a couple of grandchildren… What else can a man ask for?

John Scully: The Iceman Tapes

When people get involved with boxing, they find themselves traveling all over the world and crossing paths with a number of different people. Most of the time, they're so focused on their fights that they overlook the other opportunities that boxing gives them. There's more to being in boxing than just putting on the gloves—it's a chance to have an adventure. Born and raised in Hartford, Connecticut, John "Iceman" Scully is a trainer who fought professionally from middleweight all the way up to cruiserweight, retiring in 2001 with a record of 38–11, 21 KOs. When Scully travels somewhere for a fight, he lives the experience to the fullest, seeing all the sights and meeting new people. Being a boxer was Scully's childhood dream. This dream became a reality when he started amateur boxing at the age of fourteen, eventually turning professional. As a professional, Scully had some televised fights and he was a recognized contender, but what he wanted was to be a part of a major event on boxing's biggest stage. In 2011, he finally got his chance when he was hired to train Chad Dawson for his fight with light heavyweight champion Bernard Hopkins. Scully had known Dawson since Dawson was a kid fighting in the amateurs. He had actually worked with Dawson for a few pro fights before, but they parted ways due to logistical reasons. The Hopkins-Dawson fight, which was aired on HBO Pay-Per-View on October 15th of that year, resulted in a second round no decision due to a shoulder injury suffered by Hopkins. In October 2011, just a couple weeks after the Hopkins-Dawson fight, I called John Scully and began recording the "Iceman" tapes. At the time of this interview, Scully was hoping that an agreement could be reached for a rematch between Chad Dawson and Bernard Hopkins. The rematch took place in April the following year, with Dawson winning a majority decision.

When did you first put on the gloves? How old were you and what were the circumstances?
     When I was a kid, my mother and father were divorced, and I used to stay with my father on the weekends. I'd have to find things to do to keep myself busy, so I started reading different magazines and books on boxing. One of the books was *The Greatest*, which was about Muhammad Ali. Before I read the book, I already knew who Ali was, because I remembered when "The Thrilla in Manila" was about to happen. Our local newspaper had an iron-on decal in the paper. It was a butterfly and a bee and it was advertising the upcoming fight. My brother and I were arguing about who got it, so we could iron it on to our shirt.

I just remember wanting that decal so bad, because anybody who had their own decal must be pretty big. Who else had their own decal besides Superman? When I read *The Greatest*, I was really caught up in it. One of the things Ali said in the book is that he didn't use drugs or alcohol. I was eleven at the time and that just really caught me. To this day, I'm forty-four years old, and I've never tasted alcohol in my life. Never a beer, never a glass of wine… Nothing. I figured if a guy like Ali didn't do it, it must be a good move. That's how I've chosen to live my life and I have Muhammad Ali to thank for that.

When I was twelve, my father bought me a pair of boxing gloves. On the weekends, I would take fake Halloween blood and put it on my face, and I would put water on my face to simulate sweat. I would wrap my hands in toilet paper and put clear tape over it to make it look like handwraps, and I would box in the mirror. I'd have a timer and I would box for three minutes. I would pretend I was Ali and I would box against Jimmy Young. For some reason, I always chose Jimmy Young as my opponent. I would act out every round, and then I would score the fight and declare the winner. When I was fourteen, my father brought me to a boxing gym for the first time. My very first day, the coach put me in the ring with a kid named Mark Cyr. He was seventeen and he had a little bit of experience. When I was in there, all I did was imitate Muhammad Ali—float like a butterfly and sting like a bee. I used to watch tapes of Ali's first fight with Liston and I tried to fight like that. I don't think I hit him that much, but he didn't hit me at all. He asked me afterwards, "How long you been boxing?" I said, "About a half an hour." That was the first time I sparred with a real boxer and the coach told my dad, "If your son sticks with it, in one year, he'll win a championship." That was March of 1982 and in May of 1983, I won the Connecticut Junior Olympic Championship.

What moments stand out about your amateur career?

One of my best moments as an amateur was when I beat Otis Grant. Everybody's seen Otis in the pros. He was a WBO champion and he fought Roy Jones for the middleweight title. I fought Otis in Montreal on three days' notice. He was number two in the world and he had just won a big international tournament in Germany the month before. I was unranked at the time, so beating him on short notice in his hometown was pretty big. As it turns out, Otis and I became the best of friends. We're still great friends to this day. Another great moment for me was when I fought Darrin Allen. I had always wanted to fight Darrin, because I had seen him fight on the *Wide World of Sports* several times. Today, he would be the equivalent of a Floyd Mayweather type of guy. He was a big amateur star. When I beat him to win the eastern Olympic Trials in 1988, I really made my mark in amateur boxing. I never felt like I belonged in the upper echelon until I beat Darrin. When they announced the decision, I jumped in the air so high. It was like I was on a pogo stick. I was jumping up and down and I had no control over it. In my head, I was saying that I better stop, because I was getting close to the ropes. It occurred to me that I might actually jump over the top rope and land on the concrete.

What moments stand out about your professional career?

For better or worse, I experienced boxing. To use an analogy, if you go to Puerto Rico and you stay in the resort the whole week, you haven't really been to Puerto Rico. You have to experience where you're at. With me, I traveled all over when I was a pro, but I didn't just stay in my hotel room and focus on my fight. I was checking things out. This may have hindered my career in some way, but it was worth it. The moments that stand out about my professional years are some of the things I experienced outside the ring. I'm a curious person. Just recently, I went to Los Angeles with Chad Dawson for his fight with Bernard Hopkins. When I was in LA, I rented a car and went to see *The Brady Bunch* house. You got me? *The Brady Bunch* house! I stopped a guy who was walking by, and had him take a picture of me standing in front of it. I didn't just go to Los Angeles, I *experienced* Los Angeles.

I was at a fight the other day and Ronnie Shields was there. I remember watching him fight in 1983 when I was fifteen. He fought on *Wide World of Sports* and Tim Ryan and Gil Clancy were the announcers. When I saw Ronnie, I told him about that, and I got my picture taken with him. Seeing guys like Ronnie Shields was one of the things I liked about being a pro. I got to stand next to guys who I saw on TV. They're my heroes. I've met hundreds and hundreds of famous people and it never gets old. I never get used to it. I remember

John Scully in front of *The Brady Bunch* house, while in Los Angeles for Chad Dawson's 2011 fight with Bernard Hopkins (courtesy John Scully).

the first time I met Muhammad Ali. It was like a religious experience. I've heard stories from people before who had met him. They said it was larger than life. It was like a Biblical figure and I definitely felt that when I met him. When I was an amateur, I went to Sugar Ray Leonard's house. He let me hold his WBC belt, he let me hold his gold medal… It was like a dream and I was hoping I would never wake up.

When I went to spar with Roy Jones, Jr., for the first time as a pro, I was so excited about sparring him. He was a great fighter and I wanted to see what he had. After the first week, they gave me a paycheck. I didn't even know what it was. It caught me off guard. I said, "What's this?" They said, "That's your paycheck." I was like, "Oh, yeah, yeah, yeah…" They didn't know that I would have gone there for nothing. If they told me that they ran into some problems with the budget and they couldn't afford to pay me, I would have stayed. I was just glad to be there. There was another time I was in Las Vegas and I was in my hotel room eating ice cream. I was lying in bed watching TV and my manager called and said, "Get to the gym right now. Mike McCallum is here and his sparring partner didn't show up and he needs sparring." I got up and threw the ice cream in the garbage and went over to Johnny Tocco's and boxed with Mike McCallum. I was so excited about that!

Of all my fights in the pros, the one that always comes to mind is Michael Nunn. I out-punched him according to CompuBox and a lot of people thought I won. Michael Nunn was a guy I always admired growing up. I used to watch him on TV all the time. At one point during the fight, I was talking a little bit of trash and I was like, "Come on! Fight me!" He hit me a couple of times and I told him he couldn't hurt me and then he called me a mother eff-er. We got into a clinch and I remember thinking, "Wow! Michael Nunn just called me a mother eff-er!" In either the seventh or eighth round, I hurt him with a really good right hand. I knew he was hurt and I could see it in his eyes. I heard Al Bernstein behind me saying, "I think Michael Nunn was hurt with that shot!" In that moment, in that very instant, I was picturing Michael Nunn on HBO when he fought Iran Barkley and I couldn't believe that I was in the same ring with him. Looking back on it, maybe I should have been more focused on the fights, but I was just having too much fun.

What led you to become a trainer?

I was a trainer while I was a boxer. The first time I worked a corner for an amateur fighter, I had just turned pro. This was 1989 and I was 6–0 at the time. I worked the corner for a kid named Luis Maysonette. After the first round, I told him, "Just throw your jab–right hand right down the middle and you'll tear him up." He knocked the kid out the next round with the jab–right hand. I was like, man, this is crazy! I just told him how to knock this kid out! I thought I had something there, so I started training amateurs. After I fought Michael Nunn on ESPN, two weeks later, I was sleeping on the floor of a motel room. The kids were on the bed and I was on the floor and they were boxing in a regional Silver Gloves tournament. During my pro career, I was training and traveling and always going to national tournaments. While I was still fighting in 2001, I was asked to train Elizabeth Mueller, who was fighting for a world title. I trained her for that fight and she ended up winning the world lightweight title. In 2003, once I stopped fighting, I got a call asking me to train heavyweight Lawrence Clay-Bey. I started training him the next day and the following year I started training Chad Dawson, Mike Oliver, Jose Antonio Rivera, Matt Godfrey…

I don't consider myself a trainer who trains fighters. I consider myself a fighter who trains fighters. By that, I mean that I get in there and box with my fighters to see how good they are. Who can tell better than the guy who's in there with him? I'll box with them and I'll tell them, "You're real good with the left hook, but your body shots aren't that good." That type of stuff. I love sparring and I still spar a lot. I'm always looking to spar with people. I want to see who hits hard, who's fast, who has a good jab… Anytime there's a good fighter within a hundred miles of me, I'll go check him out and spar with him. I like to test myself and I'm a unique trainer for that reason. There's this light heavyweight I train. Two months ago, we did fifteen rounds. We were gonna do twelve, but I decided in the eleventh round that we were going fifteen. Part of the reason is that I want to lead by example. I tell them, "I'm forty-four and I go a strong fifteen. If I can do it, there's no way in the world you can't do it." Also, I think a lot of trainers who have never fought before or trainers who haven't done it in a long time—they forget or they don't know what it is to be a fighter. There are certain aspects of boxing that you cannot know unless you've actually been a fighter. That's just the way it is.

You trained Chad Dawson for his October 2011 fight against light heavyweight champion Bernard Hopkins. When did you first meet Dawson?

I met Chad when he was about eleven or twelve years old. His amateur coach Brian Clark had a gym in New Haven, Connecticut, called Ring One. He and his kids would all

John Scully holds the mitts for Chad Dawson in preparation for Dawson's 2011 fight with Bernard Hopkins (courtesy Bret Newton—ThreatPhoto.com/Pound4Pound.com).

go to the same tournaments as me and my kids and a lot of times we would travel together. If we would go to Ohio for the week, it would basically consist of boxing for part of the time and then the rest of the time it was practical jokes. It was my team against his team. We would be at a hotel and we would just terrorize the place day and night. It was just weeks and weeks of fun. I worked the corner for several of Chad's amateur fights back in the '90s. If his trainer couldn't make it to a tournament that I was going to, he would send Chad with me. As a pro, I trained him in 2004 and 2005 for his fights with Darnell Wilson, Carl Daniels, and Efrain Garcia. At the time, he was in the process of leaving his trainer and they called and asked me if I'd like to train him. I actually called his trainer and asked him for his blessings. He said, "If somebody else is going to train him, it ought to be you."

The training I did with Chad at that time was some of the best training I've ever done. It was some of my best teaching. If I brought out the best in him, he brought out the best in me. It was just a great, great relationship. When we parted ways, he was leaving his promoter and his manager at the time. The manager paid the rent at the gym where I trained him and Chad stayed at his house while he was in town to train with me. When he left the guy, that took away the gym and the living facility, so I basically had no way to train him. Chad then signed with Gary Shaw, and Gary was aligned with Dan Birmingham, who trained Winky Wright and Jeff Lacy. He sent him down to Birmingham, and from there, he went through a few different trainers. When I talked to him years later, he said that he had always wanted to train with me. I wasn't in touch with Chad after he left, but I would sometimes run into him at a fight. I would always see him and it was always a good feeling. To be honest with you, when I was asked to train him this time, I wasn't at all surprised.

What led you to become Dawson's trainer once again?

It's a crazy thing. Life is really funny sometimes. It was early in July of this year. As luck would have it, my friend Damon Feldman called me. He had a friend who wanted to reach Chad about some kind of sponsorship deal. I called Chad and said, "Hey, this guy wants to talk to you. Maybe you can make some money out of it." Chad said, "It's really a coincidence that you called me on this day in particular, because my brother and I were just talking about you this morning." When he said that, I thought they were talking about the old amateur days, but he said that he was making some changes in his training, and that he had this big fight with Hopkins coming up, and he wanted to know if I would be interested in training him. A couple days later, he was in the gym. When I trained him in 2004 and 2005, he was the most coachable fighter I've ever worked with. I was worried, because since that time he's gotten a lot of money, he's gotten fame, and he's won titles. Thirty seconds into the first round of holding the pads for him, it was like he was eleven years old again. It was exactly the same.

The Hopkins-Dawson fight was ruled a no contest due to Hopkins suffering a shoulder injury in the second round. Tell me about your experiences at this event and your perspective on what happened in the fight.

I had trained guys for championship fights before. I worked with Jose Antonio Rivera when he won a world title, but this was different. We were fighting a guy like Bernard Hopkins who was a world -wide star. It didn't really faze me though. I was excited. This was the reason I started boxing in the first place. Some people thought I was really up against it, because we're facing Bernard Hopkins and he had Naazim Richardson and some of the top trainers from Philadelphia in his corner, but I knew I belonged there. I'll tell you a little story. When I was fourteen years old, I used to talk to my wife on the phone all the time. We weren't even dating back then. I met her when we were in the sixth grade, and I used to tell her that I was going to be a professional boxer and fight on TV, and that I was going to marry her someday. This was 1983 and we didn't even get together and get married until 2007! The point is that I always knew what I wanted in my life and I knew it was going to come true. Fighting in the ring like a real boxer, beating Darren Allen for the '88 eastern Olympic Trials, meeting Muhammad Ali… It was all part of my dream. So, when I was at the center of the ring looking at Bernard Hopkins, I knew I was standing right where I was supposed to be.

Chad came out very determined and after the first round, I said, "We got it." I knew we won that round. To me, it was an easy round to score. Hopkins's whole demeanor was passive. He didn't look like a hungry fighter trying to defend his title. I think he was surprised at how strong and aggressive Chad was. Based on Chad's fight with Jean Pascal, I think he was looking for a weakness in the armor that he didn't see. Chad didn't allow himself to be manhandled. There was a point in the fight where Bernard was against the ropes and he tried to maneuver out of there, but Chad ended up with his forearm lodged in Bernard's throat. He kind of locked it there, and over the top of the forearm, he was looking right in

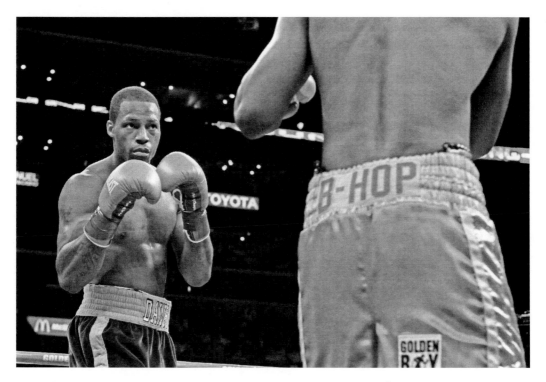

Chad Dawson squares off with Bernard Hopkins in their 2011 encounter (courtesy Bret Newton— ThreatPhoto.com/Pound4Pound.com).

Bernard's eyes. I had a clear view of it. He had this stone cold blank expression as if to say, "You picked the wrong guy. You're not going to manhandle me tonight. I'm going to man-handle *you*." I think at that moment, Bernard knew he wasn't in with a soft kid like he thought.

Towards the end of the second round, Bernard threw a jab–right hand. It was the sloppiest jab–right hand that I've ever seen. When you throw a right hand, your right leg is supposed to stay down when you extend your arm, but when Bernard threw that right hand, he catapulted himself forward and he ended up on top of Chad. Chad ducked the right hand and he had Bernard on his back. His instincts were to get Bernard off of him, so he shrugged him off. When Bernard went down, I knew at that moment that he wasn't getting back up. I just knew it. I based that on some of his past fights. Against Roy Jones and Joe Calzaghe, he was tapped below the belt and they had to call time out. He made a big ordeal of it. I knew he wasn't going to get back up. I'm not saying he faked it and I'm not saying he quit, but at that point, I knew for sure that the fight was over.

You have a quote you like to use. "The wait in the dressing room before a boxing match—that last hour—could be enough to strip a man that never boxed before of whatever pride, desire and heart he thought he had." What does that mean?

That means that it's an experience where if any man says he's not afraid, he's lying. Some of the top champions of recent years have read that quote and e-mailed me about it. Jesse James Leija called me after he read it. I had never spoken to him before. He got my number and he called me and said, "That quote is so accurate. It's so perfect." He copied it and hung it up on the wall of his gym so people could see it. That dressing room wait is the moment of truth. I actually believe that some fights are won and lost in that last hour. When that guy comes in and tells you that your time is coming and that he'll be back in twenty minutes to get you, there's no feeling like it. There's a fighter I know who had a hun-dred twenty-five amateur fights. He was one of the best amateurs in the country. After his pro debut, he told me that it was the craziest thing he had ever been involved with. He said, "I was in the dressing room and I was looking at this door that led to the alley outside the arena. It occurred to me that I could just run out that door and nobody would know I was gone. I could just escape." It occurred to him to do that, because the feeling of going out there, it's almost like you're going to the electric chair. You can't explain it. Guys box in the gym every day and they have a hundred amateur fights, but there's something about being a professional waiting for that door to open. It takes a special human being to do that.

11

Roy Jones, Jr:
Pound for Pound

In boxing, the term "pound for pound" is used to measure the quality of fighters, regardless of the weight class they are in. An average heavyweight can usually beat the best middleweight, though the middleweight is still considered to be a better fighter, pound for pound. When a fighter is referred to as, "number one pound for pound," it means that they are the best in all of boxing. Born and raised in Pensacola, Florida, Roy Jones, Jr., has won world titles at middleweight, super middleweight, light heavyweight, and heavyweight. He was named "Fighter of the Decade" for the 1990s, and he is the only man in history to start his career at junior middleweight and win a world title at heavyweight. A former silver medalist from the 1988 Olympic Games, Jones was the victim of what many consider to be the worst robbery in the history of amateur boxing. In his last fight of that tournament, Jones clearly out-pointed Korea's Park Si-Hun, though the judges scored the fight in favor of Si-Hun and denied Jones the gold medal. As a professional, Jones holds victories over living legends Bernard Hopkins and James Toney, as well as several other highly regarded fighters. After winning a heavyweight world title in 2003, Jones moved back down to 175 pounds to recapture his light heavyweight title, defeating Antonio Tarver via majority decision. In an immediate rematch, Jones lost his title to Tarver via second-round TKO. Nevertheless, Jones had already cemented his legacy as one of the best boxers who ever lived. In November 2011, I called Roy Jones, Jr., and asked him about his reign as the pound for pound king of boxing. At the time of this interview, Jones's record was 54–8, 40 KOs, and he was scheduled to face Max Alexander.

When did you first put on the gloves? How old were you and what were the circumstances?

I started when I was ten years old. When I was five, I watched Muhammad Ali and Joe Frazier fight. Ali was a great antagonizer and I knew that I was a great antagonizer. When I saw what Ali was doing, I felt like I could do that. All I needed was somebody to show me what to do with my hands. I kept nagging my dad to let me start. My dad boxed when he was in the Job Corps and he had two pro fights, but I didn't know it at the time. He taught other kids how to box and when I was ten, he started teaching me at the house. He'd have me spar with some of the kids he was working with. The first time I got in the

87

ring with an outsider, I did an exhibition with this fourteen-year-old kid. I was only ten and he was much bigger than me, but I always liked fighting bigger kids anyway. There was nobody else I could do an exhibition with, so I did an exhibition with him. After the exhibition, everybody was calling me "Little Sugar Ray" and all kinds of nicknames. I didn't understand what that meant, but I knew they were saying that because I was good.

Did you play other sports when you were growing up? If so, why did you ultimately choose boxing?
I played football before I started boxing. I was a standout before the team folded. I played basketball, too. I was all right at basketball, but boxing was where my personality fit best. I loved to fight. I was right at home inside the ring. It was hard work and I missed out on a lot of my childhood because I took it so seriously, but that was part of what I had to do.

You grew up on a farm where there were fighting roosters. From what I understand, these roosters were a passion of yours. What is it that attracted you to them?
The roosters fought and I fought. I was intrigued by their colors and how pretty they were. They believed so much that they were in charge and they would die fighting for what they believed. That was a lot like Muhammad Ali, too. Ali was willing to die for his cause.

That's what fighting is. It's life and death. It's kill or be killed. Look what happened to Duk Koo Kim. "Boom Boom" Mancini wasn't trying to kill him, but he was beating on him and that's what happened. I realized that's what this is about. I was putting my life on the line every time I fought. Nobody wants to say it, but that's what it is when you get in the ring. It's not just a sport. This *is* a real fight. This is a war. This is you get me or I get you.

You won a silver medal at the 1988 Seoul Olympic Games as a junior middleweight and you were the outstanding boxer of the tournament, despite losing a controversial decision to Park Si-Hun in your last fight. What stands out in your mind about that experience?
I wanted to fight in the Olympics since 1976, when I watched Sugar Ray Leonard and Howard Davis and Leo Randolph and Leon and Michael Spinks win gold

Former four-division world champion and Olympic silver medalist Roy Jones, Jr. (courtesy Marty Rosengarten/Ringside Photos.com).

medals. I won every round of every fight I was in, all the way till the end. In the last fight when I fought Park Si-Hung, I was robbed of the gold medal. Everybody knew I won. Even *he* said that I won. I was devastated at the time and I felt like if I can beat a guy and not get the win, why should I keep doing it? But I still had the drive. When you have talent, you can't deny it. If I quit, how could I ever explain it to the people who were behind me? There were people who would have been disappointed if I didn't turn pro. After seeing that look in their eyes after the Olympics, I couldn't quit. I learned that if I can keep going after what happened, I can come back and do other things like be one of the best pound for pound best fighters who ever lived. I think I did a good job of that.

Given your accomplishments as an amateur, you had several options when you turned pro. A lot of promoters wanted to be involved with you, but you kept everything between you and your father. He was your trainer and your promoter. Why did the two of you remain independent of the boxing world?

We, and especially me, wanted to control my own career. It started off the way I wanted, but I could see that I was becoming less and less likely to succeed because of the people I was fighting at the time. My father had an overbearing attitude about a lot of things and I knew that I couldn't become champ under that overbearing personality. I needed a change. That's why I called Alton Merkerson, who was my Olympic coach. I told him that I was having disagreements with my father and I asked him if it would be cool for me to come down

Roy Jones, Jr.'s longtime trainer Alton Merkerson, 2008 (courtesy Marty Rosengarten/RingsidePhotos.com).

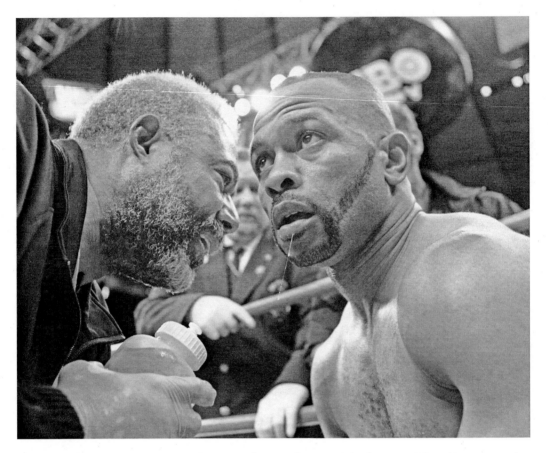

Roy Jones, Jr., in the corner with trainer Alton Merkerson, 2008 (courtesy Marty Rosengarten/ RingsidePhotos.com).

and train with him. I always knew that I was going to go back to Coach Merkerson one day. I told him that at the Olympics. I did that and I went back to doing things my way. I had no manager, no promoter, nobody telling me how to do it. I started getting the better fights and getting closer to becoming a champion.

After four years of remaining undefeated as a professional, in May 1993, you defeated Bernard Hopkins via unanimous decision for a vacant middleweight world title.

Before the fight, I basically fractured my right hand, but I had to take the opportunity because I didn't know if I would get it again. I knew Bernard was good, but I thought I could beat him with my left hand. I went in there and that's what I did. I beat him with my left hand.

After the Hopkins fight, you drifted up and down from middleweight to super middleweight, defeating fighters like Thulani Malinga and Thomas Tate. In November 1994, you challenged super middleweight champion James Toney in a fight you won via unanimous decision. At the time, a lot of people considered Toney to be the best pound-for-pound fighter in the world.

That's why I wanted to fight him. I always looked for the guy who was the best at that time. He got all the attention and everybody said he was the best pound for pound. I had to beat him if I wanted to be the best pound for pound. That's what I did. I knew I could beat him, I *told* him I could beat him… He thought he was the trash talker, but *I'm* the trash talker. He wasn't going to beat me at my own game. I was the underdog in that fight and that's what I love. I love being the underdog, because it motivates me to be at my best. That's why I had to knock him down like I did. I knocked him down with the "chicken move." I learned it from watching my roosters. I posed down like the roosters do. He tried to do the same thing, but he didn't know that I can punch from that position, so I hit him with a left hook.

After the fight with James Toney, you dominated at super middleweight against fighters like Vinny Pazienza, Merqui Sosa, and Eric Lucas, among others. What stands out in your mind about some of those fights?

Back then, there was nobody to really challenge me. I wanted a new challenge, so I started playing basketball. I love basketball and I wanted to get better, so I played in the USBL for the Jacksonville Barracudas. When I fought Eric Lucas, I played in a basketball game on the morning of the fight. After the game, I went there and defended my title.

Did you really have that much confidence going into your fights?

Hell yeah, I had that much confidence! That's how good I was!

In November 1996, you captured a world title at light heavyweight by defeating Mike McCallum via unanimous decision. The following March, you suffered your first loss as a professional via ninth round disqualification when you faced Montell Griffin. What happened in that fight?

Like you just said, I was disqualified. I hit him with this little soft punch when he was on the mat and he acted like he got knocked out. It was like round two from the Olympics. I felt like I was cheated all over again. It was the only time I ever brought RJ out. RJ is my alter ego. RJ is the kind of person I never want to bring out. I never want to see that person, because if I do, I'd probably go to jail or something. You know what I'm saying? Once you turn that switch on, you can't switch it off. There's no "off" button. I might kill somebody. Montell Griffin basically quit in the last round of the first fight. He quit and then they gave him my title and then he bragged about it! Oooooh… You quit and then you brag about it? What kind of guy are you? You're gonna pay for that! When that happens, that's when RJ comes out. RJ is the kind of guy who doesn't care. He doesn't give a damn. When we got to the press conference for the rematch, I told him he wasn't going to be able to quit this time. I was going to go out there and show him what happens when I really want to get it over with. That's what I did.

In August 1997, you knocked Griffin out in the first round of your rematch to reclaim your title. In April the following year, you knocked out Virgil Hill in the fourth round with a body shot.

Yep.

Was this a shot that you planned on landing? Did you see it before it happened?

I set it up by design. I kept throwing right hands to his head and he kept blocking with his left arm. I said, okay, if you're going to keep blocking it, next time I'm going to shoot a body shot underneath. That's what I did.

Reggie Johnson, David Telesco, Richard Hall, Eric Harding, Julio Cesar Gonzalez, Glen Kelly, Clinton Woods... What comes to mind when you think of those fights that took place at light heavyweight from 1999 to 2002?
    All superb performances!

Nobody was touching you at that time.
    Nope.

In March 2003, you moved up to heavyweight to challenge John Ruiz for his world title in a fight you won via unanimous decision. What stands out in your mind about that experience?
    I came to the ring first. I was waiting for him and he came to the ring to *Goodnight Saigon* by Billy Joel. That's a song that I loved. I was like, wow! I couldn't believe he came to the ring to a song I liked. We get in there and he thought I was going to run all night, but I had no intentions of running from him. I stood in front of him and beat the hell out of him. I became the only man in the history books to win the middleweight, super middleweight, light heavyweight, and heavyweight title. All I had to do at that point was recapture the light heavyweight title. Nobody had ever gone up to heavyweight before and then

John Ruiz, Don King, and Roy Jones, Jr., at a press conference for the 2003 Jones-Ruiz fight (courtesy Bret Newton—ThreatPhoto.com/Pound4Pound.com).

went back down to recapture a title at light heavyweight. Not everyone can do that. You know what I'm saying? Chris Byrd tried it and look what happened. It will kill you. It will drain you. This is something I had to do to complete the cycle. This is something God wanted me to do.

So, being the first man to go from light heavyweight to heavyweight, and then back down to light heavyweight was a goal you wanted to accomplish?

It's not something I wanted to do. It's something I *had* to do.

In November 2003, in your first fight back at light heavyweight, you won a majority decision over Antonio Tarver for Tarver's world title. From the start, it looked as if you were drained because of the weight loss. How did you feel going into the fight?

Losing twenty-five pounds of muscle was killing me the whole way through. That was evident, but I wasn't going to die until I got my title back. I had to get my title back first. *Then* I could die. When I fought Tarver the first time, I didn't have near the energy that I had when I fought at light heavyweight. I didn't have near the power, but God wouldn't let me stop. Not until I got my title back.

Your first fight with Antonio Tarver was a tough, close fight and it was the first time in your career that you had to dig down deep to get the victory.

Referee Arthur Mercante, Jr., points Roy Jones, Jr., to a neutral corner after Jones dropped Felix Trinidad en route to a unanimous decision victory in their 2008 fight (courtesy Marty Rosengarten/ RingsidePhotos.com).

Yep. The people who had admiration for me before that fight had even more admiration for me after the fight. There were people who told me, "You know what, Roy? I liked you as a fighter before the fight, but I didn't love you as a fighter. Now I love you as a fighter."

A lot of people feel that you could have retired after your fight with John Ruiz with nothing left to prove.

I did what God demanded of me. After the Ruiz fight, I did part of what he wanted. I didn't do everything. If I had retired, that would have been a lie. I'm not going to say I did everything with a straight face, because I'm not that kind of guy. I don't want the accolades, I want to do what's asked of me. Once I do everything that's asked of me, *then* I'll accept the accolades.

12

Emanuel Steward:
The Kronk Legacy

Most people who get involved with boxing never intend for this sport to be their livelihood. It's often just a hobby, while other trades pay the bills. But sometimes when a person is passionate about something and they are a master at what they do, their passions become their life. Born in Bottom Creek, West Virginia, later relocating to Detroit, Michigan, Emanuel Steward spent most of his early years as an electrician. When he was first asked to run the boxing program at the Kronk Gym in Detroit, he turned the opportunity down, because his work schedule was so demanding. However, Steward eventually caved in and began working with various boxers in the gym. One of those boxers was a kid by the name of Thomas Hearns, who went on to become a five-division champion. Steward also trained and guided other champions such as Lennox Lewis, Wladimir Klitschko, Michael Moorer, Hilmer Kenty, Milton McCrory, Gerald McClellan, Jimmy Paul, and Duane Thomas. In addition, Steward was sought out by a number of high profile fighters for shorter periods of time, including Ray Charles Leonard, Oscar De La Hoya, Aaron Pryor, Julio Cesar Chavez, Sr., Miguel Cotto, Jermain Taylor, and Evander Holyfield. Later in his career, Steward was a boxing analyst for HBO, where he offered a trainer's perspective and provided an education of the sport to the fans watching. In June 2012, I called Emanuel Steward to discuss when the Kronk legacy first began. At the time of this interview, he was training Wladimir Klitschko for his rematch with Tony Thompson. Later in the year, it was reported that Steward had been diagnosed with colon cancer. On October 25, 2012, Emanuel Steward passed away at the age of sixty-eight. Before Steward's passing, he predicted that Kronk fighters Adonis Stevenson and Andy Lee would win world titles. Within three years, Steward's prediction came true. Steward's teachings of the sport are now passed on to a new generation of fighters through former pupils Javan "Sugar" Hill and Johnathon Banks.

What is your background in boxing and what led you to become a trainer?

I got a pair of boxing gloves when I was seven years old. I was fascinated with this game of hitting somebody, jumping back, making them miss, and jumping in and hitting them again. I was born and raised in West Virginia. There was no organized boxing or anything like that, but I had a few fights when I was kid. My first fight was at the American Legion Hall. They matched me with another little boy. There were no ropes, but we had gloves on. It wasn't even legal. They were making corn whiskey and betting on us. I just jumped around and hit the kid in the nose. He started crying, so they stopped it. I did a few fights like that and that's how I got into boxing. I moved to Detroit when I was eleven and I started to get into a lot of street fights. There was one situation that was pretty bad. They were going to put me away in juvenile permanent, but my mother begged them not to do it. She said that when I was a little boy in West Virginia, I used to box. One of the police officers said they would try to give me a break and see if they could situate me in some kind of boxing program. That's what they did. I boxed at a recreation center called Brewster. It's the same center where Joe Louis, Eddie Futch, and Ray Robinson used to box. It's located in a well-known Harlem-type area in Detroit where a lot of black boxers came out of.

When I was fourteen, I went into the city Junior Olympic tournament and won that in the 110-pound division. The next year, I went back and won it at 120. I didn't have a chance to get into any trouble, because every time I got home, it was too late to do anything. I had to walk for almost an hour and a half to get to the gym. When I got off probation, I kept boxing. I was eighteen when I won the national Golden Gloves tournament in Chi-

Boxing trainer and manager Emanuel Steward (courtesy Marty Rosengarten/RingsidePhotos. com).

cago at 118 pounds. When I came back, the city of Detroit was going crazy. Everybody was celebrating. At that point, I was mulling over turning professional. I was offered $50,000 by a group in Los Angeles, but I would have had to move to California. I thought about it, but I didn't want to leave Detroit. I had my mother and my two sisters I wanted to take care of. I had also married, so I didn't turn pro. This was all around 1963. In 1969, my father had remarried and I had a half-brother named James, who came to stay with me. I was about twenty-six and I was working at Detroit Edison as an electrician. James wanted to box, so I took him to a recreation center that was close to my house. This center was called Kronk.

When the Golden Gloves came in January of 1970, I put my brother in the tournament representing Kronk and he won. Kronk had about six other fighters in the tournament and my brother was the only one who won. The next year, they asked me if I would be the head coach at Kronk. I said "No" because I was busy at Edison with my electrician job. After they called me a few times, I finally gave in. The next year, I put my brother and the same kids who lost the year before in the Golden Gloves and they all won the championship. There were headlines all over the country, "Young Coach In Detroit Only Produces Champions." Kids from all over wanted to come to Kronk. One of those kids was a little skinny kid named Tommy Hearns and the Kronk legacy took off from there. In 1976, Ray Leonard trained at Kronk when he wanted to make the Olympic Team. Ray was our first Kronk star, believe it or not. There's a list of names on the wall of the great fighters who trained at Kronk. Ray Leonard is on there with Tommy Hearns, Milton McCrory, Michael Moorer, and everybody else. On November 25th, 1977, when Tommy turned professional, Ray was there to help build up the fight. He was congratulating Tommy and meeting people. Little did I know that this was the beginning of what turned out to be one of the biggest rivalries in the history of boxing.

How did the rivalry between Thomas Hearns and Ray Leonard develop from that point on?

Every time Tommy fought, people said, "You look good, but the 'Sugar Man' is going to get you." Every time Ray fought, the same thing was said about Tommy. For one of Ray's fights, he was fighting a guy named Floyd Mayweather, who of course is Floyd Jr.'s father. They asked if Tommy would come in and spar with Ray for that fight, because Tommy and Floyd were both kind of rangy. Tommy had about three or four fights at the time. I wasn't there for the sparring, but word from Washington, D.C., was that it was unbelievable boxing. It was so intense that Tommy went back home after two days. After a while, people realized that they had to fight. The public demanded it. They didn't have Pay-Per-View back then, but from what I was told, twenty-five percent of the American population tuned in to the fight. After it had been built up for three or four years, I met with Mike Trainer at the airport in Syracuse. Mike Trainer was Ray Leonard's agent and manager. In fifteen minutes, we put together one of the biggest fights in history. We shook hands and that was it. There were no egos at all. I got back on the same plane that I came in on and went right back home.

Going into the fight, because of the magnitude, it was the only time that Tommy and I ever had friction and arguments. We've never had problems, other than that fight. The training camp was so big. Everybody was fighting to get close to Tommy and I had to compete with them. One guy was telling Tommy, "You should be running your own camp. Ray Leonard runs his camp. Emanuel has been controlling you since you were a kid." This was going on continually the whole time. At one point, somebody brought in a special cook for Tommy. I had always done the cooking before, but for this fight they had a special chef and everything. They brought this guy in and Tommy was eating cottage cheese, jello, tuna fish… I said, "Tommy, what are you eating this for? You look so

Thomas Hearns in the 1970s, before he was a five-division world champion (courtesy Jackie Kallen).

damn weak, man!" When I cooked for Tommy, he would eat green beans, pot roast, baked chicken, macaroni and cheese, and candied yams. That's what he was raised on. Tommy would run in the morning, but one night, I looked out the window and there he was running again with four of his guys. I said, "Tommy, what is wrong with you?" He said, "I'm the one fighting. I want to be in the best shape of my life." He was over-training and under-eating, and when he got on the scale before the fight, he was 145. He came into the fight too light. Instead of a big welterweight, he was a tall, skinny welterweight.

I learned after that camp that I had to have more control, but it happened that way and there's no room for excuses. This was one of the best fights ever and it was one of the few fights that exceeded the expectations. Unbelievable drama! The boxer became the puncher and the puncher became the boxer. They went back and forth. In the sixth round, Tommy and Ray had a good exchange and Ray hurt Tommy with a short left hook. I had never seen Tommy hurt before, so it was an emotional experience for me. From that point on, I said, "Tommy, we got to go back to the amateur days and box this guy." He became a boxer and he started coming on and taking Ray to school. Ray changed up himself and did what he had to do to become the aggressor. At about the twelfth round, I was talking to Tommy between rounds and it was like his eyes just dropped. I knew that we had run out of carbohydrates and this was right when Ray started coming on strong. Ray always knew how to close the show and that's what he did. Unbelievable fight! Anytime those two fought, it was going to be a hell of a fight. That was just the kind of competitive spirit they had.

In April 1985, Hearns was defeated by middleweight champion Marvin Hagler via third-round TKO. Hagler-Hearns is considered to be one of the best fights in the history of the sport.
I had been following Marvin on a regular basis since 1973, when I saw him in the national Golden Gloves. I was a big fan of Marvin's. He could box when he needed to box, slug when he had to slug. He was the type of fighter who could do whatever he had to do to win. He wasn't exceptional in any one area, but he was good in every area. Marvin had a chip on his shoulder. That's what made Marvin. You take away the chip and he's no longer Marvin Hagler. It was this attitude he brought and this mental strength that made him, what I believe to be, the best middleweight champion ever. I wanted Tommy to box more, but that just wasn't in his make-up in a fight like this. In the first round, Tommy hurt Marvin. When he came back to the corner, he told me his right hand was broken. We had fourteen more rounds to go and he couldn't throw his right hand like he wanted to. Marvin buried his chin and gambled and made it a very physical fight. In the third round, he ended up stopping Tommy. After all these years, people still say that this was the best three rounds in the history of boxing. With all the great fights we've had, that's a real compliment.

Thomas Hearns is best known for his fights with Sugar Ray Leonard and Marvin Hagler. Even though he didn't win those fights, he is still considered to be one of the best fighters of all time. Why do you think that is?
He gave everything he had in every fight, all the way from welterweight to cruiser-weight. Tommy never held back or laid down. Whether he hurt somebody or he got hurt himself, he performed at his best. That's why he could lose to a Ray Leonard or a Marvin Hagler, come back in the next few months, and the place would be sold out again. He was

a beautiful fighter to watch. He was a master boxer and a devastating puncher. Of all the fighters in history, I don't know anybody who had those kinds of unbelievable early knock-outs on the elite level like Tommy did. Tommy knocked out Pipino Cuevas in the second round and he did the same thing to Roberto Duran. Nobody had ever done that to Duran before or after. Look at his fight with James Shuler. This is a fighter who had never lost and Tommy knocked him out in the first round. On top of that, he out-boxed the best boxers. He out-boxed Wilfred Benitez and he out-boxed Virgil Hill. With Tommy, you didn't know if it was going to be a long fight, or if it was going to be over in twenty seconds. For me, of all the fighters I worked with, Tommy is still my favorite. Not just to train and manage, but to watch. Every time we left the dressing room and walked down the aisle, I knew he was going to give some excitement.

You trained Evander Holyfield for his November 1993 rematch with heavyweight champion Riddick Bowe, a fight that Holyfield won via majority decision.

Evander got in touch with me through MC Hammer, who was his new promoter at the time. I met Evander Holyfield and MC Hammer at the airport in Atlanta. When I saw Evander, he looked small to me. I said, "How much do you weigh?" He said, "204." I said, "Evander, let me tell you something. This guy is bigger than you. *Much* bigger. He's younger than you. He's better on the outside. On the inside, he rips you with that uppercut. In other words, he's better than you in every way." I had done resurrecting jobs before, but I didn't know what I was going to do. One night, we were out dancing. It was me, Evander, and MC Hammer. We were on the dance floor till one in the morning and I said, "I've got it. I got the strategy. We're going to beat him with your rhythm. We're going to beat him with movement. We're going to change directions, move in and out, and keep him all uncoordinated, so his height and all of his natural advantages become a handicap." I got on the mitts and emulated Riddick Bowe and had Evander follow the strategy. Later on, Eddie Futch said to me, "Emanuel, after the first round, I knew we were in trouble." In Evander's next fight when he fought Michael Moorer, he was going to make twelve million. He said to me, "I'll give you two-fifty." I said, "Evander, that isn't even two percent." He said, "I'm a world champion again. I can get anybody to get me some water." I didn't like that, so I told Evander that he could just keep his money. In the papers, he said, "If Emanuel is such a great trainer, he can go get another fighter and make him a champion." That's what I did with Lennox Lewis.

You trained Oliver McCall for his September 1994 fight against heavyweight champion Lennox Lewis, a fight that McCall won via second-round TKO. Shortly after that, you began training Lewis and helped him to become the most dominant heavyweight of his time.

Don King called me in '94 and said, "I've got this fighter by the name of Oliver McCall. He's gonna be fighting Lennox Lewis for the championship and I want you to train him." I didn't have anything going on right at that minute so I thought, why not? We went to the press conference for the fight and they introduced me and gave me a very complimentary introduction. After that, Lennox Lewis's trainer Pepe Correa got up there and said how Emanuel Steward wasn't anything special. He talked about how great he was and he went on about all the great work he had done with Lennox Lewis. He was very arrogant. I just sat there and smiled. When we got back to Detroit, I told Oliver, "We're going to win this fight, but let's go over a few facts. First of all, Lennox is bigger than you." It was Evander Holyfield–Riddick Bowe all over again. I said, "He's not only bigger, he's stronger and he's a better boxer. He's better in every way, but we'll find a way to win." Everything Lennox did was based on landing the right hand, so I told Oliver that we would knock Lennox out while he was throwing a right hand. In the second round, BAM! Oliver caught him while he was throwing a right hand.

About a month later, I got a call from Lennox Lewis's people and they said they were looking for a new trainer. I always liked Lennox. When he was a kid growing up in Kitchener, Canada, he used to come to Detroit on the weekends and train. Lennox was extremely intelligent. He was very observant about everything and everyone around him. Lennox also had a little wild streak in him. Up in Kitchener, he got in a lot of fights, so he had almost a thug mentality. What made Lennox the best heavyweight I've ever worked with was his ability to make adjustments. When he fought Michael Grant, before the fight I said, "This guy is uncoordinated and not that experienced. Just go out there and get him out of there." David Tua had an unbelievable iron chin, so Lennox out-boxed him for twelve rounds. Against Vitali Klitschko, I said, "This guy is too tall to do what you normally do. We've got to take it to the alley and make it a street fight." When Lennox fought Mike Tyson, I told him, "In that first round, we're gonna slug with him. We're gonna make it a rumble and make him respect you." From that point on, we went into the strategy—half jab, make him move his head, then throw a real jab. Time him. Whenever the referee breaks you, push him a little bit and remind him that you're big.

In April 2001, Lewis lost his heavyweight titles to Hasim Rahman via fifth round knockout. In November of that year, Lewis regained his titles with a fourth round knockout of Rahman.

Lennox didn't take Hasim Rahman seriously the first time. Instead of going to South Africa early so he could get used to the altitude and time change, he was in that movie *Ocean's Eleven*. His focus was on too many other things. In my mind, Rahman wasn't a serious threat, but I should have been more forceful with his training. That fight taught me something I already knew. You can never underestimate an opponent. In boxing, one punch can change it all and that's what happened. Rahman threw a perfect right hand and Lennox's head hit the floor right in front of me. The next thing I knew, there was a new heavyweight champion of the world. It was a horrible feeling. I said to Lennox, "It's over, baby. You got caught. That's the championship." That was one of the worst days of my life. I went up to my room and cried. About a week later, I flew down to Jamaica where Lennox was renting a house. We sat there in the yard and talked. He knew what he did wrong. He said he wanted to get the team back together and knock this boy out. That's the way Lennox was. Towards the end of his career, Lennox married his girlfriend Violet. He didn't want to get into any kind of serious relationship early on, because boxing was his love. After his fight with Vitali Klitschko, sure enough, his wife told him that she wanted him to stop boxing and that was it. It was around that time that I got a call from the Klitschkos. They asked me if I would be interested in working with Wladimir.

When you started working with Wladimir Klitschko, he had recently suffered a TKO loss at the hands of Corrie Sanders. Shortly after that, in April 2004, Wladimir lost to Lamon Brewster via fifth-round TKO. How were you able to build him back up after the losses and guide him to become a dominant heavyweight champion?

I spent a lot of quality time with Wladimir. We talked a lot and went places together. I didn't just pick up my bags after training and go home. We developed a good bond. As a result of that, we came back from the Brewster fight and got through that tough moment with Sam Peter. Sam Peter had just beaten James Toney and Oleg Maskaev, and everybody expected him to knock Wladimir out. When Wladimir and I left the press conference in New York, we were walking down the street. This drunk came up and said to Wladimir, "You're a good man! You showed heart against Lennox Lewis!" I said, "No, that's not Vitali. This is his brother Wladimir." Then this guy said, "You ain't shit! You're the one that's got no heart! You ain't got no chin!" He followed us about halfway down the block. I wanted to push him away, but Wladimir said, "Leave him alone." I could see the tears welling up in Wladimir's eyes. We sat down in this little Chinese restaurant and he said, "Emanuel, I've never been at the bottom. All my life, I've always been at the top." He said that he didn't like being at the bottom and that he was never, ever going to lose again. He was obsessed with that.

We went to camp in the Poconos for the Peter fight. Vitali, the big brother, was always protective of his little brother. He called and wanted to come, but Wladimir said, "No. You're not going to be in my camp. I have a new trainer now and he's the only one talking to me." It was just me and Wladimir. There were so many sparring partners up there and

Emanuel Steward and Vitali Klitschko before Klitschko's 2004 eighth-round TKO victory over Corrie Sanders (courtesy Bret Newton—ThreatPhoto.com/Pound4Pound.com).

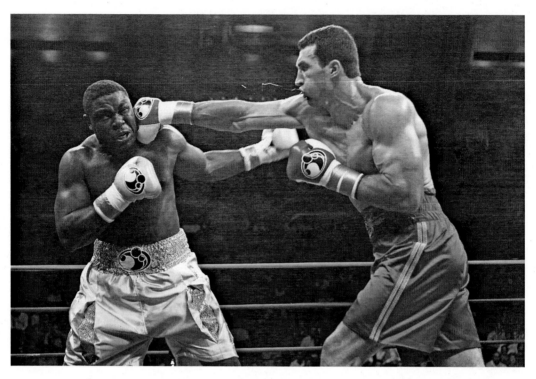

Wladimir Klitschko hits Samuel Peter with a right hand en route to a unanimous decision in their 2005 fight (courtesy Marty Rosengarten/RingsidePhotos.com).

he either dropped or knocked out every sparring partner we had. It was unbelievable. In the Peter fight, Wladimir went down twice. The first time, he came back to the corner and I told him what he did wrong. He said, "I got you." When the bell rang, he stepped out to the center of the ring and he was waiting on Sam. He took control of the fight, and in the tenth round, he went down again. Going into the twelfth round, it was the most dramatic twelfth round of my career since the second fight between Milton McCrory and Colin Jones. I looked at the crowd and I saw that all the blue and yellow flags from the Ukraine were in the people's laps. Vitali said to me, "Be honest, Emanuel. Do you think he can make it through the round?" I said, "He'll be okay." As we were sitting there, lo and behold, Wladimir caught him with a short left hook and Sam Peter was out on his feet. To me, that was one of the most dramatic finishes for him, even though he didn't knock him out. That was his turning point and he went on to dominate everybody he faced since then.

How do you feel about the state of the game today opposed to when Thomas Hearns was fighting?

I've been in boxing since the '50s and I'm now on my sixth generation. I never thought it would grow like this. I always thought I was going to stay with my job as an electrician. It wasn't until I was about forty-seven that it hit me that I was going to be in boxing for the rest of my life. When it comes to training fighters, I'm from the old school—beating the heavy bag, skipping rope, speed bag, and lifting your own body weight. I only do a certain

Top: Emanuel Steward (left) and assistant trainer Derrick Coleman (center) look on as future light heavyweight champion Adonis Stevenson shadow boxes, 2012 (courtesy Dan Graschuck). *Bottom:* Emanuel Steward speaks at a press conference to announce a boxing event planned for Detroit's Joe Louis Arena, which Steward was organizing in 2012. The event was eventually cancelled once it was learned that Steward had fallen ill (courtesy Dan Graschuck).

amount of the modern stuff. Nowadays, some of these trainers are checking the blood, checking the electrolytes… Fighters have to have a nutritionist, they have to have this, they have to have that… When we made the fight with Tommy Hearns and Ray Leonard, we put all egos aside. The public demanded it, so we made the fight. Manny Pacquiao and Floyd Mayweather has been going on for over three years and they still haven't made the fight. There are too many business issues and it's not fair to the public. These guys are arguing over who's the best pound for pound and all these little things, but it doesn't matter. When great fighters fight each other and give it their all, win or lose, everybody comes out a winner.

13

Steve Smoger: The Third Man

While officiating a fight, referees walk a fine line. Boxing is a brutal game and they must be cognizant of the fighters's safety and health. But at the same time, they must give the fighters every opportunity to display their heart and their skills. Born in Norfolk, Virginia, and raised in Atlantic City, New Jersey, Steve Smoger is known as one of the "toughest" referees in the sport in that he gives fighters the benefit of the doubt, even when they appear hurt or technically out-gunned. Smoger was issued his license as a professional boxing referee in 1982 by former heavyweight champion "Jersey" Joe Walcott, who was then the commissioner of the New Jersey State Athletic Commission. Ironically, Walcott's 1952 fight with Rocky Marciano was the first live boxing match that Smoger ever attended. Marciano-Walcott I took place thirty years prior to the very day that Smoger was issued his license. It would seem that fate has played a role in Smoger's career, particularly when you look at his involvement in the first fight between middleweight champion Jermain Taylor and Kelly Pavlik. In the second round of that fight, Pavlik was knocked down and almost out. Most referees would have stopped the contest right then and there. However, a few months before the fight, Smoger attended a medical seminar where he was given a certain piece of information that led to his decision to allow the fight to continue. Pavlik went on to win the fight via seventh-round TKO and the boxing world had a new middleweight champion. In June 2011, I called Steve Smoger to discuss his experiences as the third man in the ring for some of the most significant fights of the modern era. At the time of this interview, Smoger had just refereed the Ivan Redkach–Alberto Amaro fight.

What is your background in boxing and what led you to become a referee?
Fighters were always the heroes in my household. My dad, rest in peace, was a very knowledgeable fight fan. My earliest memories were sitting on his lap in the mid to late 1950s, watching Johnny Addie introduce the *Gillette Cavalcade of Sports* from St. Nicholas Arena. I was allowed to stay up for their version of the *Friday Night Fights*. I would see these fighters and I really, really enjoyed it. Of course, part of it was my father's influence. He said how fighters are the last vestige in one-on-one. There are no timeouts, you can't go in a huddle, and you can't ask advice. For three minutes, it's you and another guy. I boxed through high school in the lightweight division, and then I went to college at Penn State.

Professional boxing referee Steve Smoger (courtesy Craig Eagleson).

In the late '60s, boxing was strictly intramural. There was no intercollegiate at Penn State. Apparently, there was a death on the college level and they terminated any intercollegiate boxing. I went to law school in Washington, D.C., and I inquired where I could find a nice local gym where I could, not train to fight, but just work out. I used to go to a gym that was close to the armory in District of Columbia. Years later, I ended up refereeing a world title fight at that very armory. It was Simon Brown–Tyrone Trice II. Their first fight was a war and I worked that fight as well. In fact, it was the "Fight of the Year" in 1988.

Early on, I realized that my calling in boxing was in the officiating aspect of the game. From 1974 to '82, I worked as a referee on the amateur level. In 1978, I was an assistant city prosecutor with the city of Atlantic City. At the conclusion of my workday at City Hall, sometimes I would go to the Police Athletic League, so I could work on my craft in the ring, while the fighters sparred. One night, the phone rang and I picked it up. A voice said, "This is 'Jersey' Joe Walcott." I just about fell on the floor! "Jersey" Joe was the Commissioner of the New Jersey State Athletic Commission at the time, and of course, being from New Jersey, I was always a big fan of his growing up. On September 23, 1952, I was there when Rocky Marciano got off the floor to stop "Jersey" Joe in the thirteenth round. I was two or three years old and I had no concept of what just happened. What I did know is that I lived in New Jersey and that the champion was "Jersey" Joe. When I learned that "Jersey" Joe had been knocked out, it brought me to tears. While everyone in the stadium was swarming Marciano, I said, "Dad, I want to see Jersey!" My father brought me over to the former champion and I reached out and touched his robe just before he disappeared into his dressing room. Over the years as an up-and-coming referee, I had become very close to "Jersey" Joe. I told him that story and he got a major kick out of it. As it turns out, that very story led to the delay of my licensing as a professional referee.

In 1981, with all of the fights that were being staged on the casino scene in Atlantic City, they had to increase the roles of the referees. The powers that be liked me. I was pronounced ready to go pro, but I was told that they just needed the appropriate time. I said, "What do you mean?" They said, "Joe is very closed mouth." It was "Jersey" Joe who got to decide. They said, "Joe has a rhyme and a reason and you just have to sit still." One night, "Jersey" Joe called me in to see him. I got there and he said, "Come on in, Steve. Remember that little story you told me about how you were upset the night I lost my title?" I said, "Yeah. It still sticks with me." He said, "Today is the thirtieth anniversary thereof, and you will know for the rest of your career that you received your official license as a New Jersey professional boxing referee on September 23, 1982." He then said, "I would have waited until eleven o'clock at night, because that's when I got clipped, but I want you to work tonight." That night, I ended up working a four-rounder at the Tropicana. That's when I learned that as a referee, you always carry your gear. I've got my gear in my car right now. Shoes, shirt… I could get the call at any time.

On September 29, 2001, at Madison Square Garden, right after 9/11, Bernard Hopkins defeated Felix Trinidad via twelfth-round TKO in a middleweight unification bout. Tell me a little about your experience as the referee of this event.

I received the call about mid–August. There had been some talk about selection of referees and I heard my name was in, but you never know until you get the actual call. The call came in and it was set for September 15th. As you know, the tragedy of September 11th came and I absolutely knew that the fight couldn't go on in light of what had just occurred. The offices of the New York State Athletic Commission are in close proximity of the Twin Towers, and they could actually see the devastation through their windows. I sat tight and about a week after the event, I received a telephone call to circle the 29th. On the night of the fight, I reported to Madison Square Garden, all set to go. Fight time approaches, so I went downstairs from the dressing room and I made my way onto the main floor. When I saw the crowd, I was just overwhelmed with the electricity. You could absolutely feel it. I checked in with the time keeper, I checked in with the physicians and the doctors, and I entered the ring.

As I recall, someone from the fire department sang the National Anthem. Just being in the neutral corner when they sang the National Anthem gave me the chills. I said, "Steve, maintain your composure." Not only was this the first major event in the world after the trauma, but it was also a fantastic boxing match that was about to take place. Once the bell sounded, I think that we all settled in. From my perspective, it was one of the most technically sound bouts that I have ever witnessed, in that I saw Bernard slowly but surely assert his will. As the rounds progressed, there was nothing apparent, but I could see that Trinidad was somewhat wilting under the pressure of Hopkins. Bernard's shots were becoming more effective and Tito's shots were not having that much of an effect. In my view, a lesser man would have fallen much earlier. Tito went down in the twelfth round, but he made it to his feet. I still think he was capable of defending himself, but his corner elected to stop it. I'm almost in my thirtieth year as a referee and this was the most emotionally charged event I've ever been involved with. And it was a hell of a fight!

Bernard Hopkins and Felix Trinidad were bitter rivals going into their 2001 middleweight unification bout. In 2007, they share a mutual respect (courtesy Marty Rosengarten/RingsidePhotos.com).

In April 2003, you were the third man in the ring when James Toney defeated Vassiliy Jirov via unanimous decision for Jirov's cruiserweight world title. Toney-Jirov was the best cruiserweight fight of the early 2000s. What stands out in your mind about that night?

Like Hopkins-Trinidad, it was the slow progression of James taking over and asserting his skill and his will. That was Vassiliy's finest hour and he gave everything that he could. Highly competitive, highly spirited… Jirov was just about out of there in that last round. I knew it was close. He was stunned, but he was still defending himself. What I call the "signature punch" did not come and I was hoping he would be able to finish on his feet, which he did. I must say that James Toney is an absolute pleasure to work with. He's an outrageous personality and he can sometimes come across as defiant, but he's always treated me with the utmost respect. I worked with James as a middleweight, I worked with him as a cruiserweight, and I worked with him as a heavyweight when he got his shot at the heavyweight title against John Ruiz. That was a beautiful performance from James, and it was quite distressing that he tested positive for having something in his system that was in violation of the rules. He won the fight, but it was ruled a no contest.

Speaking of heavyweight boxing, you worked the Mike Tyson–Brian Nielsen fight in October 2001, a fight that Tyson won via seventh-round TKO.

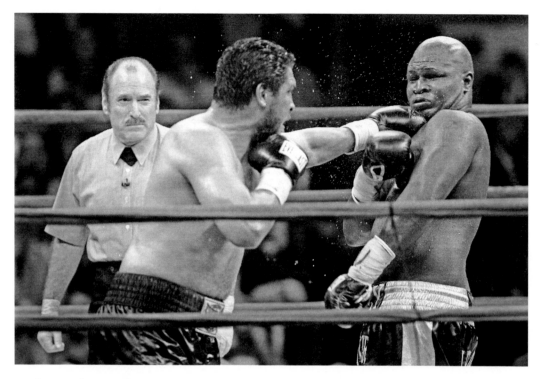

John Ruiz throws a jab at James Toney, as referee Steve Smoger looks on. Toney seemed to win a unanimous decision handily, but the bout was later ruled a no contest due to a failed post-fight drug test from Toney (courtesy Marty Rosengarten/RingsidePhotos.com).

That fight was not that long after Tyson fought Lou Savarese in Scotland. John Coyle, who is a dear friend of mine, was the third man in the ring for that fight. He's one of the finest referees in Europe and Tyson totally disrespected him. He tried to stop it in the first round. He got between the two fighters, and Tyson ignored the call and kept swinging and knocked him down. I was brought in for Tyson-Nielsen specifically to control Mr. Tyson. Before the fight, I approached Tyson's manager, Shelly Finkel. I said, "Shelly, with your permission, I would like to talk to Mike one-on-one." Shelly said, "Go ahead, Steve. Whatever you've got to do." I go to Mike and I said, "Mike, when I'm not in the ring and I'm not directly involved in what you're doing, I'm one of your biggest fans." I then said, "Now, I must turn to my role as your referee this evening. I will not tolerate any violations of the rules, specifically what you did in Scotland with John Coyle in the Savarese fight." He said, "Yes, Steve. I understand, I understand." Mike was winning the fight. He's a much stronger puncher than Nielsen. At the end of round six, he had Brian cornered. He cocked his right hand, he heard the bell, and he looked at me. He held the shot. Right then, I knew all would be well. After the sixth round, the fight was over anyway, because Nielsen didn't answer the bell for the seventh.

In September 2007, Kelly Pavlik defeated middleweight champion Jermain Taylor via seventh-round TKO. When Taylor knocked Pavlik down in round two, Pavlik appeared to be in serious trouble. Many were surprised that you allowed the fight to continue.

Everything in life is timing. In May of that year, I had the benefit of being assigned the fight between Kelly Pavlik and Edison Miranda, who were in an eliminator to fight for Jermain Taylor's middleweight championship. That was my first experience with Kelly. In the fourth round, Edison landed a series of right hands on Kelly. I thought to myself, "How the hell did he take those shots?" He shook them off and he kept coming forward. That gave me the idea that Kelly was at the top of his game at that particular time. Kelly hurt Miranda significantly in round six and ended up stopping him in the seventh. In the summer of '07, I attended a medical seminar given by Dr. Anthony Alessi, who is one of the top neurological doctors in the fight game today. The accent on this particular seminar stemmed from Zab Judah and Kostya Tszyu. The doctor said that Zab had absorbed an "equilibrium shot." They are somewhere behind the ear area and it has an adverse effect on a person's equilibrium. I recall the doctor saying, "There is an immediate effect, but there is also a relatively rapid recovery." I learned from that seminar that you have to be very careful about stopping a fight when there is a shot behind the ear or on the temple area. Sometimes the wobble effect can be misleading.

So, we have the fight between Pavlik and Miranda in May, the medical seminar that summer, and in September, I was assigned to work Taylor-Pavlik I. In round two of Taylor-Pavlik, I saw a right hand from Jermain land behind the left ear of Kelly. It was a massive shot. He flops and drops and flops. He was up by eight, but he was still very unsteady. Jermain went after him and he threw some shots that just missed. In the third minute of that

Steve Smoger counts after Edison Miranda was knocked down by Kelly Pavlik in their 2007 encounter (courtesy Marty Rosengarten/RingsidePhotos.com).

Kelly Pavlik and Jermain Taylor at a press conference, promoting their 2007 fight. Promoters Bob Arum and Lou DiBella stand behind them (courtesy Marty Rosengarten/RingsidePhotos.com).

round, Jermain looked like he was taking a breather. I don't want to say that he was gassed, but he was recouping and he allowed Kelly to hold. The next thing I know, Kelly started coming on! Toward the end of the round, he was winning! At the bell, he walked back to his corner and I heard him say, "I'm okay." I've been asked to lecture before several commissions about the non-stoppage in round two and the eventual stoppage in seven. As we've discussed previously, it's night and day. In round seven, there was an inside right hand from Kelly and Jermain was out before he hit the canvas. There were several polls that said how ninety-five out of one hundred referees probably would have stopped that fight in the second round. But with everything I had learned beforehand, I knew I had to let it go on. It was clear to me. It was so very, very clear.

You are known as one of the "tougher" referees in the sport in the sense that you will let a fight go, even if a fighter appears hurt or technically out-gunned. What are your criteria for stopping a fight?

There are no warriors like the warriors in our rings. Fighters are a culmination of a lot of work by a lot of people, and I want them to have every opportunity to display their heart and their skills. I'm very sensitive to their health and safety, but I try to balance that by giving them every opportunity to prevail. Every aspect to allow the fight to proceed to its natural conclusion must be implemented. Ron Scott Stevens, one of the commissioners, summed it up by saying, "You don't want to jeopardize the safety or the health of a fighter under any circumstances, but you don't want to take the drama out of our sport if at all

Smoger counts after featherweight Whyber Garcia was knocked down by Yuriorkis Gamboa in a 2009 fight that Gamboa won via fourth-round TKO (courtesy Marty Rosengarten/RingsidePhotos.com).

possible." The most dramatic fights of the first decade of the twenty-first century have occurred when referees have allowed the fighter to give every ounce of what he or she has. As a referee, you must react to what is before you instantaneously. There can be no hesitation. You must go with your experience and do what you feel is right. I look for the signature shot when a fighter has lost his total presence. That's the word: presence. It's that moment when he or she is incapable of defending his or herself. I find that the biggest compliment usually comes from the losing corner. When I'm on the way out, and the lights are down, and they're breaking down the ring, and Taylor's corner comes to me and thanks me for giving their fighter every opportunity, that's when I know I've done my job.

14

Monte Barrett:
The Tale of Two Gunz

Boxing can be an unforgiving sport. It's a lot easier for fighters to think highly of themselves when they win fights than when they lose. Not everyone has the character to pick themselves up after a loss and still see themselves as a winner. Born in Greenville, North Carolina, eventually relocating to Brooklyn, New York, former heavyweight Monte "Two Gunz" Barrett grew up in a broken home, surrounded by poverty and violence. Hard luck and tough times have followed Barrett his whole life, as he was once evicted from his apartment and forced to take a fight on short notice. Barrett knows what it is to be an underdog. His philosophy is that for every problem, there is an answer. In boxing, the answer is to get up and fight. Barrett got off to a late start in boxing, but he made up for it with a fighting spirit and a natural instinct for combat. His career as a professional boxer was a series of ups and downs, but every time the public wrote him off, he re-emerged out of nowhere with an eye-opening performance. In August 2011, Barrett beat the odds once again with a unanimous decision victory over David Tua, who was one of the division's hardest punchers. It was the best performance of Barrett's career and he did it at the age of forty. Barrett was featured on the major networks several times throughout the 2000s and has faced some of the best fighters of his time, retiring in 2014 with a record of 35–11–2, 20 KOs. In September 2011, I called Monte Barrett and asked him how the tale of "Two Gunz" first began. At the time of this interview, Barrett still had a wire in his jaw from the Tua fight and his plans were to get back in the ring ASAP.

When did you first put on the gloves? How old were you and what were the circumstances?
  I met a guy named Herbie Veil, who won the Golden Gloves in New York. He was a good amateur fighter and he introduced me to a guy named Al Davis. Al trained me for about a year in his basement. He took me running, he showed me how to hit the bag and jump rope… I was twenty-one at the time. I had never done anything with boxing before that. I was a late bloomer. That's why I'm so fresh now at age forty. I'm not burned out from the amateurs. After a while, Al introduced me to a trainer at Starrett City named Jimmy O'Pharrow and that's what got me in the ring. At first, I wasn't training to fight. It was just

Former heavyweight world title challenger Monte Barrett (courtesy Marty Rosengarten/Ringside-Photos.com).

conditioning. I got started with boxing because I wanted to know how to knock somebody out fast. I was already good with my hands in the street. I wasn't a bully or anything, but I was the biggest out of my crew and I was the youngest. I did a lot of fighting when I was a young kid, because I grew up in the hood. I lived in the projects where there were drugs, killings, rapes, prostitutes... It wasn't until I started traveling around the world and seeing other things that I realized there was another way of living.

You've gotta have discipline to be a boxer. It takes a lot to get up in the morning and run and do the same thing day in and day out. You have to be accountable. I already had that in me. I'm very punctual and I always handle my business. That's just the kind of person I am. When I first started boxing in the pros, I was running my own security service. It was called Rotten Apple Security. I started that in '95 and it went all the way to 2001. I was providing security to construction sites. Since I had my own business going, I wasn't stressed out financially. I was able to travel and box and do my own thing. I liked boxing right away, because I liked the contact of it. I'm a physical person and I've been in sports since I was a kid—baseball, football, I ran track… Boxing was second nature to me, especially with all the street fighting I did. I already knew what it was to get hit and get hurt. I was always ready to unleash some punishment. When I first started sparring, I used to get beat up every day. I used to be bleeding from my nose, from my ears, from my mouth… That's how it was when I was coming up. Nobody was going to take it easy on me or show me anything.

One day, this guy named Mango Bryant beat me up so bad. He was 168 pounds and he was beating up all heavyweights. I was tired of getting beat up. Jimmy O'Pharrow called me up one day and said, "Come on, Gumba." He used to call me Gumba. He called everybody Gumba. He said, "Come on, Gumba. Meet me at the gym. You're sparring Mango today." I went all the way to the gym and then I turned around. I said, "Man, I'm not taking this butt whipping today. Not today. I'm tired." I went all the way home and I was about to pull in my driveway, but I said, "You know what? This is going to make me a better fighter, so I'm just going to do it." That was the day I became a fighter. My first amateur fight was in November '93. I went on to do the Golden Gloves and the Ohio State Fair, and I was winning everything I was entering. At the Empire State Games, I stopped this guy and he was out for like fifteen minutes. It was a right hand–left hook combo. Al Davis said, "You did that like you had two guns." After that, everybody started calling me "Two Gunz."

What led to your decision to turn professional?

I had a lot of buzz from the amateurs and I was developing a name for myself. There were people courting me and giving me money. With all these people coming to me, I could see that boxing was something I could take on as a career. Jimmy Glenn was like a father figure to me. He was looking out for me and making sure nobody was taking advantage of me. Me and Jimmy went to Don King's house when King lived in New York. I didn't know much about Don King at the time. He was a very loud and charismatic person. Straight to the point. Flashy. The first time I met him, he gave me ten thousand dollars cash. He said, "I want to be involved with you, now. I see you got talent." I said, "If you give me a contract, I'll take it back and give it to my lawyer." He was like, "We got a lawyer coming here and we can sign the contract right now." Right then I knew this guy was shady.

What stands out in your mind about your pro debut?

I fought a guy named Jamal Edwards. He was from New Jersey. It was his pro debut and it was mine, too. The fight was in a barn. It was at a raceway and there were horses there. It was a pretty exciting show. I stopped him at the end of the first round. I was wearing this glittery red and gold outfit. I felt like I was in a music video. I saw these little gloves I had to put on and I said, "Somebody is gonna get hurt today! These things are small. Somebody's gonna get *hurt* and it's not gonna be me!" I was a little cocky at that time. When you're young, you feel like you're Superman. When you get older, you feel like you're Clark Kent. I always thought a lot of myself and I always felt like God had a plan for me. I believe that everything that happened to me, whether it was good or bad, it was meant to happen that way. And no matter what happened, I always thought highly of myself. Confidence starts within yourself first. If you don't think highly of yourself, who's going to think highly of you?

You were undefeated as a professional in your first twenty-one fights before facing Lance Whitaker in August 1999, a fight you lost via split decision. Your second loss came in July 2000 via seventh-round TKO against Wladimir Klitschko. Tell me about the night you faced Klitschko.

Let's first go back to Lance Whitaker. I was robbed in that fight. The fight was close, but I know I won. When I was training for Wladimir Klitschko, I was in camp with Lennox Lewis. We sparred twenty-two rounds together and it was like a fight. We were really going at it. After the first week, my trainer Eddie Mustafa Muhammad said to me, "You're out, Monte. They're not gonna box you no more. It's not what they're looking for." That was the only good sparring I had for that fight. I felt like I needed about seventy-five rounds of

Promoter Lou DiBella, Monte Barrett, and promoter Joe DeGuardia, 2007 (courtesy Marty Rosengarten/RingsidePhotos.com).

good sparring to compete with a guy like Wladimir. Wladimir was good when I fought him and he's improved since then, but so have I. Every fight I've lost has made me a better fighter. When you get a late start in boxing like I did, sometimes you lose those big fights on the way up. I've been boxing for nineteen years and I feel like I'm just now coming into my own. I have a lot of respect for Wladimir as the heavyweight champ. He deserves all the credit for what he's done, but if I ever fought him again, I know it would be a different story.

You've had moments in your career where you've lost a fight and it seemed as if your potential was realized. But then you re-emerged with an eye-opening performance. You gave an undefeated Joe Mesi a tough fight, you gave Dominick Guinn his first loss… Owen Beck, Hasim Rahman, Cliff Couser… These fights took place from 2003 to 2007.

With Joe Mesi, I was so close to winning the fight. HBO thought it was a great fight and they gave me another chance against Dominick Guinn, who was a better fighter than Mesi. People thought Guinn was the future of the heavyweight division and I beat him in his hometown. I fought Owen Beck who was an undefeated Don King fighter. I had just signed with Don King, because Lou DiBella signed me over to him. I knocked Beck out in the ninth round. I fought Hasim Rahman, who is a friend of mine. I trained really hard for that fight, but I couldn't get it going like I wanted. I just couldn't fire my guns. I had some personal problems on the day of the fight. One thing you learn in boxing, you can't stay focused when you're emotional about something. When you get into an argument with your girlfriend or your kids or whoever, you're not making the best choices. That's what happened when I fought Cliff Couser the first time. I'll never forget that day. It was July 7th, 2007. 7–7–7… Everybody that was supposed to win, lost that day. I was one of them. I didn't train right for that fight. I was just trying to get out of my contract with Don King and I took him very lightly. He stopped me, and in the very next fight, I stopped him. I showed that it was a fluke. I regret taking the fight with Rahman, and that first fight with Cliff Couser, and the fight I had with Odlanier Solis a few years later. When I fought Solis, I had just been evicted from my apartment. I took the fight on two days' notice and he stopped me in the second. In those fights, I wasn't one hundred percent in my boxing game as far as the preparation—mentally, physically, spiritually, and emotionally.

In October 2006, you challenged Nikolai Valuev for his heavyweight world title, a fight you lost via eleventh-round TKO. Valuev stood seven feet tall and he outweighed you by over one hundred pounds.

Valuev is a big dude. If you've got a nice sized ring, you can maneuver and do things. When I got there, Don King had this little ring. The WBA minimum is fourteen and three quarters. They had a fourteen-foot ring and this guy is seven feet tall 320 pounds. I thought that was ludicrous. I was so bitter and pissed at King for pulling that bull crap that I just didn't have my game plan on. My trainer said to me, "Monte, you don't have no room to move, so you're just gonna have to fight this guy." I got in there and I ended up receiving a severe concussion. I had to stay in the hospital overnight and it was a trying time for me. It took me like three months after the concussion to get back to myself.

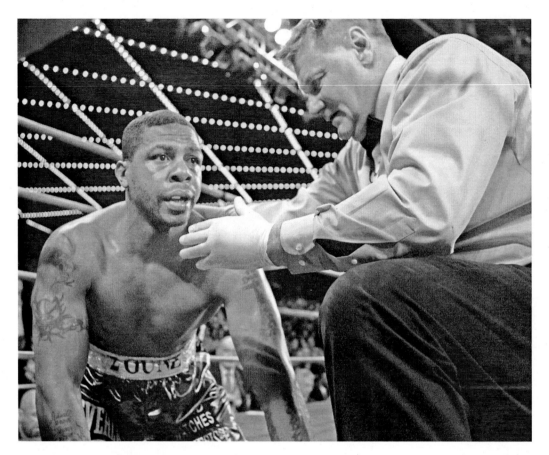

Monte Barrett tastes the canvas in his 2009 second-round TKO loss to Odlanier Solis (courtesy Marty Rosengarten/RingsidePhotos.com).

Another giant you faced was Tye Fields, who stood 6'8". It was June 2008 and you knocked him out in the first round.

I was very prepared for that fight. I trained with a guy who was an alternate on the Olympic Team. His name was Nate James. He was a big heavyweight. He was actually the first person who ever dropped me in the gym. One day, he just caught me with a straight left and that really woke me up. The next day, I wound up dropping him. He got me up for that fight. He really busted my butt in the beginning. I knew that Tye Fields was nowhere near as good as this guy. I knew Tye Fields was clumsy and methodical and that he was just going to come, come, come… I'm a counter puncher. He threw a lazy left hand, and I countered with a right, and I kept on punching and he got stopped.

Who is the hardest puncher you've ever faced?

I tell everybody Eric Kirkland. Eric Kirkland hurt me from round one to round ten. Every punch he threw, he hurt me. I never knew what heavy-handed was until I met Eric Kirkland. The guy's got stones in his hands. I stopped him in the tenth, but I got busted up in that fight. I got stitches in my mouth, under my chin, over my eye… He's just a heavy-handed guy. He's small. He's only 6'1" 220. I've fought guys like Wladimir Klitschko and

Monte Barrett knocks out Tye Fields in the first round of their 2008 encounter (courtesy Bret Newton—ThreatPhoto.com/Pound4Pound.com).

David Haye who have explosive punching power that comes out of nowhere, but Eric Kirkland is the hardest hitter pound for pound.

You're talking about getting concussions, having stitches in your mouth, and all the wear and tear that comes with being a prize fighter. How did you find it inside yourself to take this kind of punishment and keep coming back?

I've been dealing with adversity all my life. When I came out of my mother's womb, statistics said that I would probably be a failure. I'm black. I was in a broken home. I was in a situation where my mother had me at a young age. She was a kid having a kid. We lived in a basement. We were on welfare. Things were rough for me, living in the ghetto. I grew up around deprived people who were starving. That's what was in front of me, but when things go hard on me, I go harder. You might stop me. I might lose a ball game, I might lose a track meet, but I'm not going to quit. I'm going to find a solution. For every problem, there's an answer. In boxing, the answer is to get up and fight. That's what I get paid to do. I just get up. I have a tattoo that says, "The Fighting Spirit." I do have a fighting spirit, in boxing and in life. You can't do anything to me that hasn't been done to me before. I'm not a quitter. That's the best answer I can give you. I'm just not a quitter.

Going into your first fight with David Tua in July 2010, nobody in the boxing world gave you a shot. Tua is one of the biggest punchers in the division and you were coming off of three consecutive losses. What was your mindset going into that fight?

Monte Barrett is pointed to a neutral corner by referee Randy Neumann after knocking down David Tua in the twelfth round of their 2010 encounter (courtesy Marty Rosengarten/RingsidePhotos.com).

I was a 14 to 1 underdog, but I never believed that. I'm not going to give my opponent more credit than I'm going to give myself. I just go in there and handle my business. When I took the fight with David Tua, it wasn't about money. It was about me. I was content with myself. I was in a good spiritual place. I had just met this guy at the gym. His name was Luis Ruiz. He was an MMA trainer and he really took my conditioning to a new level. We weren't getting ready for anything. We were just training, but it made me feel like I wanted to fight again. I started to get that desire to compete. I was telling everybody that this was going to be my last fight. I just wanted to go out being a winner.

Your first fight with Tua was ruled a draw, but the popular opinion was that you deserved the decision. How did that make you feel at the time? Did you feel like you just couldn't get a break?

I *did* get a break. I won. Everybody knew I won. The scorecards don't always tell what really happened. When I fought Joe Mesi, I thought I won that fight. When I fought Lance Whitaker, I knew in my heart I won. I felt at peace with myself. I was all right with it, but since everybody was saying that I should have gotten the decision, they offered me the rematch. I was like, okay, let me try this thing again.

In August 2011, you had a rematch with David Tua in Tua's homeland of New Zealand. In the twelfth round, you were knocked down, but you made it to your feet and won a unanimous decision.

Jesus died for all of us. I have faith in Christ and I don't take credit for any of my victories. I give all credit to Him. That's what made me get up. Once I got up, I said, "Monte, just stay on your feet and you win the fight." It was redemption. It wasn't redemption for what happened in the first fight, it was redemption for my life. It just shows what happens when you get in the best space possible with Christ. You make the adjustments you need to make. Not just in the fight, but in life. My life and my boxing career evolved the same way. Up and down, up and down... I'm forty years old and I just put on one of the best performances of my life. I made the adjustments I needed to make. Some people get it early, some get it later on. I got it later on. I do get it now. I've grown as a person. And if you grow as a person, you grow as a boxer, too.

15

Al Bernstein:
The Origins of ESPN

In the early 1980s, most homes didn't have cable television. If they did, they had to be located in a certain places, because some areas weren't even wired for it. The early years of cable had very few stations compared to what it has today, though it did offer a sports station called ESPN. Born and raised in Chicago, Illinois, Al Bernstein was one of ESPN's original boxing analysts. At that time, ESPN was a platform for up-and-coming fighters who went on to compete at the highest level. With a background as a newspaper editor and having just written an instructional boxing book, Bernstein reached out to ESPN when they were putting on shows in Chicago and offered to provide them with information about local fighters. He was invited on the air a few times to discuss various boxing topics and his career as an announcer took off from there. Bernstein has been one of the signature analysts of the sport for the past thirty-five years, always offering reliable commentary. Since 2003, he has served as a boxing analyst for *Showtime Championship Boxing*, where he covered several major events, including the Super Six World Boxing Classic. The Super Six was a unique six-man tournament that matched up some of the best super middleweights in the world against each other for multiple fights. Bernstein also announced the first encounter between lightweights Diego Corrales and Jose Luis Castillo, a fight that many regard as one of the best in the history of the sport. In July 2014, I called Al Bernstein to discuss the origins of ESPN. At the time of this interview, his next assignment was the upcoming fight between Saul Alvarez and Erislandy Lara, scheduled for July 12th.

How did boxing first become a part of your life and what led you to announcing fights?

My earliest recollections are listening to a transistor radio when I was a little kid. It was the Johansson-Patterson fight. I had the radio under my pillow and I was listening to it really low. It was exciting to me to hear the crowd and the people talking about it. That was the first moment I realized what an exciting sport it was and from there I just got hooked. At a young age, I wanted to be a sports writer or do something involving sports. When I would hear Don Dunphy calling Sugar Ray Robinson's fights, I thought how great it would be to be him. I was the managing editor of a chain of newspapers called Lerner Newspaper.

After a while, I got burned out on hard news. I really just wanted to do sports all the way through, so I quit. I started doing freelance writing for a lot of the boxing magazines and other publications, and I ended up writing a book called *Boxing for Beginners*. It was an instructional book about boxing. When ESPN came along in 1980, they were going to four different locations for their fights. One of them was Chicago, where I lived. Chicago wasn't even wired for cable at the time. There was some in the suburbs, but in the city there was almost nothing. ESPN was only in about three million homes at that point. When they came to Chicago, I got involved any way I could. I gave them information about local fighters and they got me on the air and interviewed me about my book. For one show, they asked me to come on

Television boxing analyst Al Bernstein (courtesy Al Bernstein).

and talk a little bit. They liked what I did and they just kept hiring me and bringing me back. I did all of the fights west of the Mississippi and Randy Gordon did all of the fights east of the Mississippi.

We had a lot of characters in the early days. There was Terrence Alli who was on about twenty-four times. He would do a back flip every time he won and he would jump over the ropes when he came in. We had a fighter named "Vampire" Johnson who would enter the ring in a coffin. There were people like Kenny Bogner who was a lightweight with a big contingency of fans in Atlantic City. One night, I was interviewing him and it was very loud. I asked him a question and he said, "I can't hear what you're saying." I asked him again and he said, "I can't hear an effing word you're saying!" I repeated it again and he said, "I *still* can't hear an effing word you're saying!" So, I got really close to him and he finally answered the question. Those were the crazy things that used to happen back then. Bobby Czyz was a fighter who fought on ESPN. So was Matthew Saad Muhammad and

The announcing team of former featherweight champion Barry McGuigan, Al Bernstein, and former heavyweight world title challenger Gerry Cooney, for a 2007 Pay-Per-View card (courtesy Marty Rosengarten/RingsidePhotos.com).

Dwight Muhammad Qawi, who was then Dwight Braxton. There were a lot of fighters on there who turned out to be great. It was a spawning ground of champions. I approached announcing fights from the perspective of a journalist, not like somebody who acted like they knew everything about the sport. I did have knowledge and I boxed as an amateur, but I offered just enough analysis to augment what the play by play guy was saying. That was my way of easing in with the audience who didn't know me. People take different approaches to calling fights. Gil Clancy looked at it from a trainer's standpoint. Larry Merchant was a columnist, so "opinions" were already the tools he was using. I was an editor and my style came from someone who organized news stories. To this day, my background as a newspaper person influences what I do.

In April 1985, you announced the middleweight championship fight between Marvin Hagler and Thomas Hearns, a fight that Hagler won via third-round TKO. What stands out in your mind about that experience?

When I announced Hagler-Hearns, I was in a duel world. I did the ESPN fights, which were never of the championship level. At that time, there were three levels of boxing. There was ESPN and USA Boxing. There was the boxing that was on Saturdays and Sundays on the anthology shows, which was on free TV. They were really big fights. There was also Pay-Per-View, which was the highest level. I was involved in the lowest and the highest. I did the ESPN fights and then I started doing these big Pay-Per-Views for Top Rank. Hagler-Hearns was one of those fights. I remember sitting there looking around and I couldn't believe I had that seat for this type of event only five years into my broadcast career. In every fight before the main event takes place, I always take a couple moments to look around, assess what's going on, and realize how much fun it is. In that fight, you could feel the tension building as they came into the ring. It hit a crescendo in round one when they produced the best round in middleweight history. We had seen a lot of brawls on ESPN, but to see this was miraculous. Gary Shandling, who was a friend of mine, was working with Joan Rivers at Caesars Palace that night. He had to go on, but he came to the fight and he was hoping and praying that it would be explosive and quick because he had to leave. As he so cleverly puts it, he had just enough time for a three-round fight and that's exactly what they gave him.

At one time, boxing was considered an "American" sport, particularly by fans in the United States. Today, the sport is mostly embraced by Latino and European countries. When did this shift take place?

In the '60s, '70s, and '80s, Hispanic fighters really began making their mark in their own countries and also in the United States, especially on the west coast. They were making a huge impact with smaller fighters, all the way up to fighters on the level of Alexis Arguello. Mexico has produced some great champions. Not only did that help the sport worldwide, but it kind of started, in my opinion, what is now the "saving grace" in boxing in the United Sates, which is the continuously loyal Hispanic fan base that lives in the United States. At one time, boxing in England was an afterthought. It wasn't an afterthought *there*. It was always a major sport overseas, but in the last decade or so, fighters in the UK have fared better on the world stage. One of the seminal moments was in 2006 when Jeff Lacy went over to fight Joe Calzaghe. Jeff Lacy was a favorite in that fight and it was hard for me to really grasp that. He only had the IBF title for a short period, and some of the opponents he fought, Joe Calzaghe had already defeated them. Joe Calzaghe was underestimated in that fight and he delivered an amazing performance and beat up Jeff Lacy for twelve rounds. Another important moment was when Ricky Hatton beat Kostya Tszyu, which took place at the Manchester Arena, as did Calzaghe-Lacy. Those fights, combined with the great passion that fans in England have for the sport, has made UK boxing an important component of the success of boxing.

In May 2005, you announced the lightweight unification bout between Diego Corrales and Jose Luis Castillo, a fight that Corrales won via tenth-round TKO. Like Hagler-Hearns, Corrales-Castillo I is considered one of the best fights ever.

It's certainly the best fight I've ever covered and it's probably the best lightweight championship ever. It was Hagler-Hearns times three. Corrales had a height and reach advantage and many people thought he would use that, but he didn't. He stood inside and they just went at it for ten rounds. In the tenth round, Corrales was knocked down twice

Former two-division world champion Joe Calzaghe, a leader in bringing European boxers into the American spotlight, 2008 (courtesy Marty Rosengarten/RingsidePhotos.com).

Diego Corrales is lifted into the air by trainer Joe Goossen after his 2005 tenth round TKO victory over Jose Luis Castillo (courtesy Bret Newton—ThreatPhoto.com/Pound4Pound.com).

and it looked like he was going to go, but instead he stopped Castillo! Not only was the fight exciting all the way through, but it had this dramatic twist and turn in the final round. It was staggering. Not to denigrate the Gatti-Ward trilogy, which were terrific fights, but the difference between those fights and Corrales-Castillo is that Corrales-Castillo was fought at the highest level. The inside work these two men did was classic.

From October 2009 to December 2011, you covered Showtime's Super Six Boxing Classic, a six-man tournament consisting of some of the top super middleweights at that time: Arthur Abraham, Andre Dirrell, Carl Froch, Mikkel Kessler, Jermain Taylor, and Andre Ward. Dirrell, Kessler, and Taylor dropped out of the tournament midway through and were replaced by Allan Green and Glen Johnson. Ward ultimately won the tournament when he defeated Froch via unanimous decision in the final fight. What stands out in your mind about the Super Six?

You can't call the Super Six a failure and you can't call it a success. One thing you *can* call it is long. There have been tournaments before, but usually single elimination tournaments. What made the Super Six different is what may have been its undoing. It lasted two and a half years and you had fighters leave the tournament because of injuries and other things. It was such an appealing and compelling idea and the feeling at the beginning was pretty extraordinary. It provided more than its share of interesting moments and it also kind of reduced the barrier between American and European fighters. It drew those two together and it produced a star in Andre Ward. Even though the tournament didn't live up

Andre Ward, former super middleweight world champion and the winner of the Super Six World Boxing Classic (courtesy Marty Rosengarten/RingsidePhotos.com).

to its lofty goals, it was an important milestone. The idea that anyone could put something like this together seemed implausible.

The biggest fight in boxing that could have happened in recent times is the proposed mega fight between welterweights Floyd Mayweather, Jr., and Manny Pacquiao. This fight was first discussed by the boxing public in 2009. At this time, the fight still hasn't materialized and it seems to have missed its window. What are your thoughts on the Mayweather-Pacquiao fallout and who do you think would have been victorious had they fought when the fight was first discussed?

The reasons why this fight didn't happen are so convoluted. It's hard to say who was more to blame. In three or four years, somebody's going to write a great book about it. It could be called *The Unmaking of a Fight*. It would be fascinating to look back and see what really happened. Mayweather-Pacquiao has become the poster child for fights that didn't get made. It's too bad because it hurts the sport. I'd like to see them make this fight whether both fighters are past their prime or not, just so boxing can get that monkey off its back. I don't think it's going to happen, but it would be a good idea. When this fight was first discussed, I thought Pacquiao had a good chance to win because of his volume punching and the way he was fighting. I have since changed my opinion for a variety of reasons. Not because he was knocked out by Juan Manuel Marquez, but because of the way Mayweather has demonstrated that he can take volume punchers and limit their punch output. I think the general perception is that Mayweather would be a big favorite, but people still want to see it.

What is the difference in the state of boxing today, compared to when you first started working for ESPN in 1980?

In 1980, the sport was very big, full of talent, and some of the best matches were being made. At the end of the '80s, Gil Clancy told me that it was a special as a decade as he has ever seen in boxing. He was right, because in the '80s we had "The Four Kings," Aaron Pryor, Alexis Arguello, Larry Holmes, Michael Spinks, and you can go on and on. The sport was on free TV in the United States and it was very mainstream. As we headed into the '90s, which I call the abyss for boxing, things started to change. By the year 2000, there were mostly network fights, so the window to the world for boxing was lost, at least in the United States. The newspapers and ESPN began covering the sport very little and that was the part where the sport changed very dramatically. Right now, ironically, Floyd Mayweather, Jr., is the highest paid athlete in the world. That doesn't speak for the total health of the sport, but at the same time, for the people who want to completely write the sport off, it's a cautionary sign that they shouldn't do that. No matter what, a sport can't be completely irrelevant if its prime protagonist makes more money than anyone else in the world of sports. I will win this argument with anybody who wants to have it with me, but the actual content that boxing has been producing for the past twenty-four months, the amount of great fights, the amount of competitive fights, is as good as it's ever been. People don't pay attention to that, especially in the United States. The "boxing is dead" scenario is prodded out, because it's a simple and easy argument to make. It's propaganda. It's kind of like saying that the world will end tomorrow. But it never ends, does it?

16

Carlos Varela, Sr.:
The National School

Alexis Arguello, known as "*El Flaco Explosivo*," or "The Explosive Thin Man," was a three-division champion, having won world titles at featherweight, super featherweight, and lightweight. He is regarded as one of the best fighters of his era. But before he made history, he was just a skinny kid from Nicaragua who wanted to learn how to fight. Born and raised in Nicaragua, Managua, Carlos Varela, Sr., was one of Arguello's trainers when Arguello first put on the gloves. Varela himself fought professionally and was considered one of the best technical boxers out of Nicaragua in the 1950s and '60s. He won Nicaraguan and Central American championships at flyweight, but he never reached the top level of the sport because of boxing politics and his admitted lack of discipline. After retiring with a record of 71–18–4, Varela got a college degree and worked for various companies as an accountant. Nevertheless, Varela always had a passion for the sweet science and he remained in boxing as a trainer. Varela trained Arguello throughout the early part of his career, all the way to Arguello's first title shot against Ernesto Marcel. Upon leaving Arguello's corner, Varela maintained a strong friendship with him, until July 1, 2009, when Arguello was found shot through the heart in Managua. The death appeared to be suicide, though foul play is suspected. In June 2015, I sat down with Carlos Varela, Sr., at the Comfort Inn Carrier Circle in Syracuse, New York, to discuss his experiences working with Arguello, a relationship that began at the national school in Nicaragua. The interview was translated by Varela's son, Carlos Varela, Jr. At the time of the interview, Varela was training boxers in Toronto, Canada.

What is your background in boxing and what led you to become a trainer?

When I was eight or nine years old, I used to fight all the time in school and in the street. My uncle Hector Varela saw that I liked to fight and he recommended that I try boxing. Hector was one of the best trainers in the history of Nicaragua. He trained some of the early champions, before Alexis Arguello. My mom sent me to Hector and he taught me the rules of the sport. When I walked into the ring for the first time, I felt like it was my destiny to box. I was passionate about how to use your brain to hit and not get hit. With my uncle training me, I became one of the best technical fighters in the country. There was a national boxing school and I had to go there before I could fight. From age nine to twelve, I trained at the national school and I had my first fight at age twelve. At the age of fifteen, I turned pro. My dream was to fight on a big international show, but I never had a sponsor or anybody helping me. The highest I was ranked was number eleven in the world. One time, I had a draw and they dropped me to number eighteen. It was a big disappointment in my heart. It seemed like I wouldn't have a chance to fight for a title, so I thought about doing something besides boxing. But I don't want to blame anybody for my lack of chances. I used to drink a lot and I never took care of myself. Sometimes I wouldn't train and I just took fights. But even though I was disappointed, I always had passion in my heart for boxing. I became a trainer because I wanted to transmit my knowledge of the sport to the new generation of fighters. Some of these young guys in Nicaragua had talent, but they would get hit a lot. I wanted to teach them to not get hit and have successful careers.

When did you first meet Alexis Arguello and what was your impression of him?

I met Alexis for the first time in 1968. Alexis's father was very close to Miguel Angel Rivas, who was the director of the national boxing school. I was the assistant director. His father brought him to the gym and said, "This is my skinny son. He wants to learn boxing." What impressed me about Alexis from the start was the look in his eyes. In his mind, he wanted to go somewhere. The director asked me, "What do you see in this kid?" I said, "He seems determined, but we have to test him." We made him spar for the first time and he knocked out the two sparring partners we put him in with. These weren't bums. They

were fighters and he knocked them out cold. That's when I said, "Now, we're going to work with this kid." We did everything as a team, but the director asked me to work with Alexis one-on-one with his technique. He had good hands, but he was never agile with his legs. We tried to enforce the footwork, but he wouldn't listen. I said, "You have stupid legs! You have to work on them!" Since he couldn't dance around, we tried to make his hands better—a commanding left jab, an amazing straight right hand, and a good left hook. His head movement was okay. Good, but not exceptional. He was more comfortable blocking punches and he did that very well. We taught him basic things and he learned it to perfection.

Former flyweight boxer and boxing trainer Carlos Varela, Sr. (courtesy Carlos Varela, Sr.).

Arguello made his pro debut in October 1968 at the age of fifteen, winning via first-round knockout against Israel Medina. This was the

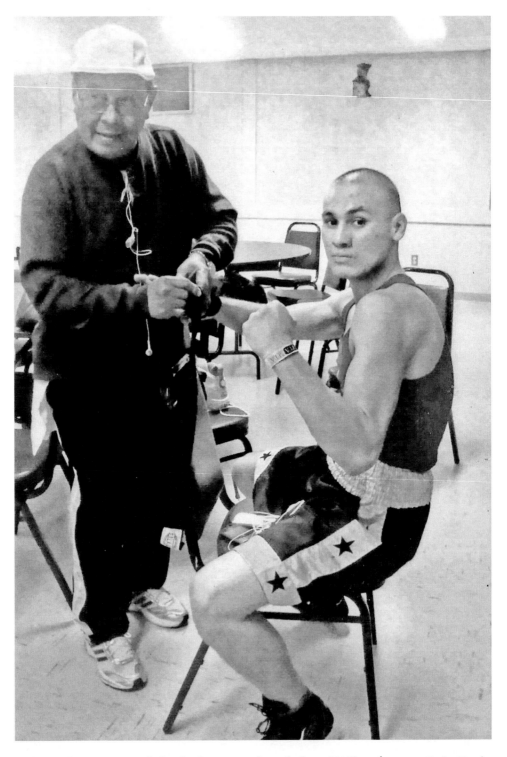

Carlos Varela, Sr. wrapping the hands of an amateur boxer before a 2014 bout (courtesy Carlos Varela, Sr.).

year that you first started working with him. Why did he turn professional with such little experience?

Alexis did a fight before that. His brother-in-law wanted to make some money, so he took him to do a pro fight in Costa Rica. He didn't tell me, he didn't tell the national school… Alexis was under the legal age and he wanted to hide it from the commission. He only had two amateur fights and he wasn't ready for that. But he learned a lot. And since he did that fight, he had to turn professional.

From 1968 to 1974, Arguello compiled a record of 31–3 before challenging Ernesto Marcel for Marcel's featherweight world title in February 1974. He lost the fight to Marcel via unanimous decision, but bounced back in November of that year to defeat Ruben Olivares via thirteenth-round knockout for Olivares's featherweight world title. What stands out in your mind about those years?

Alexis always stuck to his training and never deviated from it. He never smoked or drank alcohol. He was winning a lot and he was very popular, but he was never at parties. He went to sleep at eight or nine o'clock at night. If he fought on Saturday, he was back in the gym on Monday. What always impressed me about Alexis was his power and his ability to follow instructions. One time, we asked him to knock a guy out in the second round and he did. Another time, we told him to knock a guy out with a body shot and he did. He won most of his fights by knockout with his straight right hand. When he beat Olivares for the title, he was in amazing physical condition. At that time, Olivares was on his way out as a great fighter, but he was still the master of the left hand. It was one of the best left hands in the world. Alexis took that punch for thirteen rounds and didn't go down. Any other fighter who took that shot from Olivares would have gone down, but not Alexis.

What led to you stepping down as Arguello's trainer?

I never trained as a way of making a living. When I retired from the ring, I went back to school and got a degree. I had a good job working for a big company and I would train Alexis after work. We never had a contract and he never paid me money in any of those fights. I did it because I loved the kid. After the fight with Ernesto Marcel, the new manager told me that they were making some changes to the team and they needed someone who was more permanent. Alexis tried to fight him, but the manager wouldn't let me stay. I was fine with that. As long as Alexis reached his goals, that's all that mattered. I still had a very good relationship with him. He was very close to my family. The first car he ever owned, he brought it to our house to give us a ride. Sometimes he asked me for advice. When they couldn't find sparring partners, I would go in the ring and spar three or four rounds with him.

In November 1982 and September 1983, Arguello had two fights with junior welterweight champion Aaron Pryor. He lost both fights, the first via fourteenth-round TKO, and the second via tenth-round knockout. The first fight between Arguello and Pryor is regarded as one of the best fights of all time. What were your thoughts going into that first fight?

Alexis's coach "Pambele," who was my coach too, asked me what I thought about Alexis fighting Pryor. We saw a video and I think it was when Pryor knocked out Cervantes. I told

Carlos Varela, Sr., Alexis Arguello, and Eduardo Mojica, Arguello's brother-in-law, 2007 (courtesy Carlos Varela, Sr.).

him Alexis isn't going to beat this guy. He said, "Really? Why do you say that?" I said, "Number one, he's stronger than Alexis. Look at his body. He's fighting in his proper weight class." Alexis was going up in weight. I said, "Number two, he's fast and he has more technical abilities." Alexis lacked the footwork to deal with this guy. I always told Alexis to learn footwork, and I warned him that one day he would fight someone who was stronger and faster than him and that he would get knocked out if he ever went to the ropes. Alexis never believed that. He never emphasized working the legs. If Alexis would have learned the craft of working the ring, he still might not have beaten Pryor, but he would have had a better chance.

You trained a kid who knew very little about boxing and guided him as he became one of the best fighters in the history of the sport. What are your thoughts when you look back at the time you spent with him?

I can't take all the credit. I was only one of the people who helped Alexis. His former coach "Pambele" was a big influence in Alexis's life too. We were both father figures to him. I feel very honored and happy beyond words of the little influence I had on one of the greatest champions in the world. But I feel crushed because of the way he died. It really hurts my heart. He was one of the best human beings ever.

17

Glen Johnson: The Road Warrior

When fighters get off to a late start in boxing, they find themselves facing opponents with more skills and experience. The money they make in the pros usually doesn't pay their bills, so they have to get a day job while in training. They're behind the eight ball from the get-go, but some people thrive when they're in that position. Born in Clarendon, Jamaica, later relocating to Miami, Florida, Glen "The Road Warrior" Johnson first walked into a boxing gym when he was twenty. His intentions were to lose some weight and get in shape, but the next thing he knew, he found himself competing as an amateur. Johnson turned pro in 1993, winning his first thirty-two fights until he was defeated by middleweight champion Bernard Hopkins via eleventh-round TKO. At that point, Johnson began losing as many fights as he won. It seemed that his place in boxing was that of an opponent, but Johnson himself wouldn't be fooled. While working a construction job by day and going to the gym at night, Johnson believed that something greater was in store for him. In 2004, his time finally came. That year, he knocked out living legend Roy Jones, Jr., in the ninth round, defeated highly regarded Antonio Tarver via split decision, and was named "Fighter of the Year." Having competed at middleweight, super middleweight, light heavyweight and cruiserweight, Johnson is one of the most appreciated fighters of his time, because of his aggressive style inside the ring and his gentlemanly ways outside the ring. In July 2011, I called Glen Johnson and asked "The Road Warrior" about the path he traveled in boxing. At the time of this interview, Johnson's record was 51–15–2, 35 KO's, and he had recently lost a majority decision to super middleweight champion Carl Froch in the semifinals of the Super Six World Boxing Classic.

When did you first put on the gloves? How old were you and what were the circumstances?

I was twenty. I was getting a little bit chubby and my first wife told me that I was growing a pot belly. I was very self-conscious of it and decided immediately in my mind that I needed to start working out. I started looking around and found this gym in my neighborhood. I walked in there and spoke with one of the trainers. His name was Bobby Baker. He said that if you live in the neighborhood, it would be free. Free fit into my budget, so I jumped on it. It was just a way to work out and lose weight. I was doing it a lot and Bobby Baker asked me if I wanted to try amateur boxing. I told him that if he thought I could, I

Former light heavyweight world champion Glen Johnson (courtesy Marty Rosengarten/Ringside Photos.com).

would. He started to teach me a few more things. I started to do amateur boxing and the next thing I knew, I was hooked.

Were you already a boxing fan? Did you know much about the sport?

I grew up knowing about Muhammad Ali. He was famous and that was a name I always heard about. That's pretty much all I knew about boxing at the time. As I started training and getting involved in it, I started learning all the names like Sugar Ray Leonard, Marvin Hagler, Thomas Hearns, and "Hands of Stones." Going back further, I started learning about Rocky Marciano and those guys. I had never even seen an Ali fight to be honest with you, but I rented a lot of tapes and started watching his fights. During that time, we had Mike Tyson and Evander Holyfield and Riddick Bowe. They were coming up then and I got familiar with boxing real quick because now I was a part of the family.

Some people who take up professional fighting have hard lives outside the ring. Was that the case with you?

I don't have any horror stories as far as living on the streets or being abandoned by parents. I grew up in a poor neighborhood here in Miami. Before that, in Jamaica, I lived in a rough, tough neighborhood, which was like being in the ghetto here in America. I've been around rough neighborhoods and seen drug dealers and seen people get killed in the streets. I've witnessed and been around that, but I have a close family background. I've always had loving family members and I had good friends as a kid. I had a lot of fun. When I came here to the States, I didn't really understand the culture, so it took some getting used to. I withdrew a little bit. As a kid, when you're not around familiar territory, you're not as open as when you're in your own culture. I went through that process a little bit and then I came into my own after a while. My mother was always very much involved in what

Glen Johnson defeats Hugo Pineda via eighth-round TKO in their 2008 encounter (courtesy Marty Rosengarten/RingsidePhotos.com).

I was doing and she kept a tight rein on me. She never let me go astray or step out of line. I had that working for me and that kind of kept me out of trouble. I was never with the wrong crowd, never got arrested, never went down that path.

Before you started boxing, would you have described yourself as a fighter?

I always fought as a kid. I fought with all of my friends and family members. As a kid, I got a lot of whoopings from my elders. In Jamaica, that was our culture. When you see a child do something that he shouldn't be doing and you know the parents of the child, you give him a whooping and you tell the parent. That was our thing. Over here, it's a different culture. I still got whoopings from my mother, but for the most part, nobody else would give you a whooping because it was against the law.

Do you think these whoopings somehow toughened you up or gave you a sense of discipline?

I think the whoopings were good for me. They kept me in line. They kept me straight. I always knew what the penalty was if I did certain things. Here, a lot of the times, whoopings are not a part of the culture and I really think that's a mistake. The kids today are running wild and doing whatever they want. Parents are afraid of the kids, teachers are afraid of the kids, and the kids are going crazy right now. It might have toughened me up, but even if it didn't, it kept me in line for sure.

As an amateur, how did you feel about competitive fighting at first? Did you feel at home in the ring or did it take some time to adjust?

It took some time to adjust. Boxing is a humbling sport. It's very tiring. In my first sparring session, I certainly felt that I was going to pass out. I couldn't breath and I couldn't believe anyone would do this. The trauma that the body goes through… Not so much from the punches, but your wind and the fatigue. Fatigue I think is the first punishing thing that boxing exposes you to. If you're getting hit, that's a whole other thing. That's on top of all the other stuff. It's physical, it's mental… You're gasping and everything else. All of that is something you have to get used to. At first, I could only go two rounds. I felt like I needed oxygen or I was going to faint and die, but I would look around and I see guys with more experience doing rounds and rounds and rounds. After a while, it kicks in and you say to yourself that you are not a lesser man than the next guy. If he can do it, there must be something in me that can do it, too.

You want to quit, because you no longer can breath and your body feels like it wants to shut down. When you rest up and you go home and you start feeling better, your pride kicks in and you say you have to do better tomorrow. That's what it was for me. I always challenged myself to do better the next day. I have to do better than that guy. If that guy can do it, so can I. He doesn't have four holes that he breathes through, he only has two holes like I have. If he found a way, I can find a way. I wouldn't let up. Eventually, my lungs started opening up and my skills started coming together. I was able to do three rounds and then I was able to do four rounds. I was stuck at four rounds for a long time, but then I was able to do more rounds on top of that. That's just that. It's that no-quit attitude that was always in me and boxing just brought it out into the forefront. You never really know yourself until you get pushed to that level. That's when you find out who you really are.

You're either going to quit and stop, or you're going to find a way to continue. I never knew anything about myself until I got there and then I realized what I needed to do.

What stands out in your mind about your pro debut?

I had a typical debut. I had an "opponent." At that time, I was nervous to take the headgear off. In all of my amateur years, when I fought, I had headgear on. Now I was fighting without headgear, so it was a new thing and it was a different challenge. I got used to one thing and now I had to get used to a whole new thing. I was nervous. The butterflies were really setting in. The bell rang and the crowd was out there and everybody was cheering. I went out there and started to do my thing. I saw that my jab was working, and I started to get some shots in, and my confidence started to grow, and I got the chance to touch the guy up a few times. That's basically what it was for me. I ended up stopping him in that first round and I felt like I was on my way.

You had a great deal of success early in your professional career, winning your first thirty-two pro fights. Tell me a little about that time of your life and where you saw your career heading.

I felt like I was going to be a champion during that time. At first, I never knew I was going to have that much success early on, but then when I was in it and I was winning these fights, my confidence grew and my belief started growing and it was good times. Bobby Baker was with me for about my first twenty fights, but then he turned me on to Pat Burns, because he was friendly with Burns. Over that period of time, Burns took over and he was

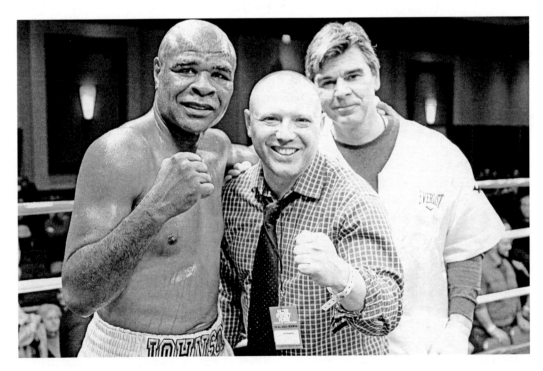

Glen Johnson, Ted Panagiotis, and Mark Vaz, after Johnson's 2014 fourth-round TKO victory over Jaime Velasquez (courtesy Craig Eagleson).

with me all the way to my fight with Bernard Hopkins. When I lost to Hopkins, Burns pulled out and then I just kind of took it on myself and kept it going.

In July 1997, you challenged Bernard Hopkins for his middleweight world title in a fight you lost via eleventh-round TKO. What stands out in your mind about that experience?

Bernard was on a different level than the people I had been fighting. I was fighting opponent-type guys and Bernard Hopkins was a world champion–type guy. As soon as the bell rang and I went out there, he hit me with a body shot. I said to myself, "Welcome to big time boxing!" Everything that I tried to do, everything that I was successful with that I would do before, it wasn't working. Every time I tried to make an adjustment that worked for me in the past, it wouldn't work. It got to this point in the fight where I just didn't know what to do anymore, so I said I'll just fight. I had no other plan. I didn't have anything to go to. All of my experience didn't work for me. In the eleventh round, they called it. To this day, I believe it was my toughest fight. Nothing that I did worked and I've never faced that before.

When a fighter is stopped inside the distance, especially if it's their first loss, sometimes they take it close to heart. How did you process what happened?

I never fooled myself. I kept reality in the forefront. I knew I was in there with a better fighter and I always thought that I was still learning. I felt that if I could learn what I needed to learn, I could beat the man who beat me. The next day, I said that I could beat Bernard if I could get the opportunity to fight him again. In my next fight, I fought Merqui Sosa. I figured that with all the things that I learned in the Bernard Hopkins fight, this was my opportunity to show the world that I can do so much better than I did with Bernard. That was my mindset going into that fight, but again, I ran into that stumbling block. I had success early, but Merqui Sosa wore me down.

You lost to Hopkins, you lost to Sosa, and you also lost your fight after Sosa to Joseph Kiwanuka. That's enough to crush some people.

You never know how you're going to react to something until you're in it. If you've never run out of breath and you're now under water and you're in survival mode, you can think about what you would do if you were in that situation, but you never know until you're actually in it. For me, once I lost three fights back to back, I had to ask myself, "Is this all you have? Is this as far as you want to go?" I felt like I could do more. I believed in my skills and I believed that I had the will to grow and the ability to learn. I started boxing when I was twenty. A lot of these guys started when they were kids. When I started, there were kids at the gym who were eight, nine, ten years old with unbelievable talent. I thought, "Wow! When they're my age, they're going to be amazing." I already knew that I was behind the eight ball.

Sometimes you have to make a conscious decision on what you're going to do with yourself for the rest of your life. I felt like I had a chance to make some money and I wasn't going to waste my time half-assing it. For me, it was a hundred percent. I was never going to quit on myself and I never let the losses break my spirits or break my belief. This was a reality thing and it was time to wake up and smell the coffee. It was time to go to work and

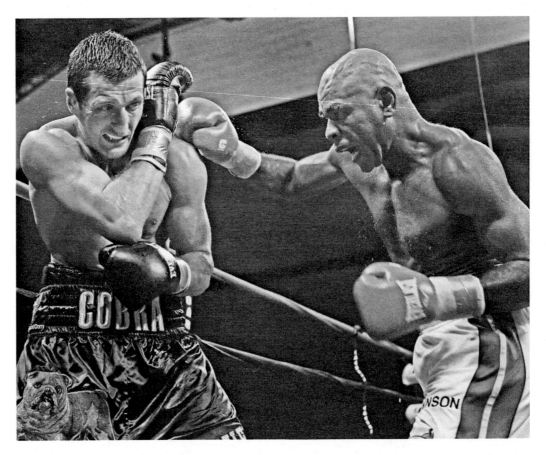

Glen Johnson battles Carl Froch in the semifinals of the Super Six World Boxing Classic in 2011, losing the bout via majority decision (courtesy Marty Rosengarten/RingsidePhotos.com).

that's what I did. I had a day job, but boxing was the thing that would take me out of the day job. I would work construction from seven to three-thirty, rush home, take a shower, and be at the gym by five. I would be tired, but I figured that all I had to do was commit myself to what I needed to do, so I could get better and learn. I knew I was still learning and that one day I was going to learn enough to win.

In February 2004, you defeated Clinton Woods via unanimous decision for a vacant light heavy-weight world title. In September of that year, you knocked out former pound-for-pound king Roy Jones, Jr., in the ninth round. Tell me about your fight with Jones.

I always admired Roy. I was his biggest fan, but I always thought I could beat him. I told a couple of my friends that and they laughed at me and told me that Roy would kill me. When I got the fight, I said that this is my chance to back up all the talking that I was doing, because if I went out there and lost the fight, my friends would mock me like crazy. I really committed myself to working hard. All the extra running that I needed to do, I did it. I knew Roy Jones was a guy who throws quick combinations, but he wasn't the guy who would throw five or six punches. He would throw a couple of shots and then create distance.

Glen Johnson (left) poses with Antonio Tarver at a press conference before their 2004 fight (courtesy Bret Newton—ThreatPhoto.com/Pound4Pound.com).

If you give him that distance, if you give him that space, he's able to relax a little bit and come back at you again. I told myself that I wasn't going to allow him to have that space. I wasn't going to allow him to relax. I was going to make him fight every second of every minute. When I trained, I prepared myself to do that. I believed that I was going to win the fight, and I went out there and fought the way that I thought I was supposed to, to beat him, and that's what I did.

The year 2004 was a great one for you. You beat Woods, you beat Jones, you went on to beat Antonio Tarver via spilt decision, and you were regarded as the "Fighter of the Year."

It was the best year of my career. We went out and did what we were supposed to do. I was finally getting some recognition. All the talk about me being nothing more than somebody's opponent kind of went away. It was an amazing run. I felt really good about myself. All of the belief I had in myself came true. All the hard work and all the years I spent working construction finally paid off. It was a great time for me. I really felt like I was going to go for a run, but it didn't happen that way. I had the rematch with Tarver and it was all downhill from there.

What comes to mind when you look back at everything you have experienced in boxing?

If it was a perfect world, if things had worked out a little bit better, I would have accomplished so much more. I would have more wins and fewer losses. I would have more titles and more decorations, but I'm very proud of myself for beating the odds like I did. I believe I've had a great career, a successful career. When you look back at the great fighters from way back in the day, they had records like mine. Back then, you didn't have to be undefeated to be recognized as one of the best fighters in boxing. They had some losses. At the end of the day, they didn't stack their records. They fought real fighters. They fought the best people who were available to them. That's what I did. My career wasn't handed to me. I had my share of opponents when I first started, because I didn't have any experience. The early part of my pro career was an extension of my amateur career, and then I had to fight. I did that at the appropriate time, and I stand tall and proud of what I was able to accomplish.

18

Mackie Shilstone: Special Forces

Boxing is a sport where the combatants often use old-school training methods. The idea has always been that the harder you work, the better conditioned you will be. The "science of intensity" worked for fighters in the past, so why change the approach? Born and raised in New Orleans, Louisiana, Mackie Shilstone is a fitness guru who has worked with thousands of professional athletes in a number of different sports. In the boxing world, Shilstone is something of a pioneer in bringing modern techniques to various training camps. In 1985, Shilstone guided light heavyweight champion Michael Spinks when Spinks moved up in weight to face heavyweight champion Larry Holmes. Spinks defeated Holmes via unanimous decision, becoming the first light heavyweight in history to capture the heavyweight crown. In 2003, Shilstone helped make history again, when he worked with light heavyweight champion Roy Jones, Jr. Jones challenged John Ruiz for Ruiz's heavyweight world title, winning the bout via unanimous decision. Shilstone's growing reputation was evident when middleweight Bernard Hopkins hired him in 2006 while preparing for his eventual unanimous decision victory over light heavyweight champion Antonio Tarver. While Shilstone is known for helping fighters move up in weight, in 1992, he helped Riddick Bowe lose weight before his unanimous decision victory over heavyweight champion Evander Holyfield. In 2015, super middleweight champion Andre Ward sought Shilstone's advice and went through his diagnostic program, as did football star Peyton Manning. In April 2011, I called Mackie Shilstone to talk about why he refers to himself as "Special Forces." At the time of this interview, Shilstone's primary athlete was tennis legend Serena Williams.

You have a strong background in fitness and professional sports, but what was it that brought you to the world of boxing?

I was working in a lifestyle management program in 1982, and I was helping, it turned out, a man by the name of Don Hubbard and his wife, who I went on to become very close with. Don Hubbard was associated with Butch Lewis Productions. Don told me, "You know, Mackie, you've helped people with this thing. I think you could be of great benefit to my fighter, Michael Spinks." Michael Spinks had just won the light heavyweight title. I was brought in to bring Michael's training to the next level. Michael had to make weight and it was hard for him, because he was 6'3" making 175. They did it the old-school way—

145

turning on the steam and sweating. Michael was always told not to drink water and I told him he couldn't do that. I got him to start drinking water and get out of the Army boots that he was running in on the beach. Joe Frazier did it, so he did it, too. I remember I got Michael his first pair of actual running shoes. They were Nikes. Anyway, he just breezed through the first fight that I helped him with and he felt very good about himself and he liked working with me. One thing led to another and I worked with him for the rest of his light heavyweight career.

When it came time to move him up to the heavyweight division to face Larry Holmes, I was the logical one to work with him. Eddie Futch could not be the trainer for that fight, because he also trained Holmes, so Nelson Brison stepped in to train Michael. That fight put Michael on the map and it did the same thing for me. After Michael won that fight, I was taken to Los Angeles and put on every major show. Michael was on the cover of Sports Illustrated and I was featured in the story. It put me all over the world, because it had never been done before. Little did I know that seventeen years later, I would do it again with Roy Jones, Jr. After working with Michael Spinks, I went on to work with Riddick Bowe. Rock Newman had Riddick Bowe. At the time, nobody really wanted Riddick because he had a foot issue, but Rock took him and brought him to me, because he knew me from working

with Michael Spinks. I helped Riddick get started with his career. I was affiliated with AMI St. Jude Medical Center in Kenner, Louisiana, and I put him on the fifth floor of the hospital to give him a break on accommodations. We trained and they went off and they didn't come back to me again until the Pierre Coetzer fight. This was an eliminator, I believe. If Bowe won this fight he was going to fight Holyfield. I worked with him and we won the fight, and lo and behold, we went on to prepare for Holyfield.

I worked with Bowe all the way along and then I sat out for a while. Finally, I got a call out of the blue from Roy Jones, Jr.'s people. They wanted to know if I was interested in doing something that hadn't been done in seventeen years, which was to help Roy Jones, Jr., move up from light heavyweight to heavyweight and take on John Ruiz. I worked with Roy and Roy is an incredible human being, both as a person and as an athlete. We developed a great relationship and we beat Ruiz. A few years later, I got a call from Bernard Hopkins's team. He wanted to move up to light heavyweight to face Antonio Tarver. The last boxing camp I did was with Bernard Hopkins. At this point in my career, I'm not going to go in there and live there as I've done in the past. I'll work with Serena Williams for an extended period, because tennis is a different world. You have to keep in mind, my strategy in boxing is that I have to perfect a way to kill the opponent. There's a paragraph in the contract that a boxer signs that says that if you die in the ring at the hands of the opponent, he doesn't go to jail. My strategy is to hurt the opponent and to create devastating pain.

I took Bernard Hopkins and I put him in the cockpit of an F-15. I did the same thing with Roy Jones. I taught them the kill strategy of an F-15 and how they track. An F-15 has never lost in combat. If the F-15 isn't outgunned six-to-one, it doesn't think it's a battle. One-on-one, it's never a fair fight for an F-15. I talked to Bernard and Roy about taking out their opponent in a cold, calm, calculated way. The F-15 just took out a person they've never seen and killed them! I want that for you! I always gave each fighter his own story. That's a technique I use. I called Bowe the story of the Trojan Horse. We're going to wheel that in and take out Holyfield at the beginning of the eighth round and he did. I've come a long way in my field. I'm sixty years old, I've worked with over three thousand pro athletes, and I've worked in every major sport. In boxing, I've worked side by side with a lot of the great trainers in the game. I've worked with Eddie Futch, Nelson Brison, Alton Merkerson, Naazim Richardson, Freddie Roach… I only get called when they're facing adversity. They

Bernard Hopkins and Mackie Shilstone, 2006 (courtesy Marty Rosengarten/RingsidePhotos.com).

have someone else to do the day-to-day. I'm not sitting there like a boxing coach who works with the guy all the time. When they get into trouble, I'm the one they call. I'm what you would call "Special Forces."

When you worked with Michael Spinks for the Larry Holmes fight, it was 1985. When you trained Roy Jones, Jr., and Bernard Hopkins, it was over fifteen years later at a time when training methods and technology had changed. Tell me about the differences that existed in your approach from when you trained Spinks and when you worked with Jones and Hopkins.

My model has never changed, but the components have. Back in 1982, I would use heart rate monitors with a company named Polar. I would actually chart the heart rate monitor as a Polar monitor. I realized that boxers didn't need to be trained off of a formula heart rate, but off of sparring and what their heart rate generated when they were sparring. I would tape and velcro these heart rate monitors to them while they were actually sparring, so I would know what level to train at. Years later, there's a computer system that does that, so I advanced to that. Right now, we use duel x-ray technology (DEXA) to look at body composition. We can measure body composition down to the gram, both in fat and bone and muscle. I use metabolic testing to measure metabolic rate. I can determine how many calories a person is burning at rest. I brought science to boxing when boxing training was archaic. I remember Angelo Dundee telling me that what you're doing is crazy, that nobody in his right mind can lift weights and not lose speed and flexibility. With the technology now, I'm not even sure if it's actually caught up. We can perform a biomechanical analysis like I did on Hopkins and Jones. We can measure the client's VO2 Max (Maximum Endurance Capacity) and their resting energy expenditure (REE). We can custom design meals. All of Bernard Hopkins's meals and all of Roy Jones's meals were based on REE testing.

You've worked with a number of athletes throughout your career. How does Roy Jones, Jr.'s athletic ability compare to some of the other athletes you've worked with?

I've tested the best athletes in the world. The greatest pitchers in the world, the greatest shortstops... Joe DeLoach, the world record holder at 200 meters, I tested him and helped him. Butch Reynolds, the 400 meter champion, I tested him. I tested the best in every sport and I have *never* met anyone like Roy Jones in three thousand pro athletes. Nobody. It was amazing what he could do, the gifts he possessed. I think Roy could have played point guard in the NBA without dropping a hat. I watched him. I think Roy, whatever he put his mind to, he could do. He's just an incredible human being.

In March 2003, when Jones challenged John Ruiz for Ruiz's heavyweight title, I understand the plan was to break his nose and then attack his chest to prevent him from breathing properly. How did this plan come about?

I always get statistics on all of the opponents. To this day, I have in-depth reports on everything about John Ruiz. I had all the research and I went over that with Roy. I told him that we have to break his nose. The reason why we could do that is because Ruiz broke his nose in his fight against Holyfield. I went to the hospital and talked to the oral and facial surgeon, and I also talked to the ENT surgeon. I said, "Tell me, if you have got a broken nose, how do you break it again?" They said, "Mackie, we're not in that business. We're in

Roy Jones, Jr., at a press conference for his 2003 fight with John Ruiz (courtesy Bret Newton—Threat Photo.com/Pound4Pound.com)

there to repair." I said, "My job is to destroy. *Your* job is to repair." They said that you're going to have to hit him with a lateral shot, a hook, because you can shatter it. They were right. In the sixth round, BAM! He broke his nose! At the time, I had just finished with a CPR certification course. I told Roy, "CPR is used to start the heart, so let's use CPR to disrupt the heart. I want to stop his heart. We've got to be able to come in and hit him right in the breastbone. It's a devastating, painful thing. If we hit him right in the breast bone, it will disrupt his heart."

What stands out in your mind about your experience working with Bernard Hopkins, when he moved from middleweight to light heavyweight to challenge Antonio Tarver in June 2006?

I got to know Bernard because he followed the path of Michael Spinks and Roy Jones in that he was going to move up and take on a bigger person. I actually remembered Bernard from before and he remembered me, because he was in the Butch Lewis training camp with Michael Spinks. We go back to when he was a very young man. Bernard had the greatest discipline of anybody I've ever seen, other than me. He ate like I ate. We were like two peas in a pod. We would battle over being OCD. Bernard and I loved each other. When I first started working with Bernard, he told me the story of when he went to prison. I'll never forget it. He was like seventeen or eighteen. He's walking through the line on Cell Block D and they're yelling, "Jail bait! Jail bait!" He said that he had to either do something about it or he was going to be dead, so he took over Cell Block D and survived. *Tremendous* discipline!

Now remember, I do all these in-depth physiological tests. After testing Bernard, what amazed me is that he literally, physiologically, survived making middleweight all those years. He had to work so hard to make middleweight, so all I had to do was let his body grow into the real Bernard Hopkins. Before we started training, Bernard told me, "Mackie, I want you to build armor. I want to fight like the turtle. I want to be able to take shots, pop my head out, and get back in." We built his shoulders up in his upper torso, and we built his legs so he could move around if he had to. Bernard told me I did exactly what he wanted. After he won, he said, "What can I give you for this fight?" I said, "I want your mouthpiece." He had this mouthpiece that said, "Tarver vs Hopkins." I wanted that because I know that the single most important thing that a fighter has is his mouthpiece. My memento of that fight is Bernard's mouthpiece. I have it at my home. That's what I asked for. He said, "You're kidding." I said, "No, I want it."

Bernard Hopkins on his way to winning a unanimous decision over Antonio Tarver in their 2006 fight (courtesy Marty Rosengarten/RingsidePhotos.com).

I understand that before the fight, the plan was to break Tarver's jaw. How did this come about?

It goes back to what we did with the nose in the Ruiz fight. I learned from a medical report that Tarver had his jaw broken when he fought Eric Harding. I went to a TMJ expert who was a friend of mine, James Quinn, and God rest his soul, he's passed away. I learned some amazing things from Dr. Quinn. TMJ joints have the same structure as knee joints. When I realized this, I realized that we could dislodge his jaw. You remember when Bernard knocked Tarver down? Tarver, we knew, came in with these big roundhouse punches and he would catch his opponents because they couldn't see them coming. It would come out of left field. When Tarver came in and threw that round house left hook, Hopkins knew it was coming, saw it, ducked under, and hit him. I put Hopkins on a balance beam of 4×4×8 (8 feet long and 4 inches off the ground with a 4-inch width) and made him balance on the balance beam and punch the mitts with me. When Tarver threw that punch, Hopkins bent over like we did on the balance beam and countered with his right. Tarver, ironically, fell off the balance beam, so to speak, when he threw his punch. When Bernard clipped him, he didn't clip him on the TMJ joint. He clipped him just on the other side of it. Had Tarver not fallen down when he threw that round house punch, we would have scored right on the TMJ joint!

You worked with Riddick Bowe when he challenged Evander Holyfield for Holyfield's heavyweight titles in November 1992. What you did with Bowe was the opposite of what you did with Spinks, Jones, and Hopkins. You helped him lose weight instead of put it on.

Michael Spinks used to keep candy under his bed only to know it was there. I would catch him and he would say, "You know, Mackie, I'm not going to eat it." I would say, "I know that." After the fight, I would get the candy and bring it to him and he would say, "Nah, I don't want it. I just wanted to know I had it." With Riddick Bowe, he wouldn't just eat a piece of pie, he would eat the *whole* pie. But he was a different man for this fight. He had the opportunity to fight for the heavyweight title, so he was as disciplined as anybody. After he won and became champion, he lost focus. It's tougher to hold the heavyweight title than it is to get it. For the fight with Holyfield, we were training out in Bend, Oregon, in a great training environment. I knew the vibes were right. Bowe respected Eddie Futch, and Rock Newman ran a great camp. The Bowe story was simple. We knew that Holyfield thought that Bowe would not survive after the eighth round, because he was too big and that he would get tired, so I used some of the technology that I used with Michael Spinks.

When Michael had knee issues, we used to have to put him on a stationary bike. I would use these elastic cords to train him, where we used this tubing and you could punch against resistance while you were riding the bike. It was unique. I put Bowe in the ring, I measured his heart rate with heart rate monitors, and I found out what he punched in sparring. I then hooked up the cord in the ring and got in front of him. As he moved away with the cord, it got tougher. As he moved up, it got easier. It's called accommodating resistance. To make a long story short, we did that and we punched over 175 punches a round with these cords. Instead of doing it for three minutes, we did it for a minute thirty with thirty seconds of recovery. On the night of the fight, Bowe was just pounding on Holyfield. Tim Hallmark, who was Holyfield's strength and conditioning coach, told me later, "We were waiting for Bowe to tire and he never tired." If you look at the punch statistics, Bowe outpunched Holyfield almost two and a half to one and just beat him senseless.

Riddick Bowe and trainer Lou Duva, 2007. Duva was in the opposite corner when Bowe fought Evander Holyfield and Andrew Golota (courtesy Marty Rosengarten/RingsidePhotos.com).

Bowe's career ended rather early. Even before he was thirty, he already appeared faded, as was demonstrated in his two fights with Andrew Golota. Why do you think this was the case?

He was carrying too much weight in between fights. It was not uncommon for Bowe to come into training camp weighing between 267 and 272. We would have to train for three months just to get the weight off. Riddick burned out of boxing. That's why he enlisted in the Marine Corps. It was his way out. Bowe and his team were over at my house during a training camp and I brought in a five-star general of the Marines, who was a friend of mine. Right there in my den, he told Riddick, "You don't want to do this, son. You're a fine young man. You're an Olympic champion. It's not the right move." I'll tell you, Bowe had innate boxing skills. He was made to fight. His downfall was his lack of discipline. You take Hopkins's discipline and put it in Riddick Bowe, I think he would knock the Klitschkos out. There has never been anybody with his raw talent in years. It's unfortunate that it didn't materialize more than it did.

When working with fighters, you often compare them to the way predators go after their prey, whether it's a shark, or a mongoose, or even an F-15. What is the logic behind this?

Fighters are in a brutal sport where you can kill your opponent and not go to jail. The reason why I did this is it gave them a distraction and gave them something else to focus on. It takes their mind away from the battle. You have to give them something to take them away, yet keep them there. By giving them an alter-ego like the F-15, or the Riddick Bowe analogy of the Trojan Horse, or with another fighter it was the cobra and the mongoose, it's a great distraction, but it keeps them focused at the same time. When you fight, there's this fear of the unknown. You're going to get into the ring and try to do something to someone else, while they're trying to do it to you, too. You keep thinking about it all the time. You don't escape. I gave them an escape.

You've got the shark, the mongoose, the cobra… If you were an animal, what would you be?
     I don't know if I would be the wise old lion or if I would be the jackal. I'm that ultimate terrorist in the sense that you see this sixty-year-old-guy running beside you. You see, I run with all of my athletes. I have the conditioning to do that, even though I'm considerably older. Early on, I was only five years older than my athletes. Hell, in Bernard Hopkins's case, I was only fifteen years older. Everybody will tell you that Mackie does everything with you. That prevents them from giving me any backtalk. What are you going to say when your coach is running along with you? I study books of great leaders. I have to live up to what my father did as a war hero. He was a World War II veteran, but I don't do anything that heroic. I just try to be the best I can. While I'm going to help you with your sport for as long as you want me, when you leave me, you'll be better off in your life.

19

Harold Lederman:
The Pharmacist

During televised boxing matches, announcers greatly influence the way viewers perceive fights. They give their own account of what is taking place in the ring and suggest who is winning, without necessarily considering the criteria of the Association of Boxing Commissions. For this reason, the unofficial scorecards announcers give might be different than what a trained judge would offer. Born and raised in the Bronx, New York, Harold Lederman is HBO's first unofficial ringside scorer. Lederman has been a boxing fan his whole life, often keeping score of the fights he watched. Since it was already his habit to score fights, he finally asked representatives of the New York State Athletic Commission if he could be a judge. Lederman began his career as a licensed professional boxing judge in 1967, going on to judge over one hundred title fights. When he wasn't sitting at ringside with a scorecard, he watched boxing on television, notably the fights on HBO. In the mid–1980s, Lederman suggested to HBO's Ross Greenberg that the network include a judge on the broadcast team to offer an unofficial scorecard and teach the viewers at home how to properly score a fight. Lederman himself got the job and he has been a part of HBO's broadcast team ever since. While boxing has always been Lederman's passion, he made his living throughout the years as a pharmacist. In January 2012, I called Harold Lederman and asked the pharmacist about his time spent as an official and unofficial ringside scorer. At the time of this interview, Lederman was awaiting his next assignment, which was the Julio Cesar Chavez, Jr.–Marco Antonio Rubio bout, scheduled for February 4th.

What is your background in boxing and what led you to become a judge?
   It started for me at a place that nobody seems to know anything about. Nobody's ever heard of it, nobody gives a damn about it… If you lived in New York in the '40s, everybody used to go to summer vacation at a place called Rockaway. During these summer getaways, every Friday night, my father would throw me in the car and take me to the fights at a place called Long Beach Stadium. It was in Long Beach, Long Island, which was the next town over from Rockaway. Long Beach Stadium was an outdoor summer arena and they used to get pretty good crowds there. For some reason, if you ask people today about Long Beach

Unofficial ringside scorer Harold Lederman (courtesy Marty Rosengarten/RingsidePhotos.com).

Stadium, they don't even know that it existed. It just got lost. It might have closed during the '60s, but I don't know for sure. There was a boxing judge in Las Vegas by the name of Bill Graham. He must have read in a boxing magazine somewhere that I used to go to Long Beach Stadium, because he came up to me one time and told me that he fought there four times. It was amazing! I had never met anyone before who had heard of Long Beach Stadium. All of the big names from the '40s and '50s fought at Long Beach Stadium at one time or another. Roland Lastarza fought there, Tony Janiro fought there… Everybody fought at Long Beach Stadium. It was a legendary place during a special time in boxing.

I used to go to the fights with my wife Eileen, and I would sit there and keep score. I thought, "What the hell? I can do this." Eileen's dad was an inspector with the New York State Athletic Commission, so I talked to them and said that I'd like to judge boxing. They told me I had to get some experience and that I should start judging amateur boxing. I started judging amateur boxing in 1965. I did that for two years and I learned an awful lot. I used to judge twenty fights a night, five nights a week. When I judged twenty fights a night, they used to pay me five dollars. There was no money in it. It was more for experience. I went to work for the New York State Athletic Commission, and after two years, I got my license as a professional boxing judge. That's when I met the chairman of the New York State Athletic Commission, a man by the name of Edwin B. Dooley. He was there for about ten years and he was the commissioner when Muhammad Ali and Joe Frazier had that first famous fight. Commissioner Dooley is also well known because he took the welterweight title away from Jose Napoles. That was really big in its day. Napoles wouldn't come to Syracuse to fight Billy Backus, so Dooley stripped Napoles of his title, which everybody thought was ridiculous. Those are the two things Dooley was remembered for, not necessarily for making me a boxing judge.

The first major bout that you judged was in September 1971. It was the rematch between lightweight champion Ken Buchanan and Ismael Laguna in a fight that Buchanan won via unanimous decision.

That's a pretty truthful statement. At that time, Laguna's manager was a real estate guy from Brooklyn by the name of Cain Young. He was a good manager and he did his homework. For one reason or another, it kept coming out in the paper that he didn't want this judge or he didn't want that judge. He was objecting to a whole lot of judges. It seemed that he objected to almost everybody in the world except me. In those days, the Commission was run by a man by the name of Frank Morris. He wasn't the chairman. He took care of all the day-to-day stuff. Frank was a big tough Irishman with a ruddy face. At one time, he was Nelson Rockefeller's bodyguard. When Frank walked into the dressing room, everybody would sit down and shut up. He was a terrific Commissioner. People that worked under Frank Morris all loved him. I certainly did.

In those days, this is how they did things… Frank Morris would walk in and he would say that the referee and the judges for the preliminaries are you, you, and you, and the referee and the judges for the main event are you, you, and you. On the night of Buchanan-Laguna, he pointed at me. I had no idea that I was going to judge the fight until about five or ten minutes before the fight started. To tell you the truth, it wasn't a bad system because of the fact that the gamblers couldn't get at you and you didn't have time to get nervous about the fight. I think the "Frank Morris System" worked perfect. Back then, we didn't use the ten-point must system. In those days, as I remembered, the fighter either won the round or he lost the round. You pick a winner and that's it. If he won the round, he gets a point. If he knocked the guy down, he got two points. It would go all the way up to four points. You follow? The ten-point must system is still fairly new. That was started by the Association of Boxing Commissions.

**Harold Lederman with fellow HBO commentator Roy Jones, Jr., late 2000s (courtesy Claudia Bocane-
gra).**

*Another fight you worked was the heavyweight match-up between Gerry Cooney and Ken Norton
in May 1981, a fight that Cooney won via first-round TKO.*

Let me tell you, I got such a kick out of hearing my name being announced over the
loud speaker at Madison Square Garden! I was in seventh heaven! Be that as it may, Gerry
Cooney was a hell of a puncher. To say the least, Norton didn't like to fight big punchers.
Ken Norton would always go into that crouch and he had that defense with his hands
crossed in front of his face and he came forward dragging that back foot. His style always
gave Ali trouble, but he didn't like to fight big punchers. Boy could Gerry crack! In the first
round, Gerry got him into the corner and he was beating the tar out of him. Tony Perez,
who I always consider to be one of the finest referees of all time, he couldn't pull Gerry off.
He wanted to stop the fight, but what the hell could he do? He was behind Gerry when
this was happening. If you get between Ken Norton and Gerry Cooney, that's it! The lights
go out! Norton just collapsed into the corner post and Tony was eventually able to pull
Gerry off. Gerry was a terrific puncher and a heck of a fighter. Today, I think he would have
been considered another Vitali Klitschko. I think he would have held onto the title a long
time if he were champion today. He was every bit of 6'4", 6'5". He was a big strong guy with
a vicious left hook.

*Of all the fights you judged, the fight you found the most entertaining was between super ban-
tamweight champion Wilfredo Gomez and Lupe Pintor in December 1982, a fight that Gomez
won via fourteenth-round TKO.*

I still maintain to this day that Gomez-Pintor was the greatest fight I ever saw. I never saw anything like that in my entire life. At the time, Wilfredo Gomez was the reigning WBC 122 pound champion, Lupe Pintor was the reigning WBC 118 pound champion, and they went at it! It was fourteen rounds of Gatti-Ward. Pick the best round of Gatti-Ward and this was fourteen rounds of it. It was the most incredible fight I ever saw. Back and forth and back and forth... It was a vicious fight, and in the fourteenth round, Lupe Pintor went down twice and Arthur Mercante waved it off. Until the fourteenth round, either guy could have won. When they walked out of the ring, Gomez looked like he had been through a meat grinder. His face was all swollen and battered and bruised. Lupe Pintor walked out looking like he had never been in a fight. It was just incredible. There was a lot of nationalism. It was a Mexican against a Puerto Rican. It was in New Orleans at the Superdome and everybody was standing and screaming and hooting and hollering. It was a semifinal to a great fight. The main event was Tommy Hearns and Wilfred Benitez. When Hearns and Benitez went on, nobody was screaming because everybody was so drained. They were breathless. You just couldn't follow an act like Gomez-Pintor. If anybody ever left it in the ring, it was Gomez and Pintor. That's for darn sure. Two guys who gave it everything! I've never seen anything like that. Nothing could ever top Gomez-Pintor. Nothing!

Another great fight that you judged was the first fight between Evander Holyfield and cruiserweight champion Dwight Muhammad Qawi (then known as Dwight Braxton) in July 1986, a fight that Holyfield won via split decision.

That was just a great, great fight. It really was. Probably the best cruiserweight fight ever. It was two guys who were in incredible condition who were just murdering each other! Evander was the taller guy and the better boxer. He would get up on his toes and box and punch, and Qawi was one of those flat footed guys who came in low. Every time he landed a left hook, it was enough to knock over a telephone pole. He was just a vicious banger. The question was, did Qawi's left hook do enough to win the round when Evander was landing all those jabs? In my mind, Evander out-boxed him, but it was a tough call. This was the "Thrilla in Manila" of cruiserweights. You could compare Evander to Ali and you could compare Qawi to Frazier. It was very hot in there and the two of them were just going at it.

At what point did you transition into the role of HBO's unofficial ringside scorer and how did this come about?

Ross Greenberg was pretty much running boxing on HBO at the time. If you worked an HBO fight as a referee or a judge in those days, you certainly got to know Ross Greenberg. I was sitting there one night, watching a fight at home. I called Ross on Monday morning and I said that what I was watching Saturday night and what his announcers were saying were two different things. I suggested to him that he get a boxing judge to keep score and tell the public what the rules are. He said, "Harold, that's not a bad idea. I'm going to get back to you about it." Two weeks later, he called me up and he said, "Harold, how would you like to work a fight for us?" I said, "Sure, Ross. No problem." WBC heavyweight champion Pinklon Thomas was fighting Trevor Berbick. They sent me a plane ticket and I was all excited, but I said to my wife Eileen, "Pinklon Thomas is a 7 to 1 favorite. What's going to happen is that Thomas is going to whack this guy out in the first round and my career at HBO is going to be over right then and there." Little did I know that Trevor Berbick hired Eddie Futch, who was one of the greatest trainers in the history of boxing. Sure as the devil, Berbick goes out and out-boxes Pinklon Thomas and wins a twelve round decision. HBO liked hearing what I had to say about the fight and I've been there ever since.

In April 1987, you were HBO's unofficial ringside scorer for the fight between Sugar Ray Leonard and middleweight champion Marvin Hagler, a fight that Leonard won via split decision.

I agreed with twelve out of twelve rounds with Dave Moretti. If you look at Dave Moretti's scorecard and you look at mine, we agreed on every single round. The shocking score in that fight came from Jose Juan Guerra. I liked Jose Guerra. I knew him when he was a boxing commissioner in Mexico. He was also a boxing judge and he ended up working Leonard-Hagler. He gave it to Ray by a lot. He gave it to Ray by eight points. There were rounds there where Ray was laying on the ropes and Marvin was just pounding on him. I'm thinking, how can you give those rounds to Ray? Marvin was just beating him up in those rounds and that's all there was to it. Dave Moretti and I had it for Ray by two points and Lou Filippo, of course, had it for Hagler. It was a sensational fight. It really was. People always say that Ray stole some of those rounds, because he would flurry in the last thirty seconds. It's hard to say. Maybe he did, maybe he didn't. I don't know. Looking back, I think Ray just boxed a beautiful fight.

In November 1993 when Evander Holyfield defeated heavyweight champion Riddick Bowe via majority decision in their second fight, a man known as "Fan Man" parachuted into the ring during the seventh round.

That was amazing! I mean think about it. How in God's name can a guy parachute

Harold Lederman at the Paramount Theater in Huntington, New York, 2015 (courtesy Craig Eagleson).

out of an airplane and be so accurate that he lands in the ring? Looking back, that guy was pretty darn good at what he did. But boy, did Rock Newman sure beat the hell out of him! That was probably one of the most unusual things I've ever seen in boxing. That was a crazy scene to say the least to have a guy come flying in and land in the middle of a tremendous fight. Of course, Evander Holyfield ended up winning that second fight, which he certainly deserved. Bowe and Holyfield went on to have just an unbelievably great trilogy. Riddick Bowe was something special. People don't realize how good he was in those days. Maybe he never did take on Lennox Lewis. Maybe Lennox would have beaten him. Heck, if I were Riddick Bowe, I probably wouldn't want to get in the ring with Lennox either! That was Riddick's prime. In those days, he beat Herbie Hide and Evander Holyfield twice and Jose Luis Gonzalez and Jesse Ferguson… Riddick was a pretty darn good fighter. He really was. He had a great uppercut. He was big, he was strong, he could box, he had a real good left jab… If he had gotten out before the Golota fights, he might have been recognized as one of the really fine heavyweight champions.

In March 1999, the heavyweight unification bout between Lennox Lewis and Evander Holyfield is considered to be one of the worst decisions of the last fifteen to twenty years. It was ruled a draw, but most observers felt that Lewis won the fight convincingly.

It was a bad decision, but the worst decision I've ever seen was Tyrone Everett and Alfredo Escalera at the Spectrum in Philadelphia. It was for Escalera's WBA 130 pound title. We're talking 1976. Tyrone won that fight. I was sitting ringside, maybe five rows back. In giving every break in the world to Alfredo Escalera, I still scored it ten rounds to five for Tyrone Everett. He just beat up Escalera, but Escalera retained his title in a split decision. They didn't announce the decision till the day after. They said that they were working on the scorecards or some bologna like that, but what they were doing—they were trying to prevent a riot, because it was in Philadelphia where Everett was from. This was just highway robbery. By far the worst decision I ever saw. But back to Lennox Lewis and Evander Holyfield at Madison Square Garden—I thought Lennox clearly won the fight, but there are a couple of things you can point to. Eugenia Williams, who scored it for Holyfield, claimed that she was looking at Lennox Lewis's back the whole time. In other words, if you're sitting in a stationary position and a guy is on the other side of the ring and he's got his opponent against the ropes, it's hard to see the punches because all you're looking at is one guy's back. She maintained that she was blocked in a lot of instances and that's understandable.

Larry O'Connell had a very interesting score. He was the British judge. After five rounds, he said that he had it four rounds to one for Lennox Lewis. Now, first of all, you're not supposed to keep track of your own score. In other words, if you're a judge, you're supposed to score a round, hand in your card, and forget how you scored the previous round. You're not supposed to keep track of your own score. Okay? Larry O'Connell, obviously, in my mind, wasn't doing that. He knew that he had Lennox Lewis winning it four rounds to one after five rounds. Being that Larry O'Connell and Lennox Lewis are both British, I'm guessing that he thought to himself that he didn't want to show favoritism, so I think he deliberately evened it out. In round six, he gave it to Evander Holyfield! Evander certainly didn't win round six! He didn't even come *close* to winning round six! In round seven, he scored it even, which was another round that Lennox clearly won. You follow?

Left to right: HBO commentator Max Kellerman, Harold Lederman, and Lederman's wife, Eileen Lederman, 2009 (courtesy Marty Rosengarten/RingsidePhotos.com).

Larry knew how he had the fight scored early on and he was looking to keep it close and that was obvious. Somewhere along the line, I think he lost track of his scoring and accidentally scored it even, because he was afraid of giving Lennox Lewis too big of a lead. When the decision was announced and O'Connell's score was announced a draw, the first thing he said was that he thought he had Lennox winning the fight. Now, if you're not keeping track of the scoring, which you're not supposed to do, how the hell did you know that you had Lennox winning?! Stanley Christodoulou scored it 116–113 for Lennox Lewis, Eugenia Williams had it 115–113 for Evander Holyfield, and Larry O'Connell, as I mentioned, had it even at 115–115. I've studied those scorecards and I listened to every word that all of the judges said. I don't think it was a horrendous robbery. I think it was a bad decision, but it was nowhere near as bad as Escalera-Everett. That was way worse.

The trilogy between junior welterweights Arturo Gatti and Micky Ward has become legendary. Ward won a majority decision in the first fight and Gatti won unanimous decisions in the second and third fights. Those were three great back-to-back fights that took place from May 2002 to June 2003.

Micky Ward was one incredibly tough guy, and he made me look really bad one night.

I'll tell you a story. Lou DiBella used to put together the fights for HBO. I'm one of these guys who watches whatever fight happens to be on TV. I don't care who it is. If it's on, I'll watch it. I used to watch the Spanish station all the time. I noticed this one guy who was a junior welterweight. He was a good-looking guy with long black hair. He'd come to the ring with a big sombrero and a mariachi band and he's knocking out one guy after the other. His name was Alfonso Sanchez. I said, "Holy shit! Look at this!" I called up Lou DiBella and I said, "Lou, you gotta see this guy! You gotta put him on!" They put together a fight between Alfonso Sanchez and Micky Ward. Sure as the devil, the fight starts out and for six rounds, Alfonso is looking like a million dollars. He's winning every round. I don't think Micky Ward won one second of any round of that fight.

In the seventh round, Micky Ward hit him with a shot to the liver and Sanchez went down just like Oscar De La Hoya did when he fought Bernard Hopkins. I thought, holy shit! Micky Ward just ruined me, because I'm the one who recommended Alfonso Sanchez to HBO! To get back to the Gatti fights, they were just sensational. Some guys don't like to fight through pain. Look at Floyd Mayweather's fights with Carlos Hernandez and Victoriano Sosa. He hurt his hands in those fights and he went straight backwards. He was boxing and running. Gatti was just the opposite. If he was hurt, it didn't stop him. He broke his right hand in that third fight with Micky Ward, but he kept throwing it. You knew it was killing him, but he threw it anyway. His ability to fight through pain was incredible. Same with Micky Ward. You could hit Micky with a 2 × 4 and he wouldn't stop punching. He was that kind of fighter. Those were just three unbelievable fights!

Your daughter Julie followed in your footsteps and became a professional boxing judge. How did this come about?

When Julie was a little kid back in the early to mid–'70s, I used to work fights all over the world–Argentina, Chili, Colombia, Venezuela, Panama, Paris… No matter where I went, I always took Julie with me. If there were fights in Albany for example, we would take a ride up there together. When the fights were over, Julie would jump into the back of the car and fall asleep on the ride home. I took Julie all over the place. She loved boxing. She was a good student, so I didn't have a problem pulling her out of school for a few days, so she could see the fights. One night, a man named Tony Russo, who was an executive for the New York State Athletic Commission, he said to her, "Julie, why don't you judge?" She said, "No, I don't want to judge." Tony said, "You go to all the fights anyway. Why wouldn't you want to be a judge?" I said, "Listen, Julie. If you want to judge, I'll pay all your expenses. I'll pay all your fees and you can keep whatever money you make." She said, "I like that idea."

Boxing is a passion of yours, but for most of your life, you have worked as a pharmacist. How did you balance your passion for boxing with your responsibilities as a pharmacist?

It's just something I've always done. I'd be working in the drug store and all of a sudden I'd get a call, "Hey, Harold? Can you judge a fight in Colombia next week?" I'd say to my boss, "I need to take seven days off." He'd say, "You take off seven days and you'll need to find a new job." I'd have to go out and find another job, and that's just how it went. My wife Eileen put up with me for all those years and I don't know how she did it. There were a lot

Harold Lederman and daughter Julie Lederman, 2012 (courtesy Julie Lederman).

of times when I should have been in the drug store, but I was out catching a fight somewhere. I was always on the run and it could be very difficult at times. Eileen was a teacher in the South Bronx for forty years, so at least one of us had stable income. She loved boxing, too, so she understood. It's not like we were starving to death. We had a boxing family and we made it work.

$$\boxed{20}$$

Joe Goossen:
Ten Goose Boxing

The Goossen family made their mark in boxing the old fashioned way—from the ground up, with nothing but a strong work ethic and lots of belief. Dan Goossen, who passed away in September 2014, was the president of Goossen-Tutor Promotions. He promoted numerous world champions, while other family members labored in the trenches. Born and raised in San Fernando Valley, California, Joe Goossen is the eighth of ten children. As the Goossens were coming up in boxing, Joe Goossen took on the role of trainer. The Goossens's first champion came in 1988, when Michael Nunn scored a TKO over Frank Tate for the middleweight championship of the world. However, Joe Goossen is best known for training Gabriel and Rafael Ruelas when they were kids and guiding them all the way to world championships. Goossen also helped to resurrect the career of Diego Corrales. Before he started working with Goossen, Corrales had just lost to super featherweight champion Joel Casamayor via sixth-round TKO. Ironically, it was Goossen who trained Casamayor for his victory over Corrales. Following Casamayor-Corrales I, Casamayor began working with a different trainer. Goossen wound up training Corrales for their rematch, a fight that Corrales won via split decision. Under the guidance of Goossen, Corrales went on to score TKO victories over lightweight champions Acelino Freites and Jose Luis Castillo. Corrales-Castillo I, which took place in May 2005, is considered to be one of the best fights in the history of the sport. In addition to the aforementioned fighters, Goossen has also worked with Shane Mosley, Terry Norris, David Tua, Riddick Bowe, Ben Tackie, Lance Whitaker, Frankie Liles, Lionel Butler, Wilfredo Rivera, James Toney, Azumah Nelson, Vanes Martirosyan, Edison Miranda, Juan Lazcano, Alex Ramos, and Julio Cesar Chavez, Jr., among others. In June 2012, I walked into Joe Goossen's gym, Ten Goose Boxing in Van Nuys, California, where he told me how his family got their start in boxing. At the time of this interview, Goossen's top fighter was John Molina, Jr.

What is your background in boxing and what led you to become a trainer?

My mother and father were dedicated parents and they had ten children. Out of those ten, there were eight boys. My dad was the son of Russian Jewish immigrants. My mom's parents were Irish Catholic. Back in those days, it was culturally unacceptable for a Jewish man to marry a *shiksa*, a Catholic girl. He ultimately converted to Catholicism when he married my mom, hence the ten kids. My dad was a big, strong, rough, but compassionate person. He was LAPD and he worked the Hollywood division. He rose to the ranks of detective and eventually ended up on the Special Intelligence Squad, which was solely dedicated to Mafia control here in Los Angeles. He grew up in Boyle Heights. Back in those days, in the '20s and '30s, every block had a boxing gym in somebody's garage. My dad's love of sports, including boxing, was part of our upbringing. A lot of the kids in my family played sports. My brother Dan played basketball in college. My brother Greg signed with the LA Dodgers right out of high school. My brother Pat fought professionally. My brother Gordon was an outstanding high school pitcher. My brother Tommy is a football coach. My brother Larry fought in the amateurs and played a little ball. We were all kind of big guys with a strong sportsman ethic.

In the early days, my dad would sometimes clear the furniture out of the living room and have boxing matches between us. He never let anybody get hurt, but he taught us some of the finer points of the fundamentals of boxing. One day, my brother Pat came home and told me that there was a kid my age who could beat me up. This kid was an amateur boxer who probably had about fifty fights. At that particular time, I was playing football in high school. I was in great shape, I thought I was tough, and I was always throwing punches at home. I had never been in the ring before, but I was full of confidence. It didn't matter to me if it was in the ring or out of the ring. I thought I could beat this kid up. His name was Randy Shields. It took me three days to track him down. I showed up at his school and somebody pointed him out to me. We went to his gym and we went three three-minute rounds, which is pretty tough for somebody who has never been in the ring before. He taught me a couple lessons that day, but I hung in there and did well. When it was all over, Randy and I became the best of friends. I was sixteen, he was fifteen, and I've pretty much been in the gym ever since.

I went on to help Randy with his amateur career, whether it was sparring him or helping him with his training. Randy turned pro, and at one point, my brother Dan did some business with his dad. Through a twist of fate, Dan helped settle a money issue between Randy and his promoter. The promoter of the event was Top Rank. The vice president of Top Rank at the time was Akbar Muhammad. Dan stepped in and he knew how to speak Akbar's language. Within five minutes, he cleared the whole thing up. The next thing we know, we're out having a good time, riding around in a limo with Akbar. That was our introduction to big-time boxing. Within months, we started our own organization. We built a homemade ring from scratch and formed Ten Goose Boxing. My dad took out a promoter's license, Dan was the manager, and Pat, Greg, and I were trainers. It was a family thing. One thing my mom and dad instilled in us is that if you don't have a family behind you, you have very little.

At what point did you begin training Gabriel and Rafael Ruelas?

In 1984, this little twelve-year-old kid walked into the gym one lonely Saturday afternoon. That kid just happened to be Gabriel Ruelas. He walked over to me and he said, "I want to be a fighter." I kind of chuckled and said, "Look, you're a kid and I don't train kids. If you want to learn how to box, I'll give you the address of another place." I was trying to start a business and I didn't want to digress back to the amateurs, especially with a twelve-year-old. At the time, I was training Alonzo Gonzalez, the number one flyweight in the world. Alonzo was standing right there and he said, "You should train him, Joe." I gave Alonzo a dirty look, as if to say, please don't do this to me. I turned to the kid again and I tried to send him on his way, but Alonzo said, "Come on, Joe. I like what I see in his eyes." I asked the kid what his name was and where he went to school. He had a little bit of a haul from where I was. I told him what time to be here and I said that if he was a minute late, he needn't bother coming in. Sure enough, he showed up on that exact minute.

I could see from the first day that Gabriel was going to be a world champion. When he threw a 1–2 for the first time, I couldn't believe it. This was no ordinary twelve-year-old kid. I had him spar with Frankie Duarte, who was a 118-pounder, and Alonzo, who was a 112-pounder. It was good work for him, but I wanted to see him in with a kid who was his own age and size. This whole time, he kept telling me about his brother Rafael, who wanted to start boxing. Finally, I said, "Fine. Bring him." I figured we would just use him as a sacrificial lamb. Rafael was eleven at the time and he didn't have the strength or the physique of Gabriel. He was kind of a skinny kid. I put gloves on them and I put them in the ring. When the bell rang, Gabriel just tried to destroy him. He had him pinned against the ropes, but he couldn't hit him square. Rafael kept his hands up and his elbows in. It was natural for him. When Gabriel would swing, Rafael would bend back and dip to the side. He was frustrating Gabriel! I was watching this with Frankie Duarte and we were kind of elbowing each other, saying, "Look! We've got another world champion!"

In February 1993, Gabriel challenged Azumah Nelson for Nelson's super featherweight world title in a fight he lost via majority decision. In September the following year, he got another chance at the super featherweight world title when he faced and defeated Jesse James Leija via unanimous decision.

Gabriel lost to Azumah Nelson on a Don King card. King was Azumah Nelson's promoter and it was a razor thin decision. He fought Azumah Nelson with one arm and I thought he beat him. A few years before that, he broke his arm in his fight with Jeff Franklin. He had five bolts in his right arm and he couldn't straighten it out at the elbow. It was bent at a three quarter angle. Before he broke his arm, he would send guys sliding on their asses across the ring with that right hand. When you lose your extension, you lose your snap. He could still throw the right, but it wasn't even close to what it was. When he fought Jesse James Leija, he dropped him with a right hand, even though he couldn't straighten it out. Before that, he dropped him with a right uppercut. Most guys can't win a world title with two hands, but Gabriel did it with one.

In February 1994, Rafael challenged Freddie Pendelton for Pendelton's lightweight world title in a fight he won via unanimous decision.

The months leading up to the fight, at the press conferences, Freddie Pendelton was disparaging Rafael, disparaging Gabriel, disparaging Mexicans… I kept my mouth shut, because I knew what we were going to do on fight night. When we were having public workouts the week before the fight, I was approached by many, let's say, rabid fans who gave me fair warning that if we didn't beat this guy, there would be some repercussions.

Rafael Ruelas, Joe Goossen, Gabriel Ruelas, and Angelo Dundee (front), early 1990s (courtesy Joe Goossen).

They wanted retribution and they insisted that I do it through Rafael. The first round didn't go too well. Rafael was dropped twice by Pendelton and he was dropped hard. When Rafael walked back to the corner, we locked eyes and he kind of shrugged his shoulders as if to say it was no big deal. When he sat down, I said, "You just took his two best shots and you got up! He's not going to hit you any harder than that! You took it and you got up, baby! That's why you're going to be champion tonight!" Rafael went out there and he won the title and he sent Freddie Pendelton to the hospital via ambulance. At the press conference, his promoter, Bob Arum, said something I'll never forget. He said, "Freddie Pendelton has severe lacerations of the mouth and he's going to have to get that stitched up. One might say that's poetic justice."

In May 1995, Gabriel faced Jimmy Garcia in a fight he won via eleventh-round TKO. Thirteen days later, Garcia tragically died of brain injuries. On the night of Gabriel's fight with Garcia, Rafael faced Oscar De La Hoya in a fight he lost via second-round TKO.

The fight with Jimmy Garcia happened before Rafael's fight with De La Hoya. It had an effect on the whole vibe and aura of the evening. Instead of celebrating this exhilarating win, we were faced with a tragedy and it took all the air out of the balloon. I knew Jimmy Garcia was in dire straits when he collapsed. I knew something was wrong when he went down in that corner. I'm not going to make excuses, but if that hadn't happened, I believe that things might have been different in Rafael's fight. Gabriel went to the hospital and tried to comfort Garcia's family. Garcia's mother had a few harsh words for him, but she eventually understood that he was sorrowful and distraught about her son. She embraced him after he died. After that, I don't think Gabriel ever fought the same again. I really don't. I knew it haunted him. I knew something was missing, but there was nothing I could do.

At what point did you begin working with Michael Nunn?

I started working with Michael Nunn in September of '84, right after the Los Angeles Olympics. Nunn was a little bit of a "cut up." He was from the streets of Davenport, Iowa, and it's a rough town. He was a street fighter, but he was a clean-cut kid for the most part. Bob Surkein, who was a mentor and father figure to Nunn, wanted to get him out of that environment and into a family setting. It was apparent that there was something special about Michael Nunn from the start. Al Bernstein said it best. He said, "Michael Nunn not only doesn't lose fights, he doesn't lose rounds." He was 35–0 with 26 knockouts before he walked out on us. As he was climbing up in the ranks, people would come out of the woodwork from everywhere. They wanted to get in on the gravy train after all the work had been done. After two years, his star was shining so bright that I had to pack everything up and take everyone to a mountaintop in the middle of nowhere, because there were too many temptations in LA. If I hadn't done that, I don't believe he would have reached the heights that he reached.

When Nunn was really ready to step up, it was toward the end of his run with us. At that point, he had already beaten Sumbu Kalambay, Iran Barkley, and Frank Tate. When his contract was up with Dan and I, some of the people who were hanging around him told him that he shouldn't re-sign with us. Two fights removed from us, after hardly getting hit let alone losing a fight, he was knocked out by James Toney. Guess who the announcers were for that fight? Len Berman and Joe Goossen. I was the announcer for a guy who had just left me. We were right there in his hometown of Davenport, Iowa, under the big lights. He was knocked out in the eleventh round and I saw six years of my life go down the drain. It was all undone. I didn't rip him like a lot of people expected me to. I was actually very complimentary toward Nunn during the fight, which he deserved. It was my job to interview him afterwards and that was not an easy thing for me to do. It was like interviewing a family member. This guy and I were tight. As I look back on it now, it's really disturbing to see what could have been and what actually happened. He could have been a legendary fighter, but he was led down the primrose path and now he's doing time in federal prison.

In October 2003, you were in the corner of Joel Casamayor when he successfully defended his super featherweight world title against Diego Corrales via sixth-round TKO. In March of the following year, you were in Corrales's corner for their rematch in a fight that Corrales won via split decision. What do you recall about those two fights, and how was it that you ended up working with Corrales after their first fight?

When I found out that Joel was facing Diego Corrales, I knew we had to devise the right game plan. Diego was a devastating puncher and I had to make sure that Joel didn't get hit. As I studied tapes of Diego, I saw that he had certain limitations that Joel could

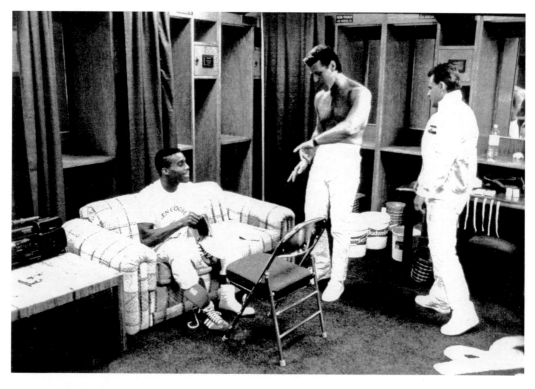

Michael Nunn, Joe Goossen, and Goossen's nephew Jimmy Buffo in Reno, Nevada, for Nunn's 1989 fight with Iran Barkley (courtesy Joe Goossen).

capitalize on. I knew we could pick him apart for the first six or seven rounds and then go in for the kill. As it turned out, I was right. We dropped Diego early on. Everything was so easy that Joel went in for the kill too soon and he ended up getting dropped himself. It took him a while to recover from that, but he went on to cut Diego pretty bad. You could see Diego's mouthpiece through a hole in his lip, so they stopped it. The rematch was made and because of business complications, I found out that I wasn't going to be Casamayor's trainer anymore. He was going to be trained by Buddy McGirt. Casamayor was my money-maker at the time and I told my wife that we were at the end of the road, money-wise. I didn't know what we were going to do.

One of my assistants took it upon himself to call Diego and ask him if he wanted to train with me. Diego promptly hung up on him, thinking it was a practical joke. After a few attempts, Diego realized that he was serious. I spoke with Diego's manager James Prince, who was delighted at the prospect of Casamayor's former trainer working with him. When Diego flew out here to start camp, it was a little awkward at first, because I was the guy who engineered his demise in the previous fight. To put his mind at ease, I told him how deathly afraid I was of him going into that fight. I also told him that he did not do several things that I thought he should have done and that we were going to work on that for the rematch. Everything we did worked and I thought he won nine out of twelve rounds. That started Diego Corrales's and Joe Goossen's two-and-a-half-year run together, capturing four world titles in two different divisions.

Joe Goossen laces up the gloves of Joel Casamayor, 2007. After parting ways in 2003, Goossen and Casamayor reunited for Casamayor's eventual split decision victory over Jose Armando Santa Cruz (courtesy Bret Newton—ThreatPhoto.com/Pound4Pound.com).

In August 2004, Corrales defeated Acelino Freites for Freites's lightweight world title via tenth-round TKO. In May of the following year, Corrales faced Jose Luis Castillo in a lightweight unification bout, defeating him via tenth-round TKO. The Corrales-Castillo bout was an all-action contest and is considered to be one of the best fights of all time.

Somebody interviewed Bert Sugar at the press conference after the fight and asked him if it was one of the greatest fights he had ever seen. Bert said, "No. It was the *greatest* fight I've ever seen." I knew it was going to be as intense as it was. I could see it coming. When we started camp, I brought in about three or four rugged guys for Diego to work with. We put in close to two hundred rounds of sparring, which is extraordinary. We trained very, very hard for that fight. Had we trained one round less, I believe we could have lost it. My idea was for Diego to go right at Castillo and fight inside. I figured they were expecting us to box since Diego was so tall and long, but Diego had a great inside game. A short left hook, a short right uppercut, a little chopping right hand, which we killed him with all night long… Jose Luis Castillo was not ready for a full frontal assault from Diego Corrales. It was a nose-to-nose fight from rounds one to ten. Both fighters were surgical geniuses in that ring. Everything they did was calculated, precise, accurate, and forceful. That fight literally exhausted the gas tank for both guys. Neither of them were ever the same after that.

Had it not been for referee Tony Weeks in the ring that night, it wouldn't have been the classic that it was. He let them fight and he didn't panic when Diego went down in the tenth round. Diego went down twice and people from our camp were screaming, "Stop the

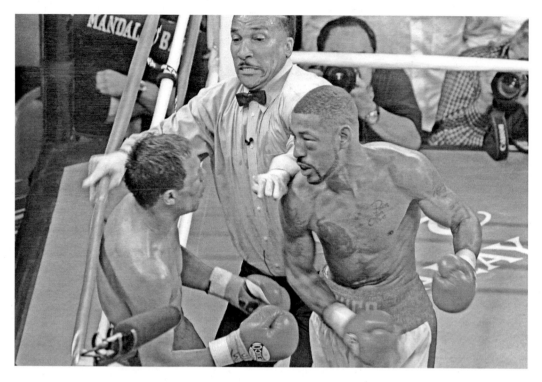

Diego Corrales hammers Jose Luis Castillo against the ropes in their epic 2005 battle, as referee Tony Weeks steps in to stop the fight (courtesy Bret Newton—ThreatPhoto.com/Pound4Pound.com).

fight! Stop the fight!" After the second knockdown, Diego came back to the corner. I put his mouthpiece back in and I gave him one set of instructions. I told him to get back inside. He looked right into my eyes and he gave me this look that affirmed that he would do what I was telling him to do. Diego went out there and he turned it around and it was one of the most fantastic, incredible, mind-blowing moments I've ever seen. It was one of the highlights of my career and it reminded me of what my parents used to tell me. When I was a kid, my parents told me that anything is possible. With everything I've seen and done in my career, I know that they were right. My parents grew up in the Depression era where you had to work for the things you wanted. In America, you can aspire to be anything. All it takes is a dream, a strong work ethic, and a lot of self-belief. Treating people well is important, too. That might be what's most important, and I try to pass that on to my kids. I've got friends for life from this game. I was sixteen when I first walked into a boxing gym. I'm almost sixty years old now and I can't believe how fast it went by. I wouldn't trade these experiences for anything.

21

Peter McNeeley: The Hurricane

In March 1995, former heavyweight champion Mike Tyson was released from prison. Although he had been incarcerated for the past three years, he was still considered "the baddest man on the planet." His next fight was going to be the most anticipated sporting event in the world, but his team needed the right opponent. Born and raised in Medfield, Massachusetts, "Hurricane" Peter McNeeley is a third-generation fighter, as his father and grandfather had notable boxing careers. McNeeley wanted to follow in their footsteps, but the city of Medfield offered him few opportunities to pursue his dream. While in college, McNeeley found a gym where he learned to fight the old school way—jumping right in and going to war with the toughest guys around. He eventually gained the attention of trainer Vinnie Vecchione, who went on to train and manage him throughout his professional career. Under the tutelage of Vecchione, McNeeley built a record of 36–1, 30 KOs, which put him in a position to face Mike Tyson. To this day, Tyson-McNeeley is the biggest non-title event in the history of the sport. While the focus of this match-up was supposed to be the return of Mike Tyson, it was McNeeley's colorful personality that carried the promotion of the fight. In August 1995, Tyson won the fight via first round disqualification when Vinnie Vecchione entered the ring after McNeeley was knocked down from a vicious Tyson uppercut. Some feel that Vecchione should not have interfered, but McNeeley is comfortable with his trainer's decision. In December 2014, I called Peter McNeeley and asked him about his fight with Tyson and the hurricane that led to his eventual nickname. At the time of this interview, McNeeley was communicating with an author about writing a book based on his life story.

When did you first put on the gloves? How old were you and what were the circumstances?
    When I was seven, I crawled up in the attic and found an old *Sports Illustrated* with my dad on the cover. It was before his fight with Floyd Patterson. When I saw that I thought, "Maybe someday I could be a fighter like my dad!" My dad got a free ride to Michigan State for football and for boxing. There was a guy who was killed in a collegiate boxing tournament, so the head honchos decided to drop boxing as a collegiate sport. When that happened, my dad turned pro. As a pro, he had a lot of unsavory characters around him wanting to manage him—underworld guys, crime figures… My grandfather, Tom McNeeley, Sr.,

was on the 1928 Olympic Boxing Team. He had a very brief pro career, but he knew the sport very well. When he saw that this is what my dad wanted to do, he took him and said, "I know you're serious about this, so let's do it right." He introduced him to the right people and he went undefeated all the way to his first title fight. He fought Floyd Patterson fifty-three years ago last week—December 4, 1961. They fought with six-ounce gloves on. That's like a sock or a mitt. A featherweight today doesn't wear six ounce gloves, never mind a heavyweight. In four rounds, my dad got knocked down twelve times. He knocked Patterson down once. This was Patterson's fight right before he lost the title to Sonny Liston.

Growing up in Medfield, we always had a heavy bag and a speed bag in the cellar. There were four of us McNeeley boys. I'm the third one and I'm the only one of the boys who became a boxer. If they hit the bags ten percent of the time, I hit them ninety percent of the time. I would buy boxing magazines off the shelves, watch fights on TV… It was my dream to be a fighter, but where the fuck are you going to box when you live in Medfield, Massachusetts? We were in the middle of white picket fence America. It was a beautiful place to raise a family, but there were no boxing gyms. When I was in high school, my parents split up. My dad moved to Choctaw, Massachusetts, and there was a gym nearby. On the weekends, I would box there with my brother "Snubby." It was a place where I could start getting my feet wet and learn a few things. When I was sixteen, my dad took me to a gym in south Boston, so I could spar. The night before, I had been out partying with my friends. Before the bell rang, I said to the guy I sparred with, "Take it easy on me. I was out drinking last night." We boxed a couple of rounds and when it was over, I told my dad about the drinking. Me and my father had a very open and honest relationship. At this time, he was sober and going to AA. He said to me, "Peter, if you're not going to do boxing right, don't do it at all." I respected his opinion, so I stopped. I knew I wasn't doing what I was supposed to be doing, so I didn't box again until I was nineteen.

After high school, I went to Bridgewater State University, which is right next to the city of champions—Brockton! I flunked out my freshman year because I was partying. They let me back on academic probation, but I couldn't play sports. I had played football all through high school and this was the first year in a long time that I didn't play a sport. There was a gym nearby, so I started boxing and working out. After less than two months, they put me in an amateur fight. I had no business being in a boxing ring at that time, but they had me in the main event because of my dad's name. I stopped for a while after that and then I asked my dad to take me to this other gym, which was run by the Petronellis. It was the home of "Marvelous" Marvin Hagler. I told my dad, "Instead of partying in the dorms, I'll spend my free time in the gym." The first night there, they threw me in with Kilbert Pierce, Jr. I was an 0–1 amateur and weighed about 190 pounds soaking wet. He was 225 and on his way to the Olympic Trials. We went six rounds and he beat me up good that night. When we left the gym, my head felt like a soccer ball. My dad said, "Good thing you're in condition or he'd have *really* caved you in." I looked at him like he was completely nuts. When I got back to the dorm, I sat down at my desk and I thought, "What the fuck am I doing?"

The Petronelli gym was like a war zone. Every night was like a real fight. You hear about the famous Philadelphia gym wars? It was the same shit there. They could have sold tickets. People were killing each other for nothing. The famous Hagler-Hearns fight had just happened a few months earlier and all these young killers were trying to follow in the

Former heavyweight contender Peter McNeeley (courtesy Peter McNeeley/hurricanepetermcneeley. com).

champion's coattails. I fought every vicious motherfucker in there! Thank God I survived it. I did this for four years while I was at college. The other kids were going to the library, while I was driving to the ghetto in Brockton. I would come back with a broken nose and concussions, and my friends would say, "How was your night, Peter?" I would say, "Great. How was the library?" Sometimes when people hear me talk, they say, "Have you been drinking today?" I say to them, "If you took as many punches as I did, you would be lucky to talk as good as me!" Boxing is insane. It's controlled insanity—that's what this sport is. There's no rhyme or reason to do what we do to ourselves. A lot of people think I'm a punch drunk retard. I've taken some shots and it definitely shows, but that being said, I would hate to see where I would be if it wasn't for Vinnie Vecchione. When I met Vinnie, it was like God said, "Let me do you a big fucking favor and put this guy in your life." The guy rescued me. Before I met Vinnie, I was headed straight to Palookaville.

Vinnie Vecchione trained and managed you throughout your career, and was something of a father figure in your life. How did you first connect with him?

One night, I came out of the Petronelli gym and Vinnie was there waiting for me. Vinnie had been involved in pro boxing for years. He had got out of boxing in the early' '80s, but he was getting back into the game because of a fighter named Paul Poirier. Paul trained with Vinnie back in the 1970s and retired at age seventeen with a record of 21–0. He saw George Foreman making a comeback and he wanted to see if he could come back himself. Paul used to be a middleweight, but he was now a small heavyweight. They were looking for a young heavyweight in the area who Paul could spar with to see if he had anything left.

Sparring partner Paul Poirier and Peter McNeeley, 1990s (courtesy Peter McNeeley/hurricanepetermc neeley.com).

Vinnie told me about Paul and said that he would give me a couple bucks to come down and spar with him. I said, "Yeah. Great." So, I went down there and I didn't know anything about sparring. I only knew how to fight. The Petronelli gym turned me into an animal. When the bell rang, I went right at Paul and tried to knock him out. Vinnie watched me and he said, "Do you see this kid? He's got balls, he's got heart, he can punch.... I want this kid!" In September of 1990, me and Vinnie started building a relationship. I liked the guy. He acted like he cared. He actually taught me things. Vinnie broke me down and showed me all the basics. He did a textbook job training me, managing me, promoting me... I'd come in and I'd say, "So, Vinnie, what are we doing today?" He'd say, "You're gonna do what I tell you to do!" He was amazing. He taught me so much. He was a best friend. He was like a father. He was awesome. He was unbelievable.

From August 1991 to April 1995, you built a professional record of 36–1 (30 KOs). Tell me about this time in your life.

I had thirty-seven fights in forty-four months. Old school! Of those thirty-seven fights, I had twenty-one first round knockouts. I had long legs and I used to watch the time keeper. By the time the bell rang, I would be out there in one big step. I didn't fuck around. It was either me or you. One guy I knocked out in six seconds. It was Frankie Hines in Hot Springs, Arkansas. I hit this kid with a left hook and his head spun around like *The Exorcist*. We got to 24–0 and we fought this fighter named Stanley Wright. He was 6'10", 279 pounds. I was winning every round, but he cut me over my left eye with an illegal punch. He swatted me with the laces and I ended up getting sixty stitches. They stopped the fight in the eighth round, but I was back in the ring two months later. We fought three fights in three weeks in three different states. Finally, Don King said, "These guys mean business! Sign them up!" That's when I became a part of DKP—Don King Productions!

On August 19, 1995, you faced former heavyweight champion Mike Tyson in Tyson's first fight since spending three years in prison. How did this fight come about?

I knew Tyson was getting out in March of '95, so I started beating the drum for this fight to happen. Who wouldn't want this fight? Why would you go to the gym and toil and take punches for chump change? Vinnie's idea was to take the least amount of risk and make the most amount of money. On paper, I was the perfect opponent. I was the white kid with the glossy record. My family had a history in the fight game, so King knew he could use that as an angle. I had been following Tyson since he was a young pro. When I was in high school, I used to have his poster on my wall. I caught Tyson at the best time and the worst time. The good news was that he had been in prison for three years. The bad news was that this was a different Tyson. Remember in the late '80s and early '90s when Tyson had that boyish man-child look to him? Now he was a hardened man who had done time. He didn't have that same look to him anymore. He was ripped and angry and rock hard. Legend had it that while he was in prison, he was doing a thousand push-ups and a thousand sit-ups every day. We signed the contract at a press conference in Las Vegas. Everybody was there. It was huge. There were more people at the press conference than there were at any of my other fights.

We were on the stage at the MGM Grand. I was on one end and Mike was on the other. Because I was a Tyson fan, I kept looking over at him. It didn't matter that we were fighting. I was like a kid. I kept looking over, trying to get a peek at him. Don King was at the podium and he called us over to sign for the fight. After we signed, Mike looked me right in the eye, stuck his hand out, shook my hand, and said, "Good luck." You know what? I fucking respected that. He didn't try to intimidate me or show any machismo that a lot of other guys might have done. After the fight was announced, we did a press tour across the country. I was on David Letterman and Larry King. Come on! I grew up watching those guys. During training, people descended on my mom's house in Medfield from around the world. The streets were lined with cars and vans and trucks from the media. After I did my roadwork, there was always a pack of reporters in my mom's driveway. It was a really exciting time. Ten days before the fight, we did a final press tour in LA. Don King put me in a limousine and they carted me around, going from show to show to show. That's when I said I was going to "wrap Tyson in a cocoon of horror." That became one of the best pre-fight lines ever! During this time, it was known that Tyson wasn't doing many interviews, so I had to carry the whole promotion myself.

Having previously faced relatively unknown opposition, you were about to get in the ring with a fighter who few men in history would stand a chance against. What advice did Vinnie have for you?

Peter McNeeley next to a heavy bag that features a photograph of Mike Tyson, 1995 (courtesy Peter McNeeley/hurricanepetermcneeley.com).

Look… Vinnie knew. We *both* knew. I had been watching Tyson his whole career and I knew what I was dealing with. We didn't really talk about it. We just trained our buns off.

When the bell rang, you ran straight at Tyson and made it a brawl. After suffering two knock-downs, you lost via disqualification in the first round when your trainer, Vinnie, entered the ring. What happened from your perspective?

From the day I signed the contract, I said I was going right at him. If nothing else, "Hurricane" Peter McNeeley is proud that I did what I said I was going to do. I didn't fold under pressure. Fear is a funny thing. Did I have fear inside my head? Yes. I felt fear before all of my fights, but I used it as a high to go forward. It's the story of the hero and the coward. It's what the hero does that makes him a hero, and it's what the coward *doesn't* do that makes him a coward. That's what Cus D'Amato used to tell Mike Tyson. I've got a special DVD from Showtime that has all of the close-up shots from the fight that you can't see on YouTube. On the DVD, you can see me wink at Tyson during the pre-fight instructions and blow him a kiss. I was trying to mess with him all the way till the last second. I was rocking back and forth trying to stay warm, and Tyson's eyes were following me like a caged animal. He was like a pit bull ready to strike. It was a vicious, ugly staredown. I got back to the corner and the last thing I said to Vinnie was, "Fuck it. I'm going right at him." The first time he knocked me down, there was some nerves and excitement. Mike did catch me, but I was off balance. I bounced right the fuck up before Mills Lane even started to count. He signaled us back in and I went right back at him again. I'm the only one to ever attack Mike Tyson like that.

Now, my style is tailor-made for the right uppercut. In the end, that's what Mike caught me with. His whole career, his right uppercut was his best punch and he caught me point blank on the chin. I got up from that and a lot of people thought I could have continued, but in one of the angles on the DVD, you can see that my pupils were dilated. That meant that I had a concussion and some sort of damage was done. I was up at three or four, but I went right to the ropes. If the ropes weren't there, I would have been sitting on somebody in the front row. My legs were gone. Vinnie saw that and he jumped in and stopped it. At the time I was pissed, but when I saw the replay, I knew why he did what he did. Mike Tyson's only loss was to Buster Douglas and Douglas was a way better boxer than I ever could have been. I'm proud of what I've done in my career and I do have a bit of an ego, but my ego isn't so big that I can compare myself to guys like that. I was simply not as good of a boxer. I've had to live with this fight for nineteen years and I have no regrets. I did the best I could with what I had.

How did you get the nickname "Hurricane"?

I made my professional debut at Boston University on Nickerson Field. It's right on the Massachusetts turnpike. I used to drive past the field when I was growing up and I always looked at it. My pro debut was on August 23, 1991. A hurricane hit Boston on August 19th, which is also the day I fought Tyson. It almost postponed the fight and it got me thinking—"Hurricane" Peter McNeeley! I gave myself the nickname. People used to want to call me "Irish" Peter McNeeley, but I was already wearing green trunks. Why overstate the obvious? "Hurricane" suited me best because I came in low and fast, just like a hurricane.

┌─────────┐
│   22   │
└─────────┘

Melvina Lathan:
The Chairwoman

At one point in time, people of authority and influence were strictly male Caucasians. That's what society expected and there were no exceptions to the rule. But as time went by, minorities refused to sit down and people began opening their hearts and minds to other possibilities. Born and raised in Philadelphia, Pennsylvania, Melvina Lathan was the first female African American Chairperson of the New York State Athletic Commission. Boxing is something that has always shown up in Lathan's life, whether it was a friendly encounter with heavyweight champion Sonny Liston, marrying a ringside physician, or finding herself being licensed as a professional boxing judge. In the 1990s and 2000s, Lathan was a judge for some of the most memorable fights on the east coast. She never saw herself becoming a boxing judge, nor could she have expected a random phone call from the Appointments Office one afternoon, requesting a meeting that would lead to her becoming a commissioner. Opportunities led to opportunities, and the next thing Lathan knew, she was the Chairperson. Lathan held this position from 2008 to 2015, where she regulated all of the boxing matches in the state of New York, including the December 2011 rematch between Miguel Cotto and Antonio Margarito. This was a controversial match-up for a number of reasons—one that required the leadership of Lathan to see that everything was legal, balanced, and fair. In July 2015, I called Melvina Lathan to discuss her experiences as a boxing judge, a commissioner, and eventually, the chairwoman. At the time of this interview, Lathan had just returned from a trip to General Santos City, Philippines.

What is your background in boxing and what led you to become a judge?
My grandmother and my father were both big fight fans, so I was exposed to it at an early age. When I was young, my grandmother introduced me to Sugar Ray Robinson, although I had no idea who he was. Years later, I asked my grandmother about that meeting and she confirmed that it was indeed Sugar, the Champ. "He was always one of us," she said, "with his pink Cadillac to boot!" I watched a lot of fights with my grandmother, especially during the *Gillette Cavalcade of Sports* era. A lot of us grew up with that. I was a dancer and always thought the two went hand and hand. There's a real art to it and I developed a

179

gradual appreciation. I grew up in Philly, a real fight town, where there were gyms all over. When I walked home from school, there was one gym in particular where I would stop and look in the window. One evening in the winter time when the window was fogged from the outside, I used my hand to clear it so I could look inside. The door opened and this big black dude came out. He said, "Why don't you come in, little lady? It's cold out here and you can see better inside." I went in and it was amazing—the rhythm of the fighters hitting the bag, the music… There were all these different sounds blending together and it was wonderful. If I could pick one time that I fell in love with boxing, that was it. The man who opened the door was Sonny Liston. There was a guy there with one of those old Polaroid cameras and I had a photograph taken with him. That photograph probably saved my life, because my mother wanted to kill me for coming home late. I gave the photograph to my dad and he thought it was the coolest thing.

My husband, Dr. Billy Lathan, was the ringside physician for the Golden Gloves. I went with him to almost every fight and would sit during the pre-fight preparations and read my book while he was doing his thing. If you know anything about the amateurs, you know that they need all the help they can get. They would ask me to help with a variety of things—set up chairs, hand out flyers, sweep the ring, collect passbooks… One day, the timekeeper got lost on his way to the show, and someone gave me their watch and the bell and made me the designated timekeeper. It seemed like every time someone didn't show up, I was "it." I spent about four or five years in the amateurs, learning everything I could. Eventually, my husband transitioned into the professional boxing arena and once again, I tagged along. I used to sit ringside and score fights for fun. One day, a guy named Randy Gordon, who just happened to be the Commissioner, asked me if I would be interested in being an official judge. I wasn't, but Randy

Chairperson of the New York State Athletic Commission (2008–2015) Melvina Lathan (courtesy Marty Rosengarten/Ringside Photos.com).

didn't quit. He stayed on me, so I said I would ask my husband about it. He said, "Don't bother. I already talked to him and he agrees with me." I "trailed" the judges for about two years, and again, I did a show because one of the judges was ill and I was there. Randy said, "You're working tonight." I said, "No, no, no…. I don't have my license." He said, "Raise your right hand." It was like he deputized me. He swore me in right there and I became a judge. I really dedicated myself to it. I watched so many fight films and trained and studied. When I do something, I don't do it halfway. I just throw myself right into it.

In May 1996, you judged the ten-round heavyweight fight between Lennox Lewis and Ray Mercer, a fight that Lewis won via majority decision. What do you recall about that fight?

I thought it was a marvelous match-up. The two of them were made for each other and it was a very tough fight to score. When Lennox would throw a punch, Mercer would have an answer. It was tit for tat. I was intrigued for those ten rounds and I didn't take my eyes off that ring for one second. I believe I had it a draw, but remember feeling very comfortable with my score. It was a very even, very close fight. I was unbiased and detached, and I always prided myself in my ability to do that. I look at a fight as a blank canvas. The painting has yet to be created and it will be painted one round at a time.

What do you recall about your experience as a judge for 1998's "Fight of the Year" between light-weights Ivan Robinson and Arturo Gatti? The fight occurred in August of that year and Robinson won via split decision after ten rounds.

It was an amazing fight! My friend Steve Weisfeld was also one of the judges and working with Steve was such a pleasure. We used to spend hours talking about boxing. It's really cool when you have someone who speaks the same language and sees the same picture. I remember sitting across the ring from him after the fight and thinking that we just had the privilege of judging one of the most incredible fights ever. It was obvious that Ivan Robinson was coming in as the underdog, but he was having none of it! The two of them just seemed to bring out the absolute brawl in each other and they both absorbed some of the most intense head and body blows ever. Near the end of the fight, they were neck and neck with each other and Gatti caught him with a fabulous blow. It stunned Ivan. He froze for a moment and you could see that he was hurt. His knees buckled and he swayed and looked like he was going down, but amazingly, he recovered and made it through the round. This was truly a knock-down-drag-out fight. It might have been the best fight I've ever seen. When we left, Steve and I were walking out of the arena saying nothing. There were no words necessary. Finally, I said, "My God, I can finally breathe." He laughed because he was thinking the same thing. I don't think I breathed for ten rounds.

You were a judge for the heavyweight title eliminator in November 1999 between Michael Grant and Andrew Golota, a fight that Grant won via tenth-round TKO. You were also a judge when Grant went on to face heavyweight champion Lennox Lewis in April of the following year. Lewis won via second-round knockout.

With Grant and Golota, Golota was winning big and having very little problem controlling the ring. I was totally stunned that he decided not to continue. He was knocked down and he got up pretty easily, obviously unhurt. He turned around and said something to Randy Neumann, and I heard Randy ask him incredulously, "Are you sure?" Then Randy came around to everybody and said, "Fight's over." I was like, are you kidding me?! That was amazing. There was no reason for him to quit. He was ahead on points. Even with the knockdown, he would have won if he had just finished the fight. It was known that the winner of the fight was supposed to go on and fight Lennox Lewis. And because Golota quit, Michael Grant got the opportunity. They called that fight "Two Big." When Grant and Lewis got in the ring, I felt the fight could not possibly go the distance. These were two huge dudes! It was a brutal first round and I kind of felt bad for Michael Grant. He came out strong, but then Lewis hurt him and knocked him down a few times. I felt it when he went down. I mean I literally felt the ring shake. I saw the look of surprise on his face. Then I saw a look of resignation. He tried to continue, but I could see what was happening. Thinking about it now, maybe he wasn't supposed to be in the ring with Lewis. Golota was beating him handily and he went on to have a fight that maybe he shouldn't have had.

In May 2001, you judged the fight between Felix Trinidad and then middleweight world title holder William Joppy. Trinidad won the fight via fifth-round TKO.

Trinidad had amazing power. He usually took a couple of rounds to get warmed up, but I don't think that happened with this fight. He came out and he seemed to know that he had to do something right away. It was pretty dramatic. I was there when Joppy fought Julio Cesar Green. I thought he beat Green with one hand. Green got the decision, but Joppy beat him in a rematch. Joppy was one of the best middleweights in the world, which is why it was a total surprise that he was no match for Trinidad. This set the stage for Trinidad and Hopkins, and I was there for that fight, too. I worked one of the fights on the undercard. It was amazing to see Trinidad on the receiving end. You could see the anguish on Papa Trinidad's face. During the minute rest in the corner, he had such a look of concern. They knew they weren't going to beat Bernard Hopkins. Boxing is so much more than the physical. There's so much emotion involved. You can see it and feel it.

You were a judge for 2003's "Fight of the Year" between James Toney and then cruiserweight world title holder Vassiliy Jirov. The fight occurred in April of that year and Toney won via unanimous decision.

Oh my god, another amazing fight! What was even more amazing was that all three judges had all twelve rounds scored almost exactly the same. We had Toney winning most of the rounds, but it was so close. These rounds could have gone in different directions, depending what you were looking for. I believe it was Toney's body punches that made the difference. He was very smart. What most fight fans don't understand is that you can have the closest of fights, but the scorecards read like it's a one-sided fight. We're looking at each round one round at a time. It could be so close, but one little thing makes the difference. Sometimes you have these close, almost even rounds, and you're thinking, "Come on, guys! Somebody do something! Give me something to work with!" It could be the matter of one combination or one telling punch that makes the difference in a very close round.

In 2008, you became the chairperson for the New York State Athletic Commission. How did this come about?

I got a phone call from the Appointments Office asking me to meet with someone. It was all a blur. My mom had just passed away, and I was standing in a store buying dresses for my granddaughters to wear to the funeral. When the phone rang, I had no idea what they were talking about. I even thought it might be a joke. I told them that if this was important to please call me back. They called again about a week later and I met with two women. One was an appointments secretary and the other was this very vivacious, inquisitive bundle of positive energy. Her name was Lorraine Cortez Vasquez and she turned out to be the Secretary of State. They asked me a lot of questions about boxing, and at the end of the conversation the Secretary of State said, "I think we want to work with you." They asked

Melvina Lathan at a press conference for the 2009 fight between Manny Pacquiao and Miguel Cotto (courtesy Marty Rosengarten/RingsidePhotos.com).

me if I would consider being a commissioner. That was kind of dramatic, because being a commissioner meant that I would have to give up judging fights. But my mom always said that sometimes opportunities come in disguise, and being able to recognize them is key. All of the pieces to the puzzle may not come together at the same time, you just have to go with that other sense that God gives you. I thought about it and I thought, why not? It would be a change of pace. At this point, I was one of three commissioners. There was one main one, the chairperson, who was responsible for the day-to-day activities. The other two were voting policy makers. I was one of the two. After I had been there a year, the Secretary of State asked me if I would entertain the idea of being the new chair. One minute, I was a commissioner with very little responsibility, and the next minute I was the chair with *all* of the responsibility. Like everything else, I just dove right in and tackled it.

One high-profile event that called for your attention was the rematch between junior middleweights Miguel Cotto and Antonio Margarito. In their first encounter, Margarito defeated Cotto in July 2008 via eleventh-round TKO. In Margarito's next bout against Shane Mosley, plaster was found in his handwraps before the fight and many suspected that Margarito had been using plaster in some of his previous bouts, though no proof has ever been found. This was a source of controversy before Cotto-Margarito II, as was the fact that Margarito suffered a severe eye injury in his 2010 fight against Manny Pacquiao. The rematch between Cotto and Margarito occurred

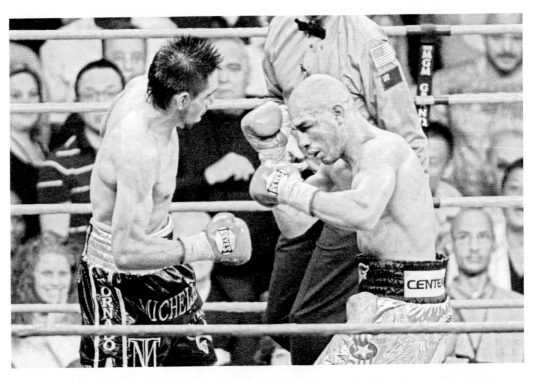

Antonio Margarito (left) batters Miguel Cotto in 2008 en route to an eleventh-round TKO victory. This victory proved to be controversial, as plaster was found in Margarito's handwraps before his next fight against Shane Mosley (courtesy Bret Newton—ThreatPhoto.com/Pound4Pound.com).

in December 2011. Cotto won via TKO when a ringside physician stopped the bout after the ninth round due to swelling around Margarito's eye.

At this time, Margarito had already served a suspension and had two fights since that incident in California. He had fought in New York before, so it was just a matter of renewing his license. However, there were legal, medical, and moral issues to be settled. These issues were put before the Commission for a vote, and it was determined that we couldn't legally prevent him from fighting since he was already licensed and actively fighting elsewhere. The clearance of the eye was a separate issue. It was known that Margarito had suffered damage in his fight with Pacquiao and we needed to know that he was healthy enough to fight again. The Commission waited months for medical information that was requested far in advance of the fight. When we finally got the requested information, Margarito's license was denied by our Medical Director, and a hearing between Top Rank and the Commission ensued, but the damage was already done. It was mere weeks before the fight and the media had a field day due to the mounting pressures of a sold-out megafight at Madison Square Garden. It was also a grudge rematch that the fans were undeniably hungry for.

Melvina Lathan holding granddaughter Lyra Lathan, with son Dr. Edward Lathan and daughter-in-law Sing Lathan, 2008 (courtesy Melvina Lathan).

Finally, it was mutually decided that additional required testing would be done by an independent ophthalmological specialist, who was not affiliated with New York, the state of Nevada, nor Top Rank. The decision of the unknown independent MD would be final and was ultimately good enough for us to allow the fight to go on. As it turned out, it was a great night for boxing. Top Rank was satisfied because the fight went on as planned, the New York State Athletic Commission was satisfied that it could uphold its safety requirements, Madison Square Garden was satisfied because it was the biggest boxing event held in the Garden for a few years due to renovations, Cotto was satisfied because he did what he believed he could do all along, Margarito was satisfied because he had a chance to fight, and the crowd was satisfied because their hero won in stunning fashion.

You were the first ever female African American Chairwoman of the New York State Athletic Commission. There was a time in history where the public never thought that could be possible. How do you feel about this, and who are some people who have inspired you to make this possible?

My parents. My children. My husband. My parents showed me what it was to be free and secure and loved. Growing up in my home was an amazing experience. My parents always encouraged me to do my thing. They exposed me to art, music, spirituality, and please, by all means, dare to be different. And my children—they teach me patience and humility and stand beside me with everlasting joy and pride. My husband always gives me love, encouragement, and understanding. He is my friend, my critic, and my rock. About the "first African American woman" label—it is significant. It is who and what I am, and I couldn't be more proud to represent my people. I also represent the strengths of the many women—of *all* woman with whom I've come in contact with over the years. I implore every young woman to recognize her strengths and her talents, and I truly hope that in some way I have inspired and encouraged and motivated. As Chairwoman, I energized the New York State Athletic Commission, and when it was time to leave, I was ready to move on. There's a rhythm to life and a time for everything. God has blessed me with amazing strengths and gifts and opportunities, for which I will be eternally grateful.

23

Exum Speight: The Ex-Files

When building a fighter's record, handlers want to match them against opponents they know they can beat. They want someone who might test their fighters and give them experience, but it needs to be someone who doesn't pose a serious threat. This type of matchmaking is common when grooming a fighter for the upper echelon of the sport. Born and raised in Whitakers, North Carolina, Exum Speight is a Cherokee-Jamaican-Guyanan-American, who competed at cruiserweight and heavyweight from the mid–1980s to the early 2000s. At age sixteen, Speight began competing as an amateur in Rochester, New York, winning about half of his fights. From there, he moved out to California to pursue his professional career. With nobody looking after his best interest, Speight was often mismatched and used to pad the records of up-and-coming fighters. He was well aware of how he was perceived by the boxing world, but he continued with his career because he wanted to prove people wrong. Throughout his career, Speight was defeated by the likes of Wladimir Klitschko, Chris Byrd, and John Ruiz, among other top fighters of his time. Despite a pro career that spanned fifteen years where he often found himself on the losing end of the stick, Speight still remembers almost every detail of every fight he has been in. Speight retired in 2001 with a record of 9–39–2, 5 KO's. In May 2012, I met with Exum Speight at Ono Hawaiian BBQ in Hollywood, California. At the time of this interview, Speight was living in Los Angeles, California. In September 2013, Speight was arrested for the 1987 murder of his former manager, Douglas Stumler. He pled "no contest" to a voluntary manslaughter charge in July 2015 and was sentenced to eleven years in prison. Exum Speight died of a stroke on March 7, 2016, at the age of fifty-two.

When did you first put on the gloves? How old were you and what were the circumstances?

My mother used to tell me about my uncle who was a boxer. His name was Thaddeus Williams. He fought pro in the late '20s. I would tell my mother, "I'm gonna fight one day, Mama." She said, "Boy, you're going to get your head knocked off!" I used to beat up on my baby brother Randy. He was my first opponent. I would practice on him. When I was about ten or eleven, my uncle came down to the farm, and he taught me a little bit. He showed me how to hold my hands, and block punches, and throw my jab. My mother taught me how to box, too. My mama was tough. She had seventeen children, all by the same father. There were ten girls, and seven boys. I can name all of them right now. I grew up on a farm in North Carolina. I come from a family of sharecroppers. My parents were hard workers. All they taught us was to love each other. I'm a Cherokee-Jamaican-Guyanan-American. I speak Patwah [Jamaican Creole], Cherokee... I speak excellent German. I speak a little Yiddish, too. When it comes to different languages, I can pick up on them real quick. It doesn't take me long.

I graduated high school, and I went to RIT for a while, Rochester Institute of Technology. I used to study theology and learn about the scriptures in the Bible. I was going to be a priest. That still ain't off the table, but I've had so many hard fights that I'm pulling myself together. I talk very well for a fighter. I don't stutter at all. I take Aricept to help restore my memory, but I'm very competent and aware. It's just that I don't know what else to do in life now that I'm not fighting. The first time I went into a boxing gym was in Rochester, New York. When I was sixteen, I was up there staying with my sister. I was on the street one day playing football, and I saw this truck drive by, and it said, "Main Street Boxing Club." We flagged it down, and this white guy was like, "What do you kids want?" We said, "We want to box!" He said, "Well, come on then!"

The first time I got in the ring, they put headgear on me. I didn't want headgear, but they made me wear it. Back then, I didn't think anybody could hurt me. I trained for about a year before my first amateur fight. It was at the Syracuse Dome. Some Italian kid beat me on points. I had about thirty amateur fights and I won about fifteen of them. When I was nineteen, I moved to San Francisco to find my half-brother. I also went out there to fight. I ended up moving to Hollywood, and I trained with all the early champions at the gym at 108th and Broadway. My coaches were Royan "Destroyan" Hammond and Terry Sorrell. Terry fought George Foreman in 1972. I did amateur boxing in California for about a year, till I turned pro in 1986. I never fought because I needed money. Fighting made me feel confident. It was something that most people couldn't do. Fighters have to be a certain way. Boxing actually knocked some sense into my head. I was always a little foolish from the time that mule kicked me. I'm more attentive now than I was before I boxed.

In March 1986, you lost your pro debut to cruiserweight David Graves (3–0) via six-round unanimous decision.

I remember it like it was yesterday. We fought at Rosita Country Club. David Graves was a top amateur. Nobody fights six rounds against a top amateur in their pro debut. I was just a country boy from North Carolina. In my second fight, I fought in Las Vegas at the Showboat Hotel. I lost on points to Marcellus Allen. He was another undefeated fighter. I was like, what are these guys doing to me? They were just trying to find an easy win for their fighters. Once they saw that I could fight, they started treating me better. I was 4–2 for a little while, but these promoters, these handlers, they tried to piss in my face and tell me it's raining. When you start fighting, you get a mentality that nobody can hurt you. You get mad and you want to prove everybody wrong. If I could rectify it, I would have done things differently.

In October 1992, you faced light heavyweight Lou Del Valle (6–0) in a fight you lost via first-round TKO. Del Valle is best known for being the first man to knock down Roy Jones, Jr. Going into the fight, your record was 4–4–1.

I had to lose three pounds before the weigh-in. The night before, I had some plastic on and I went running to get the pounds off. It made me weak, but I didn't want to forfeit the fight and have to pay them money. Lou is a southpaw and I didn't know how to fight southpaws. He hit me with a left hand and I went down. I got up and the referee asked me where I was. I told him, "Madison Square Garden." My knees sort of locked up on me and he said, "Come back and fight another day."

In June 1993, you lost an eight-round unanimous decision to John Ruiz (13–0), who went on to be the first Latino heavyweight champion in the history of boxing. Going into the fight, your record was 5–7–1.

Ruiz had a big forehead. He was tough, man. Real tough. He was in condition. I was in shape, but he was in "condition." There's a difference. Your body looks different when you're in condition. It's hard to build your offense with Ruiz. He held me a little bit. He knew how to hustle the rounds. He knew how to make the judges give him more points. Ruiz is a good gentleman. He's real, real humble.

In March 1994, you lost a six-round unanimous decision to Chris Byrd (2–0) in a cruiserweight contest. Byrd went on to capture two world titles at heavyweight. Going into the fight, your record was 6–10–1.

Chris beat the shit out of me! I used to train with Chris and his dad. He told me before the fight, "You know I'm going to beat you, Exum. We work together all the time." I couldn't do anything with him. He was so fast. You saw him when he fought the older Klitschko. You saw how slick he was.

In August 1994, you lost to Shannon Briggs (17–0) via first-round TKO. Briggs went on to win a world title at heavyweight. Going into the fight, your record was 6–12–1.

Shannon Briggs with the dreadlocks! That guy was real strong. Real physical. Real good balance, I noticed. He beat George Foreman. A lot of people think George beat him, but

Former heavyweight world champion Chris Byrd defeated Speight via unanimous decision (courtesy Marty Rosengarten/Ringside Photos.com).

I've seen that fight three times. George is massive, but Shannon beat him on points. Before the fight, they told me not to mix it up with him, to stay on the outside. How was I going to stay on the outside? I had to come to him. He was taller than me. I tried to bob and weave and get under his shots, but he got me.

Throughout 1995, all the way to August 1996, you lost fourteen fights in a row. What was going on with your career at that time and what compelled you to continue boxing?

I had a reputation as a guy from a farm. I came out to the big city to do this and I didn't have a manager a lot of the times. I was a road fighter. I was always on the road. I never had a home. I would sleep in hotels. I knew a lot of promoters around the world. They had numbers where they could get in touch with me and they would call me if they needed someone. When I fought, I would hire a second and a cutman. There were times I'd show up at a fight and I wasn't supposed to fight, but they had to fill up the card, so they put me in. Naturally, they thought I was there to make their guy look good. A few times, I was asked by promoters to take it easy on their guy or some bullshit. Easy? Are you crazy? Is he going to go easy on me? I didn't have a winning record, but I was crafty. Sometimes, I'd beat one of their guys, but they would give him the decision. It was so dirty. They would treat you like a whore. A lot of people were taking money from me. Managers and promoters sometimes signed my name for me on the contract. They would have me fight at heavyweight and sometimes I'd fill my pockets just so I made 200 pounds. People asked me, "Why are you fighting these guys, Exum?" I knew I was getting mistreated, but I wanted to prove them wrong. I wanted to show them I could do it. I always thought it would be my night. I felt like shit when I lost. It wasn't something I ever got used to, even when I lost a bunch of fights in a row. I remember all my fights. I remember who I fought and where we fought. My family thought I was going to get hurt or handicapped. They were worried that one day they would have to take care of me and put me in a home, but I survived all that.

In November 1996, you lost to Wladimir Klitschko (1–0) via second-round TKO. Klitschko went on to be one of the dominant heavyweight champions of his time, along with his brother Vitali. Going into the fight, your record was 8–30–2.

Wladimir was tall as I don't know what. When I saw him, I was like, whoa! This is a big guy! I knew who he was. He had just won the gold medal. On TV, he looked smaller than he did when I saw him. He was kind of stiff, but he hit hard. I worked with Wladimir and some other European fighters after that. I tried to help them bend their knees and be less of a target, not so straight up. When you stand up straight, you ain't got no rhythm. When you bend your knees, your arms are longer and you move better. The Klitschkos have a different regimen than we do. When we sleep, they're working out. Those guys are in condition.

In January 1997, you defeated heavyweight Lyle McDowell (18–3–1) via second-round TKO. Going into the fight, your record was 8–31–2. This was a dramatically different result than you normally produced against an opponent with a respectable record. Did anything change in your preparations for this fight?

I was training out there in Ohio in Don King's camp. I had a hard camp and I came in with a more intense attitude. I was in condition, but a lot of it was mental. The fight was in Illinois and it was cold. I had real good running the night before. I ran up this hill and I was like, I'm gonna get this guy! After that, I thought I was moving on up. In my next fight, which was only ten days later, I fought Vassiliy Jirov. That guy was tall and lanky. He was wide on top and small around the waist. We fought at cruiserweight. He was hitting hard. He was counter-punching me and I was counter-punching him, but it was his fucking night! I went down in the first and I got up. The referee looked at me a certain way and I always hated that! He said, "Come back and fight another day."

In June 2001, you lost to cruiserweight Chris Thomas (8–2) via second-round TKO. After the fight, you retired with a record of 9–39–2. What finally led to your retirement?

As I got older, the punches got harder. It wasn't a decision I made. It just kind of went there. A lot of times, I still think about fighting. I start training, I start making plans… I feel good. I'm competent and aware

Former heavyweight world champion Wladimir Klitschko defeated Speight via second-round TKO (courtesy Marty Rosengarten/RingsidePhotos. com).

of what's going on. Sometimes, though, I have headaches and my hand hurts from blocking punches. I seen my doctor lately and he said I'm fine. I'm doing all right. It's just that I don't know what to do sometimes. I go for a lot of walks. A couple of weeks ago, I was down at Manny Pacquiao's gym watching them train and I just left. I miss fighting. When I was a pro, people knew me around the world, because they saw me on TV. I was a fighter. People came to see a fight and that's what I did. I'm just a country boy they tried to take advantage of. Nobody cared what happened. People are mistreated in boxing. I've been behind the doors. They didn't think I knew what they were doing, but I did. But with everything that happened, I'm still happy. I'm still content. Maybe it's because of the time that mule kicked me. When it's daytime, it's daytime. When it's night, it's night. God made me, so there must be something about me that's just like Him. Even though I'm in the flesh, there's a spirit about me and everyone else. We're all the same, we just look different.

24

Angelo Dundee: Final Words

The 5th Street Gym in Miami, Florida, is one of the most iconic boxing gyms in the world. It was started in 1950 by Chris Dundee, a successful promoter who turned Miami into a major boxing city. In addition to his own achievements, Chris Dundee was also the older brother of one of the greatest trainers and motivators in the history of the sport. Born and raised in Philadelphia, Pennsylvania, Angelo Dundee dabbled as a cornerman while he was in the Air Force. After the Air Force, Dundee planned on pursuing a career as an aircraft inspector. When the local aircraft factory moved out of town, he switched gears and moved to New York City to work in the fight business with his brother Chris. While in New York, Dundee learned about boxing from watching legendary trainers such as Charlie Goldman, Chickie Ferrera, and Ray Arcel. The first world champion Dundee cornered for was Carmen Basilio. He was with Basilio when Basilio defeated Tony DeMarco for DeMarco's welterweight title, as well as Basilio's victory over Sugar Ray Robinson for the middleweight crown. Dundee is best known for being the trainer of Muhammad Ali. He also trained Sugar Ray Leonard for most of Leonard's career. In addition, he was with George Foreman when Foreman knocked out Michael Moorer to become the oldest man in history to win the heavyweight championship of the world. Other champions Dundee trained include Jose Napoles, George Scott, Jimmy Ellis, Luis Rodriguez, and Willie Pastrano, among others. In January 2012, I called Angelo Dundee and he shared with me just a few of his final words. The interview with Angelo Dundee took place on January 23rd, 2012. He passed away on February 1st. At the time of this interview, he was just as energetic and enthusiastic as he was known to be.

How's it going, Angelo?
I'm doing fine, thank God! I'm happy to be rapping with you.

Did I catch you at a good time?
Every time you call is a good time.

Well, good. Shall we talk a little boxing?
Sure. We can cover the whole synopsis of boxing in twenty minutes! I've been doing

it for a few years, you know. *Quite* a few years.

Let's start at the beginning. What is your background in boxing and what led you to become a trainer?

When I was a kid, my brother Joe would take me to the fights. I knew nothing about boxing, but my brother Chris was involved in the fight game, so I was around it. I was familiar with it. This was in the early '40s. After high school, I joined the Air Force. I was stationed in Germany when I saw a jet land

Boxing trainer Angelo Dundee (photograph by Jeff Julian, courtesy Tom Tsatas/5th St. Gym).

for the first time. This thing didn't have propellers and I thought I was going crazy! When I got out of the military, I spent some time in Europe. My brother Jimmy and I used to work the USO tournaments over there. We were seconds. God help us if the fighters needed us. We were sticks in the mud. We were just standing there. I was an aircraft inspector before I went into the military. When I came back home to Philly, they wanted to send me to school to teach me more about aircraft, but the aircraft factory moved from Philly to Johnstown, and it would have been a hassle to travel back and forth. Meanwhile, my brother Chris was up in New York, working in the fight business. I called him up and asked him if I could get a shot at it. I already had a taste of boxing, so I moved to New York and lived in my brother's office on 51st Street and 8th Avenue. This was at the Hotel Capitol, caddy corner from the old Garden.

When I was living in New York City, I ate, slept, and drank boxing. That was my college. I learned from watching the best, trainers like Charlie Goldman, Chickie Ferrera, and Ray Arcel. All the biggies. I watched how they talked to fighters, how they stopped cuts... I got an education on how to give an interview. I learned about public relations. I learned from my brother Chris, who was the greatest promoter alive. I listened to him in his office, how he would talk to people. You see, I learned the little things in this business. The little things are big things. After a while, I developed a feel for it. Chris, at this time, had moved down to Miami Beach. He was promoting fighters down there. I went down there with him and the 5th Street Gym became a reality. I was there seven days a week, training fighters of all shapes and sizes. The place was packed! We'd have fights three or four times a week. I took fighters to Cuba, the Bahamas, Aruba, Argentina, Peru... You name it, I was there. I got my first big break by accident. Carmen Basilio came down to Florida for a fight, but his trainer couldn't make the trip. They asked me to work the corner. I figured I was going to be the bucket boy, but I go in the dressing room and they tell me to get him ready. I was the guy running the corner! After that, Basilio wanted me with him, so I worked with him for the Baby Williams fight all the way to Sugar Ray Robinson.

In boxing, you're going to learn something new every day of your life. Did you know

Boxing manager and promoter Chris Dundee, founder of the 5th St. Gym (courtesy Tom Tsatas/5th St. Gym).

Angelo Dundee (front center) and his champions at the 5th St. Gym, 1960s (courtesy Tom Tsatas/5th St. Gym).

that Joey Maxim was scared to death of flying? This is a guy who fought every tough sucker alive and he was afraid to get in an airplane. Try to figure fighters out. You can't figure them out, but I knew how to talk to these guys. I knew how to straighten my guys out. I had Johnny Holman when he fought Ezzard Charles. All Johnny Holman wanted was a house for his wife, with shutters and air conditioning. He's fighting Ezzard Chares and I said to him, "What are you doing, Johnny? This guy is stealing your house from you for Christ's sake!" Johnny went out there and stopped Charles. What about Ray Leonard with Tommy Hearns? "You're blowing it, son! You're blowing it!" Thank God the mic wasn't on me before that, because I said to him, "You're slowing down, you dumb son of a bitch!" They missed that one. There are things you can do with fighters that work, but only certain types of fighters. Some of them will react, some of them won't. I'll give you the best story in boxing. This kid came down to Miami and I get him a fight in Las Vegas. Guess who his corner is? Eddie Futch, Freddie Roach, and Angelo Dundee. Guess what happened? The kid lost the fight. A trainer is only as good as the guy he's training. You can't tell me any different. You can only bring out the best in the individual you're working with. Thank God I've had a lot of guys who brought out the best in me.

Front six: Angelo Dundee, Tom Tsatas, Matt Baiamonte, Muhammad Ali, Alex Damjanovich, Dino Spencer, and other friends at the grand re-opening of the 5th St. Gym, 2010 (photograph by Jeff Julian, courtesy Tom Tsatas/5th St. Gym).

When did you first meet Muhammad Ali and how did you eventually become his trainer?

Sheraton Hotel. 1958. I'm up in the room with Willie Pastrano and the phone rings. It's this kid whose calling from down in the lobby. He says his name is Cassius Marcellus Clay. He's a Golden Gloves Champion and he wanted to come up and talk about boxing. This kid walks in and it was a very good conversation. He wanted to know how many miles my fighters ran, how many rounds they sparred before a fight… He was a very inquisitive kid. I enjoyed talking to him. The kid goes on to win a gold medal, and after the Olympics, Archie Moore had him. Archie Moore tried to get him to sweep the floor and he told Archie, "I don't even sweep the floor for my mother!" He broke off from Archie after that and he asked me to work with him.

Ali had a lot of natural talent, but some of the things he did in the ring are considered technically incorrect. As his trainer, how did you know when it was okay to let him do things that weren't by the book?

You do what's going to win for you. That's the name of the game. Win. Nobody hangs around a loser. Everybody loves a winner, so let's have everybody love us. In boxing, they say kill the body and the head dies. With Muhammad, you kill the head and the body dies. It didn't work for everybody else, but it worked for him. You know what I did with Muhammad? Nothing. I left him alone. You couldn't train Muhammad like a regular guy. It was impossible and I knew that. I did my homework on this kid, I knew my limitations with this kid, and I knew what would work with this kid. His first day in the gym, he says, "Okay, Ang, line up all your bums. I'm going to beat them all." Muhammad was the first superstar who talked. A lot of guys tried to copy him, but they couldn't. He was unique, he was different, he was sincere… As much as he talked, that's how hard he trained. He was the first guy in the gym and the last guy to leave. This kid never ceased to amaze me at any time in his career. I remember when he worked with Ingemar Johansson. When Ingemar was getting ready for Floyd Patterson, Whitey Bimstein came down to Miami Beach and he wanted somebody to work with Ingemar. I said, "I got a kid you can work with." Let me tell you, to this day, Johansson is still trying to hit him. He just out-boxed him, out-smarted him. With this kid, I was never concerned. This kid and I have been friends for over fifty years. We never had an argument. We never had a beef. Every day was like going to a picnic.

In February 1964, Muhammad Ali (then known as Cassius Clay) defeated heavyweight champion Sonny Liston, when Liston wouldn't answer the bell for the seventh round. What stands out in your mind about that time?

A lot of people thought Muhammad would get beat, but I had been studying Sonny Liston for a couple of years. I went to his fights and I saw that certain guys gave him problems. Runners. If runners gave him problems, what's my guy going to do? My guy will punish you while he's boxing, so I knew he would beat Sonny Liston. When they got in the ring, he looked down at Sonny and said, "I gotcha sucker!" Sonny thought my guy was

Muhammad Ali hitting the speed bag at the 5th St. Gym, 1964 (photograph by Chris Smith, courtesy Tom Tsatas/5th St. Gym).

nuts. He was the baddest man on the planet. Who's gonna talk back to Sonny Liston? A screwball!

In March 1971, Ali suffered his first loss as a professional to Joe Frazier via unanimous decision. Frazier was the champion at that time, because Ali was forced to relinquish his title due to his refusal to fight in the Vietnam War (Frazier defeated Jimmy Ellis for the vacant title).

It was the biggest thing that ever happened. Muhammad Ali and Joe Frazier brought out the best in each other. What they did for boxing can't be replaced. Early on in the fight, Muhammad was frustrating Joe. He's tappin' him on the head and pitty-patting and he gets himself hurt. In the fifteenth round, Joe hits him right on the chin. I knew my kid could take a hell of a shot, because of the fight with Sonny Banks. Sonny caught him and when he was going down, his eyes were closed. When he bounced off the canvas, he woke up. That's the mark of a great fighter! Let me tell you, Eddie Futch and I were so close it was scary. Joe was a very dear friend of mine, too. We're all from Philly! I knew every guy in his corner. We were friends forever. We were working against each other, but that's the business we're in.

In October 1974, in Kinshasa, Zaire, Ali recaptured his title when he defeated George Foreman via eighth-round knockout in a fight known as "The Rumble in the Jungle." In that fight, Ali used a technique called the rope-a-dope, where he laid on the ropes and allowed Foreman to beat on him until he punched himself out. Did you know that was his strategy going in?

Oh, no! He did it all wrong and he still won! I don't know how he kept his balance, because the ropes were so loose. The heat loosened the ropes and I thought he was going to fall out of the ring. When he would come back to the corner, I'd hit him on the butt and tell him, "Get out of there!" I could see George starting to get tired. He had completely run out of gas, the poor guy. I knew we would get him, but I had no idea it would be as dramatic as it was. My God! He hit him in mid-air for Christ's sake! It reminded me of the Cleveland Williams fight.

Ali's fight with Cleveland Williams is regarded as one of his best performances.

That I know. But how did he look with Zora Folley? Folley was a dangerous sucker and my guy destroyed him. I still say that we never got to see the best of Ali. When he fought Cleveland Williams and Zora Folley, he was just starting to peak.

In February 1978, Ali won the heavyweight championship a third time when he defeated Leon Spinks in their rematch. Shortly after the Spinks fight, he retired until he decided to make a comeback in October 1980 against heavyweight champion Larry Homes, a fight that you elected to stop after the tenth round.

Larry Holmes would try to knock my guy out in the gym every day. He was Muhammad's sparring partner and Muhammad used to play with him. The thing is, I never made my guys fight in the gym. That's my theory. You *work* in the gym. You practice what you're going to do the night of the fight. Muhammad never won a decision in the gym. I thought he was going to beat Larry Holmes, but his body was empty because he was taking thyroid pills. I thought he was taking vitamins, but he was taking these pills to lose the weight. I'm not making excuses. I thought it would be different on the night of the fight, but it wasn't. I stopped it because my guy wasn't answering back. My guy *always* answered back! My guy is such a resilient guy, but he had nothing to come back with that night. This happens to fighters. They have one night and they can't do it no more.

At what point did you begin training Sugar Ray Leonard and what stands out in your mind about the years you worked with him?

I met Ray in New York. The 1976 Olympic Team was making an appearance at Madison Square Garden and I went there with Muhammad. When we were there, Muhammad told Ray, "If you want a good trainer, get Angelo." They called me when they needed a trainer and thank God they did. Look at all the fun we had! Ray is my buddy and he was a great fighter. He had a great fight with Wilfred Benitez. Benitez was an extremely great boxer, but Ray had more strength than Benitez. Ray punched better. In that first fight with Roberto Duran, my kid was ready to fight him like he fought him in the second fight. That's the way we were planning to fight him, but Duran abused him when we were walking the streets of Montreal. Me, my wife Helen, Ray and his wife—we were walking the streets and Duran came up and he told Ray's wife that he was going to beat the hell out of her husband and then come after her next. Ray wanted to street-fight the guy right there. How about Ray's thirteenth pro fight? He fought Dickie Eklund, but he was supposed to fight Tommy Hearns. I was in Europe and the matchmaker tells me he's fighting Tommy Hearns. I tell him, "No, *you're* fighting Tommy Hearns!" I waited on that fight, because I knew it wasn't ripe. It happened when it was supposed to happen. Sometimes people ask me about the Hagler fight. They say, "Angelo, do you think your fighter won?" I say, "Whose hand was raised in the air for Christ's sake?" My guy out-punched him, out-speeded him, out-fought him, out-thought him! He beat Hagler! Period!

In November 1994, you were George Foreman's trainer when he defeated Michael Moorer via tenth-round knockout, becoming the oldest man in history to capture the heavyweight title at age forty-five.

When George was working at HBO, he had lunch with my wife Helen. He said, "Mrs. Dundee, do you know why Angelo is working with me?" She says, "No." He said, "When I was in Zaire, I was getting ready to hit Muhammad with a right hand. I set him up and I hear this squeaky voice tell him to get out of there. I knew that was the guy I wanted with me." This is a true story. If you talk to George, he'll tell you. George Foreman was the smartest man I ever worked with. He trained his body, an old body, the right way. Look at the shape he was in. That night he won the title, he was taking a licking from Moorer. I kept telling him, "He's dropping his hands! He's dropping his hands!" In the tenth round, BOOM! Moorer was out and I mean *out*! George deserved to be champion. Here's a guy who was a street guy, but he learned religion, he became a preacher, and he learned how to deal with people. George was a better fighter when he was older. When he was a young kid, if you bent down, he beat you. If you stayed tall, he had problems with you. Muhammad stood tall, even when he was on the ropes. I knew what he was gonna do to poor Joe Frazier and poor Ken Norton. They were made to order for George. Mike Tyson wouldn't go a half a round with George.

Speaking of Mike Tyson, you were in Trevor Berbick's corner in November 1986 when Tyson defeated him via second-round TKO. That night, Tyson became the youngest man in history to win the heavyweight championship at age twenty.

What can I say? I was there. We tried, but he hit him on the temple and the legs went completely out of him. Berbick was so much bigger than Tyson. Tyson was a little guy, but he was slick inside. I tried to counter that by making my guys move the same way he moved, to take away the force off his punches. I tried that with Pinklon Thomas, but he got caught. I know Tyson real well. He was a small man. If Tyson was a bigger man, forget it!

You observed Oscar De La Hoya's training camp and offered him tips when he faced Manny Pacquiao in December 2008, a fight he lost via eighth-round TKO. What were your thoughts on what you saw from De La Hoya while he was training?

De La Hoya left all of his fight in the gym. He trained like a twenty-one-year-old and he was thirty-five. You cannot do that. The only words of advice I gave De La Hoya before I left was, "Don't leave it on the mountain." That's all I said. De La Hoya had a great shot to beat that guy, but he left it all in the gym. I liked Oscar. He was a terrific fighter. Boxing needs more people like him.

How do you feel about the state of the game today opposed to when Muhammad Ali and Sugar Ray Leonard were fighting?

Boxing will be the way it's supposed to be when the fans know who the fighters are. The problem today is that people don't know who's who or what's what. When I was in Philly, everybody knew all the fighters. We need for the promoters to promote these kids. We need for the managers to manage these kids. Our world is a smaller place. The worst thing that can happen in this business is silence. Right now, boxing is having a lot of silence, but I'm not the least bit concerned. Boxing is always going to come back. You can't repeat the old days, and in twenty years, it's gonna be completely different than it is today. It's evolution. I would never have guessed that there would be great fighters coming out of Europe, but look at what's happening. You never know where the next great fighter is going to come from. I've been doing this for years and I learn something new all the time. Right now, I'm working with about four or five kids who are getting ready for the next Olympics. For the first time, I'm training amateurs and teaching them the amateur style. Let me tell you, I'm having a lot of fun. I go to the gym a couple days week. I'm still in action, I'm still moving, I'm still scheming… I haven't worked a day in my life. I do something I love and I still have a feeling for it. I'm a very fortunate individual.

Epilogue: Once Upon a Time in the Suburbs

While having lunch with HBO boxing analyst Larry Merchant, the last question I asked was, "Is there anything you would like to say in closing?" Merchant sat quietly and thought about it. After a long moment of contemplation, the man who is never short of words merely said, "Keep punching!" At that, I turned off the recorder. With this interview complete, I could scratch one more item off the things I wanted to do in life. This was a day I had been looking forward to for many years. Like the highly anticipated Ali-Frazier and Leonard-Hearns fights, my "lunch with a legend" exceeded all expectations. We sat and talked for a little while longer. Merchant eventually turned the questioning around and said, "So, how did *you* become a boxing fan?" There wasn't enough time to tell him everything, but if we had another twenty minutes, I would have told him the following story.

When I was nine years old, I asked for boxing gloves for Christmas so I could stage boxing matches with my friends. I used to wrap my hands with white medical tape, wear a bathrobe, and make grand entrances. Without headgear or mouthpieces, my friends and I hit each other to the body and head. Sometimes I would fall to the ground in dramatic fashion and make it to my feet at the count of nine, just like Rocky Balboa did in the original *Rocky* movie. At some point, I stopped playing *Rocky* with my friends, but I never gave up the idea of being a fighter. It was always in the back of my mind to one day get into the ring and compete. In my eyes, boxers were superheroes and I wanted to be just like them. However, I was an unlikely candidate to be a boxer. I grew up in the suburbs of St. Louis, Missouri, where boxing was not a part of the culture. I had been in a few fights growing up, but for me, it was just a thrill. I didn't really want to hurt anybody and I wasn't what you would call a "tough guy." It was the romanticism of fighting that appealed to me, probably inspired by all the violent movies I used to watch as a kid.

I'm a movie fanatic. One of my passions in life is filmmaking. When I was twenty-one, I was casting actors for a movie I was making. On one of the resumes, I noticed an actor who listed that he was a former boxer. I cast him in hopes that he would show me what I had to do to get in the ring. This man, who was about twenty years older than me, ended up being my first teacher. We would get together on weekends, hit the heavy bag, and trade body shots. I learned how to throw all the basic punches and I spent a lot of time studying tapes. After a while, I heard about an amateur boxing event that was in the works, so I signed up for it. I still hadn't sparred at this point or discovered what being a fighter is all about. Nobody told me that I was ready for this, but it didn't matter. I thought that since I knew so much about boxing from outside the ropes that my knowledge of the sport would somehow translate inside the ring. Unfortunately, it didn't work out that way. I was TKO'd in the second round and I didn't have the guts to give it another try until three years later.

After the fight, I started training at a gym that had just opened on the north side of St. Louis. I wanted to fight again, but I was very unsure of myself. One day, the owner of the gym asked me if I would work with some of the neighborhood kids in exchange for waiving my gym dues. Ironically, I had always wanted to train fighters. This was an aspect of the game that intrigued me, but with a record of 0–1, I felt I had no business being in that position. Despite my insecurities, I gave it a shot. I began teaching the kids the fundamentals of boxing, gradually finding myself working with them six days a week. The kids started fighting and they did quite well. In fact, one of them won the Ringside Tournament in Kansas City. After about a year of coaching amateur boxers, I switched gears and began teaching boxing fitness classes at a gym in Clayton, Missouri—right in the heart of the suburbs. I was removed from the competitive aspect of the game and I figured that I missed my window to get back in the ring. But it was at this proper and pristine location that I learned what it was to be a fighter.

Doveed Linder with his boxer Demetrius Johnson, an eleven-year-old 65-pounder, who won the Ringside Tournament in 2005 (author's collection).

Doveed Linder (left) after he won his second amateur fight via third round TKO over Eric Hall in 2007 (courtesy Bob Barton).

One of the owners of the gym wanted to learn how to box, so I showed him a few things and we started sparring. It turned out that he was a beast. This was the only time that I taught someone how to box, who turned the lesson around and gave *me* a beating! We formed a little two-man "fight club" and went to war on a daily basis. After a while, a real estate agent who had a background in boxing started coming around the gym. He wanted to start training fighters, so we all got together and it was the perfect fit. With the encouragement from my new boxing family and with the faith I gained by training the kids on the north side, I got back in the ring and stopped my opponent in the third round. Winning a boxing match was something I had dreamt about since I was nine years old. When it finally happened, it didn't seem like a big deal. It should have been, but it wasn't. Somewhere along the line, I learned that there's no difference between winning and losing. My first teacher told me that when I was just getting started. I didn't believe him at the time, but it's true. Once you step in the ring, you've already won.

Synchronicity: The Invisible Connection

Sometimes when you're passionate about something, everything just seems to work out. The right people show up at exactly the right time. I'm sure everyone reading this has had those moments where you might be thinking of someone, and then shortly after that you bump into them in the grocery store or they happen to call you out of the blue. These moments often happen to me when I write about boxing. My desire to sit down and talk to Larry Merchant existed well before I began dabbling with boxing journalism. Once I started writing for Boxingtalk.com and speaking with people in the fight game, I thought that a conversation with Merchant could actually happen. What I didn't expect is that I would meet his son-in-law by pure chance, who would then arrange for the interview to be done over lunch.

After I interviewed Merchant, the idea for this book started to come to me. As I pursued the various interviews, similar encounters to the meeting of Merchant's son-in-law continued happening. I would think about the next person I wanted to approach, then before I could act, I would receive a random e-mail with their contact information or I would cross paths with someone who would point me in the right direction. It happened again and again, notably when I met Exum Speight, the former cruiserweight and heavyweight who retired with a record of 9–39–2. At this point, I had interviewed several well-known figures and accomplished champions. For my next interview, I wanted to speak with someone who nobody had heard of—someone who has labored at the lower levels and has seen a side of the sport that is seldom discussed. One afternoon, I walked into the In-N-Out Burger on Sunset and Orange in Hollywood. The only available seat was right across from Speight. I had no idea who Speight was, but we chatted over lunch and I learned his history. It didn't occur to me until after I left the restaurant that he fit the profile of the very person I was looking for. However, Speight picked up on the "invisible connection," as he asked me for my phone number and called me twenty minutes after we parted ways.

All of the encounters I experienced while writing this book could be described as "synchronicity." By definition, synchronicity is the experience of two or more events that are apparently casually unrelated or unlikely to occur together by chance, yet are experienced

Doveed Linder on an airplane with former heavyweight world champion Riddick Bowe, 2015.

as occurring together in a meaningful manner. I don't really know what that means, but I love to write about boxing. And when I write about boxing, sometimes good things happen.

My Brush with an Accused Murderer

After I interviewed Exum Speight, we spoke on the phone about every six weeks. One morning in September 2013, I saw a headline on a boxing website that read, "Former Klitschko Foe Charged in Cold Case Murder." I read that Speight had been arrested for the 1987 murder of Douglas Stumler, who was thirty at the time of his death. The cause of death was stabbing and strangulation. This murder had remained unsolved until a forensics test linked Speight's DNA to the scene of the crime. Stumler was Speight's manager. At this point, Speight had only one professional bout. When I heard the news, naturally I was shocked. I looked back at my experiences with Speight to see if I could identify a side of his personality that would allow him to commit such a horrendous act. Speight had always treated me with a great deal of kindness and respect. I never sensed anything evil or menacing. I spoke with Speight a few times after his arrest and he maintained his innocence. Despite the facts of the case, I refused to pass judgment and still viewed him as a friend. I don't know what Speight was like back in 1987, but the guy I met was a very spiritual person. In his interview, he said, "God made me, so there must be something about me that's just like Him. Even though I'm in the flesh, there's a spirit about me and everyone else. We're all the same, we just look different." I'm not a religious person, but I have always believed the same thing. With everyone we meet, we can see a part of ourselves in them. Maybe that's why I found a connection with Exum Speight, despite our very different life experiences. Shortly before this book went to print, Speight died of a stroke. My heart goes out to the Stumler family, as well as the Speight family, and I hope everyone involved in this incident has a sense of peace and closure.

Index